Genocides by the Oppressed

GENOCIDES
BY THE OPPRESSED

Subaltern Genocide in Theory and Practice

Edited by

Nicholas A. Robins
and Adam Jones

INDIANA UNIVERSITY PRESS
Bloomington and Indianapolis

This book is a publication of

Indiana University Press
601 North Morton Street
Bloomington, IN 47404-3797 USA

http://iupress.indiana.edu

Telephone orders 800-842-6796
Fax order 812-855-7931
Orders by e-mail iuporder@indiana.edu

The paper used in this publication meets the minimum requirements of American National Standard for Information Sciences—Permanence of Paper for Printed Library Materials, ANSI Z39.48-1984.

Manufactured in the United States of America

Library of Congress Cataloging-in-Publication Data

Genocides by the oppressed : subaltern genocide in theory
and practice / edited by Nicholas A. Robins and Adam Jones.
p. cm.
Includes bibliographical references and index.
ISBN 978-0-253-35309-2 (cloth : alk. paper) —
ISBN 978-0-253-22077-6 (pbk. : alk. paper)
1. Genocide. 2. Ethnic conflict. I. Robins, Nicholas A., 1964– II. Jones, Adam, 1963–
HV6322.7.G488 2009
364.15'1—dc22
2008043164

1 2 3 4 5 14 13 12 11 10 09

Contents

Introduction
Subaltern Genocide in Theory and Practice

ADAM JONES AND NICHOLAS A. ROBINS

etween 1780 and 1782, Peru and Upper Peru (present-day Bolivia) were
ravaged by an Indian uprising in which over 100,000 people perished,
and which would haunt the land with the specter of race war for years to
come. Long exploited, the Indians had been subjected to mounting economic
pressures as a result of the Bourbon Crown's efforts to increase colonial reve-
nues and restrain the power of the Catholic Church. Not only were they forced
to purchase often useless goods at highly inflated prices from Spanish gover-
nors, but parish priests also charged increasingly onerous fees for saint's day
celebrations, marriages, funerals, and other services. Combined with widespread resentment over forced labor, the imposition of unprecedented taxes
on Indian staples, a lack of viable judicial recourse, and prophecies concerning
the return of Indian rule, the region exploded in violence. Between September
1780 and February 1781, in what is today central Bolivia, followers of the
Indian Tomás Catari (and, after his death, his brothers Dámaso and Nicolás)
called for an end to civil taxes, religious fees, forced labor, and coerced purchases. Initially killing Indian and Mestizo leaders who opposed them, the
rebels soon unleashed their forces on the lighter-skinned in general, resulting
in a brief and ill-fated siege of the regional capital of La Plata.

Throughout the region, non-Indians were systematically slaughtered. In
February 1781, the town of Tapacari was overrun by insurgents. The Spanish,
Creoles, and their Mestizo allies found that the church in which they had bar-
ricaded themselves offered little physical protection. According to the few survivors, once inside, the rebels killed all those they could find in the "altars, choir
and tower"; "the blood ran like streams" from the victims.[1] In San Pedro de
Buenavista, those inside the church, despairing after their resistance had been
broken, simply opened the doors of the church and "hand[ed] themselves over
to the arms of death."[2] Similar events played out in the region of Cuzco, where
in November 1780 Túpac Amaru, the chief of the village of Tungasuca, executed
the local Spanish governor and sparked a mass uprising of Indians which culminated in an unsuccessful siege of Cuzco in January 1781. Between March and

1

October 1781, another rebel, Túpac Catari, dominated the area around La Paz and laid siege to the city. Approximately ten thousand people, or one-third of the city's population, perished. Other rebel leaders with exterminatory aims overran scores of villages in the region.

In many cases, rebels in the field went beyond the call of their nominal leaders. This was especially the case with Tomás Catari and Túpac Amaru, both of whom were more conservative than those who operated in their names. While Oruro was the only sizable town to fall to the rebels, villages had much less protection, and the victims were generally killed in or near the churches where they had sought physical and spiritual refuge. While some women and men with certain skills were spared to serve their new masters, the rebels generally did not take prisoners. Many insurgents were inspired by prophecies foretelling the return of Indian rule to the land, harbored a belief in resurrection, and believed that native gods, long dormant, had finally risen up to expel the Christian god and those who oppressed them in his name. The native utopia that they sought to create had little use for their erstwhile masters; indeed, the continued presence of Spaniards, Creoles, and even Hispanicized Indians was antithetical to their aims.[3]

A scant decade after the Great Rebellion was finally quelled, an even more destructive rebellion—indeed, the greatest slave revolt in human history—erupted in the French colonial territory of Saint-Domingue (today's Haiti). The slave trade had turned Saint-Domingue into the jewel in France's colonial crown, producing nearly one-third of the world's sugar. The twin forces of rampant mortality among slaves and burgeoning global demand for their products resulted in a constant influx of human chattel—such that by 1791, fully half the slaves on the fertile Northern Plain had been born in Africa. These same forces, however, when combined with the cultural and linguistic bonds among the slave population, contributed to the success of the organizing efforts that produced the uprising.

In a matter of weeks, the Northern Plain went up in flames. In a volcanic outburst of racial violence, slaves systematically murdered nearly every white they could set their hands upon:

> They murdered white men in their beds and raped the women atop their husband's corpses. They nailed one member of the slave-catching militia alive to the gate of his plantation and chopped off his arms and legs. They tied a carpenter between two planks and sawed him in half. Two sons of a white planter and a slave woman stabbed their father to death. Planters had been meting out similar violence to their slaves for generations, but news of these atrocities sent waves of horror through Europe because for the first time white people were being killed by the hundreds, a toll that would soon mount into the thousands.[4]

The insurgency waxed and waned over the course of thirteen years of highly complex national and international maneuvers, but its culmination in 1803–1804, with the final and successful struggle for Haitian independence, was accompanied by parallel outbursts of indiscriminate racial murder by whites and blacks alike. General Leclerc, desperately seeking to recapture Saint-Domingue for Napoleonic France and reinstate slavery there, soon found his troops wasting away from disease and rebel attacks. He wrote in exasperation to Napoleon that to secure victory, it would be necessary "to exterminate all the blacks in the mountains, women as well as men. Except for children under twelve. Wipe out half the population of the lowlands, and do not leave in the colony a single black who has worn an epaulet." Among Leclerc's genocidal innovations was the creation of "what may have been history's first gas chamber," when black captives were forced into the hold of a ship and suffocated by burning sulphur.[5] When the French effort finally collapsed, independence leader Jean-Jacques Dessalines responded not by extending a hand of mercy and reconciliation, but with a final racial bloodbath. Dessalines declared that he "need[ed] the skin of a white to serve as a parchment, his skull as an inkwell, his blood for ink, and a bayonet for a pen." He called for "one last act of national authority, forever assur[ing] the empire of liberty in the country whose birth we have witnessed." The whites, "this people of executioners," had to be destroyed—and several thousand French citizens who had returned to the territory under Dessalines' more moderate predecessor, Toussaint Louverture, were slaughtered.[6] According to Philippe Girard, "when the genocide was over, Haiti's white population was virtually non-existent."[7] Overall, several hundred thousand people—black, white, and mulatto—had been killed in one of the most destructive conflicts of the early modern era.

The Great Rebellion and the Haitian slave uprising are two examples of what we refer to as "subaltern genocide": cases in which subaltern actors—those objectively oppressed and disempowered—adopt genocidal strategies to vanquish their oppressors. By "genocidal strategies," we mean those indiscriminately targeting a population for extermination on the basis of a collective identity, whether actual or imputed. This identity may be national, racial, ethnic, or religious, to cite the four variables mentioned in the United Nations Genocide Convention of 1948; or it may be founded on political affiliation, social class, or gender identity, to list three further variables that have gained a firm foothold in the literature of comparative genocide studies. This reworked definition of genocide—the Convention phrasing, supplemented by political, social, and gender groups, and with an emphasis on the physically exterminatory dimension of genocide—anchors the present volume, though individual authors may have their preferred definitions.[8]

Subaltern Genocide in Comparative Genocide Studies

From its original conceptualization in 1944 by the Polish jurist Raphael Lemkin, "genocide" has overwhelmingly been depicted—and prosecuted—as a crime committed by state actors against vulnerable minorities, on the state's territory or beyond its borders. The Nazi Holocaust against European Jews and others is often cited as the prototypical genocide. This was a systematic, well-coordinated, bureaucratically sophisticated campaign that directed the agencies and capacities of the state toward the end of mass extermination. A somewhat similar, and certainly state-directed, dynamic was evident in the Armenian genocide in the Ottoman Empire during World War I—the first genocide beyond the Nazi case to attract sustained scholarly attention. Analyses of other "classic" twentieth-century genocides, notably those in Cambodia and Rwanda, have tended to emphasize the element of careful organization by an extremist cabal that first seizes national power, then uses state instruments to consign victims to mass death.

The emphasis on state perpetration is also integral to many of the alternative definitions offered by genocide scholars, which seek to compensate for the ambiguities, shortcomings, and complexities of the UN Genocide Convention. The sociologist Irving Louis Horowitz, for example, defined genocide in 1976 as "a structural and systematic destruction of innocent people by a state bureaucratic apparatus."[9] For Jack Nusan Porter, genocide is committed "by a government or its agents"; Isidor Wallimann and Michael N. Dobkowski deploy identical language in their own definition.[10]

Even where definitions of genocide are not conditioned on state power, they exude a strong sense that genocide is something that socially and politically dominant groups inflict on subordinate ones. Thus, an early definition by Vahakn Dadrian (1975) depicted genocide as "the successful attempt by a dominant group, vested with formal authority and/or with preponderant access to the overall resources of power, to reduce by coercion or lethal violence the number of a minority group . . . whose respective vulnerability is a major factor contributing to the decision for genocide."[11] In their widely cited book *The History and Sociology of Genocide,* Frank Chalk and Kurt Jonassohn emphasize that "genocide is a form of one-sided mass killing,"[12] while Israel Charny cites "the essential defenselessness of the victim" as a key consideration.[13]

There are good reasons for these emphases on state power, and on perpetrators who occupy a position of structural domination over others. States have long been defined by their monopoly, or at least disproportionate control, over the means of coercion. The infliction of one-sided mass death is less likely in the absence of these disproportionate capacities. States, moreover, are generally best positioned to coordinate, logistically and bureaucratically, the large-scale campaigns of systematic killing that we usually associate with genocide.

However, a state-centric perspective tends to obscure instances where subaltern actors themselves adopt genocidal strategies and the ideologies that underpin them. Consider, for example, the sub-genre of *retributive genocide* proposed by Vahakn Dadrian and also adopted by Helen Fein. The notion of retributive genocidal killing appears to capture the dynamic of subaltern genocide, in which an oppressed group seeks to gain revenge and liberation by waging genocide against their oppressors. In fact, however, all the exponents of the concept depict retributive genocide as *imposed by the dominant upon the dominated:* it is "confined to localized atrocities as a form of meting out punishment to a segment of the minority, challenging or threatening the dominant group" (Dadrian); it subsumes cases "in which an elite of a dominant ethnic group destroys a significant part of another group which it fears will take its place as the dominant group" (Fein).[14] Subaltern genocide, though, evinces a rather different retributive dynamic, one that emerges substantially from below, as we will explore in detail in these pages.

It is worth pointing out that the closest thing we have to a consensus definition of genocide—that of the UN Genocide Convention—includes no statement about the nature of the perpetrator, and nothing about the necessary power relationship (e.g., dominant versus subordinate) between perpetrator and victim. In addition, a number of genocide scholars have been careful to frame their definitions to allow for cases where state agents are not paramount, and the "essential defencelessness" of victims does not obtain. Barbara Harff and Ted Gurr, for example, emphasize "sustained policies by governing elites or their agents," but also refer to "the case of civil war," in which "either of the contending authorities" may be guilty of genocide (or "politicide").[15] John L. Thompson and Gail A. Quets define genocide as the "destruction of a social collectivity by whatever agents, with whatever intentions."[16]

The role of subaltern actors in perpetrating genocide is largely unexplored in the genocide studies literature. But an attentive reader of that literature can nonetheless trace a skein through studies of genocide and crimes against humanity that supplies a great many insights and useful analyses. Perhaps the most insightful accounts have concerned two of the most recent genocides to enshrine themselves in the "canon" of genocide studies: Cambodia from 1975 to 1978, and Rwanda from April to July 1994.

In Cambodia in 1975, the Khmer Rouge—"Red Khmer"—regime took power in the capital, Phnom Penh, after many years of combating government forces and gradually extending their power over the bomb-shattered Cambodian countryside. By the time they vanquished the U.S. client regime, they had developed a potent ideology of class revenge—this despite the fact that their leaders overwhelmingly were not of peasant stock but, like Pol Pot, were educated urbanites who had studied overseas (and bonded) in Paris. One of their first actions was to empty refugee-swollen Phnom Penh and force its 2 million residents into rural areas, where they toiled on ill-conceived mega-projects and, in many cases, starved to death or were simply executed. As the paranoia of the ruling clique mounted, entire regions of the country—notably the Eastern Zone along the Vietnamese border—were depicted as traitorous and subversive. Some 150,000 people were killed in the region for imputed crimes in 1977–78, prompting many middle-level Khmer Rouge leaders to flee into exile in Vietnam. They would form the core of the proxy force that accompanied Vietnamese soldiers into Cambodia at the end of 1978, toppling the Khmer Rouge in January 1979 and pushing the remnants of the movement into the west of the country, where they remained a destabilizing terrorist threat for years afterward. Between 1.5 million and 2 million Cambodians, out of a population of 8 million, died during the Khmer Rouge period. But it was some time before genocide scholars readily accepted the Cambodian events as a clear-cut case of genocide. In part, this was because the victims were generally of the same Khmer ethnic stock as the victims (though ethnic and religious minorities were ruthlessly targeted, in one case—that of the ethnic Chinese—to the point of total extermination). It may also have reflected the fact that, in an Orwellian turn of events, the communist Khmer Rouge after their overthrow became valued protégés of both the United States and China; regardless of their communist ideology and genocidal past, they were seen as a useful obstacle to "Vietnamese expansionism," which was considered the main priority.

Rwanda in 1994 stands as the fastest and most intensive genocide in the historical record, and, prior to the crisis in Darfur, the shameful nadir of the international community's (in)capacity to intervene. Thousands of foreign peacekeepers were on the ground when Hutu Power extremists launched their "final solution" against ethnic Tutsis and moderate Hutus on April 7. But the foreign troops acted only to evacuate the few whites in the country, and themselves thereafter. The skeleton force that remained in the capital, Kigali, could do little to stop the slaughter. With stunning rapidity, the genocidal impetus spread to every corner of the country; only Butare, in the south, held out until its moderate leadership was murdered and the genocide was extended to that prefecture. Tens of thousands of Tutsis at a time were herded into places of supposed refuge, especially religious and educational institutions, and killed there in acts of close-up carnage that recalled the worst months of the Nazi rampage in eastern Poland and the Soviet Union in 1941–42. Other Tutsis were hunted down singly and in small groups, in their urban hiding places and in fields, forests, hills, and marshes. The genocide only ebbed when the Tutsi-dominated Rwandan Patriotic Front (RPF) pushed government forces out of Kigali, into the southwest of the country, and thence into exile across the border in Zaire; by then, a million people had been murdered. The events have begun to assume something of the centrality, for a new generation of genocide scholars and activists, that the Nazi Holocaust held for an earlier generation.

Both the Cambodian and Rwandan holocausts were state-initiated and state-directed, following the familiar pattern. Both, however, featured an unusually high degree of popular participation in genocidal killing. It is at this level of popular involvement that the element of subaltern genocide is most powerfully evident. In the Cambodian case, by the time the Khmer Rouge took power, their forces were composed of hundreds of thousands of peasant cadres, who had spent the previous years enduring the terror and dislocation of saturation bombing by U.S. B-52s—part of the most concentrated bombing campaign in history.[17] The only parts of the country spared destruction were the cities, whose populations came to be viewed as being in traitorous league with the foreign superpower, and as lazy, corrupt, and decadent, in contrast with the noble but hard-pressed Cambodian peasant. When urban residents were forced into the countryside, they found themselves at the mercy of a population that, even if it was not formally integrated with the Khmer Rouge administration, regarded them with hostility—both for their presumed luxurious living while war raged in the countryside and for the strain they placed on scarce resources at the village level. Urbanites, the so-called "new people," contrasted unfavorably with the "old people"—the peasants—who were the true backbone of Khmer identity and the communist revolution it had produced. The "new people" were assigned the harshest work for the longest hours and with the scarcest nutritional resources, and were widely perceived as receiving their comeuppance under the new order: "Sometimes the peasants, as well as the Khmer Rouge themselves, would say to the newcomers, 'You used to be happy and prosperous. Now it's our turn.'"[18] Haing Ngor, a genocide survivor whose performance as Dith Pran in the film

The Killing Fields did much to establish Cambodia as an accepted case of genocide, recalled an occasion during his time in the countryside:

> At mealtime . . . I heard one nurse calling out to another, "Have you fed the war slaves yet?" It was a chance remark, but it stuck in my ears because it explained the Khmer Rouge better than anything else. All the talk about being comrades in a classless society, building the nation with our bare hands and struggling to achieve independence-sovereignty didn't mean anything. The Khmer Rouge had beaten us in the civil war. We were their war slaves. That was all there was to it. They were taking revenge.[19]

Refugee testimonies like the preceding are matched by scholarly evaluations that emphasize the role of subaltern peasant ideologies and actions as central to the suffering that swept the country between 1975 and 1978. Michael Vickery contended that the revolutionary terror of the peasantry was the dominant dynamic of the post-1975 period.[20] Elizabeth Becker's account depicts the peasantry as "form[ing] the visceral basis of the revolution and the totalitarianism it produced."[21] The most sophisticated analysis of the phenomenon, though, was produced by an anthropologist—and is featured in this volume. In a groundbreaking essay, originally published as "A Head for an Eye" and here excerpted as "Oppression and Vengeance in the Cambodian Genocide," Alexander Laban Hinton set the subaltern vengefulness of Cambodian peasants and Khmer Rouge authorities against a cultural backdrop emphasizing the "model of disproportionate revenge" alluded to in the title. As a result of these contributions, we now have a more nuanced understanding of the Cambodian genocide as generated *both* from above and from below.

Likewise, in Rwanda, the Hutu masses—composing about 85 percent of the population—had long chafed under Tutsi overlords, whose domination deepened under the colonial order that the Belgians imposed after World War I. Even when the Belgians switched sides to support the Hutu majority, and Rwanda attained independence in 1959 under a Hutu-dominated regime, the taint of subaltern status lingered for the Hutu population. A powerful image endured of Tutsis as physically taller and more refined than Hutus, more intelligent, and more prosperous and successful. Tutsi women were stereotypically seen as more attractive and sexually alluring. While Tutsi ethnic domination was suppressed in Rwanda, it was alive and well in next-door Burundi (where a genocide by the Tutsi-controlled army in 1972 destroyed most of the Hutu educated and professional classes). It also seemed to be encapsulated in the Rwandan Patriotic Front, which invaded Rwanda from their Ugandan exile in 1990. Exponents of Hutu Power found it relatively easy to depict the RPF, which occupied substantial areas of Rwanda at the time the genocide broke out, as seeking to reestablish Tutsi hegemony and return Hutus to their subaltern status—or exterminate them outright.[22]

These subaltern frustrations and hostilities were a key ingredient in the apocalypse that descended in April 1994. As Mahmood Mamdani writes, "When political analysis presents the genocide as exclusively a state project and ignores its subaltern and 'popular' character it tends to reduce the violence to a set of meaningless outbursts, ritualistic and bizarre, like some ancient primordial twitch come to life." For Mamdani, although the genocide was "organized by state functionaries," it was "carried out by subaltern masses," and this "salient political fact" must be represented in any nuanced analysis of the events.[23] Gérard Prunier has provided a vivid image of the explosive energies unleashed during the genocide:

> In Kigali the [militias] . . . had tended to recruit mostly among the poor. As soon as they went into action, they drew around them a cloud of even poorer people, a lumpenproletariat of street boys, rag-pickers, car-washers and homeless unemployed. For these people the genocide was the best thing that could ever happen to them. They had the blessings of a form of authority to take revenge on socially powerful people as long as these [victims] were on the wrong side of the political fence. They could steal, they could kill with minimum justification, they could rape and they could get drunk for free. This was wonderful. The political aims pursued by the masters of this dark carnival were quite beyond their scope. They just went along, knowing it would not last.[24]

The killing strategies employed featured a potent symbolic dimension, again attesting to the subaltern energies unleashed by the genocide. The Nyarabongo River, a tributary of the Nile, was choked with Tutsi corpses; the killers saw themselves as returning Tutsis to their supposed Nilotic origins in classical Egyptian and Nubian civilization. Tutsi victims were frequently decapitated, or had arms, legs, and genitals hacked off by machetes, thereby physically reducing them in size (recall that their average greater height had been viewed as a marker of their superiority). Cutting victims' Achilles tendons while leaving them alive likewise meant cutting them down to size and reducing them to crawling like cockroaches, the way they were depicted in Hutu hate propaganda. The extraordinary sexual savagery, including ritual mutilations inflicted on Tutsi women, was a similarly vengeful way to bring about the comeuppance of Rwanda's erstwhile sexual elite. The notable, indeed unprecedented, participation of women as agents of the kidnapping, rape, torture, and murder of Tutsi women seems to have been imbued by a gendered sense of class revenge.[25]

As these treatments of the Cambodian and Rwandan holocausts suggest, attention to the subaltern strain has not been entirely lacking in genocide studies. Hinton's analysis of the dynamics of the Cambodian violence provides a multifaceted portrait of subaltern energies unleashed with the authorization and direction of state authorities, and in the context of longstanding cultural traits that encouraged them. The title of Mahmood Mamdani's study of Rwanda, *When Victims Become Killers,* is as succinct a summary of the dynamics of subaltern genocide as exists in the literature, and represents the most explicit framing of a genocide's subaltern component anywhere in genocide studies. Arguably the most sustained exploration of genocides committed by subaltern actors, as expressions of revenge and millennial yearnings, is offered by the lead editor of this volume, Nicholas Robins, in his study of three Indian uprisings in the Americas: the Pueblo Revolt of 1680 in New Mexico, the Great Rebellion of 1780–82 in Peru and Upper Peru, and the Caste War of Yucatán of 1847–1900 in Mexico.[26] While separated in distance and in time, the rebellions were all millennially inspired, charismatically led subaltern movements in which the elimination of Hispanics and their culture was seen as the means of establishing a native utopia. In each case, the rebels were fighting a well-organized and generally better armed, if poorly disciplined, army. Furthermore, for the rebels, genocide was not an expression of state policy, but rather was aimed at establishing an independent state—which in the cases of New Mexico and Yucatán, it did. With the exception of New Mexico during the rebellion, what is also notable is the decentralization of leadership in Yucatán and Peru and Upper Peru, where it was highly fragmented, confederational, and anything but bureaucratic.

Reading beyond the literature that has a self-declared focus on genocide, a number of other sources provide notable insights. John Sack's provocative 2000 book *An Eye for an Eye* describes the often brutal actions of Jews, including former concentration-camp inmates, who were placed in positions of authority in detention facilities for officials and functionaries of the vanquished Nazi regime (see further in chapter 9).[27] Alfred-Maurice de Zayas's study *A Terrible Revenge* focuses upon the mass uprootings and systematic atrocities perpetrated against ethnic-German populations in the former Nazi-occupied territories of Central Europe.[28] The case is explored in detail in this volume by Eric Langenbacher.

Contributions from other literatures are cited and explored by the various scholars represented here. Before closing this section, however, it is important to mention the field that, at first glance, would seem to offer a rich wellspring of material: that of subaltern studies. As Mohammed Ayoob notes, "The dictionary definition of the term *subaltern* denotes those that are weak and of inferior rank"; first employed as a social-scientific concept by Antonio Gramsci, the field of subaltern studies drew as well on "the subaltern school of history, composed primarily of historians of India, that is engaged in studying the role of the less powerful elements—peasants, artisans, and so on—within societies, elements that form a majority within their societies but whose histories are ignored by elitist historiography of the traditional kind, which tends to focus on the activities of the powerful."[29] Another classic text of subaltern studies is Frantz Fanon's 1961 work, *The Wretched of the Earth*. Fanon, who was born in the French colony of Martinique, eloquently sketched the material and symbolic means by which colonial oppressors maintained the colonized in a state of subaltern oppression. Subaltern violence, in Fanon's scheme, was millennial in nature, "a cosmic force needed to cleanse the universe in order to achieve salvation," as Eric Wolf summarized it.[30] It was also a reaction against deeply ingrained psychologies of humiliation and subjugation—a means of throwing off the chains of oppression, and reclaiming dignity and autonomy. In his famous preface to Fanon's book, the French philosopher Jean-Paul Sartre summarized this vision of subaltern violence:

> The native cures himself of colonial neurosis by thrusting out the settler through force of arms. When his rage boils over, he rediscovers his lost innocence and he comes to know himself in that he himself creates his self. Far removed from his war, we consider it as a triumph of barbarism; but of its own volition it achieves, slowly but surely, the emancipation of the rebel, for bit by bit it destroys in him and around him the colonial gloom. Once begun, it is a war that gives no quarter.

You may fear or be feared; that is to say, abandon yourself to the disassociations of a sham existence or conquer your birthright of unity. When the peasant takes a gun in his hands, the old myths grow dim and the prohibitions are one by one forgotten. . . . The child of violence, at every moment he draws from it his humanity. We [colonizers] were men at his expense, he makes himself man at ours: a different man; of higher quality.[31]

Fanon's work provides exemplary insights into the psychology of subaltern violence. The field of subaltern studies that took its inspiration in part from Fanon, however, has focused far more extensively on the material and symbolic violence done to subaltern populations, and hardly at all on the violence committed by them. The former is a highly worthwhile inquiry, and has produced work that ranges from the valuable and memorable to the stilted and opaque. In general, it has contributed relatively little to the examination of the theory and praxis of subaltern revolt and violent retribution.

Challenges and Conundrums

One of the greatest difficulties in exploring subaltern genocide is differentiating between objective subaltern status and subjective perceptions of that status. The difficulty arises from the fact that genocidal perpetrators rarely perceive themselves in a position of unchallenged dominance. They usually feel—or claim to feel—vulnerable and under imminent threat of destruction. Paranoia, after all, is almost a universal feature among elites who inflict genocide. Even in the case of the Nazi Holocaust—the case that is often cited as exhibiting the "essential defenselessness" of victims in the starkest terms, and the widest possible power gap between killers and their victims—Nazi leaders apparently fervently believed that Jews constituted an all-powerful and all-pervading threat. In the summary of Raul Hilberg, the doyen of Holocaust studies:

The Jews were [seen as] inciters of revolt; that was why they had to be deported. . . . The Jews were the organizers of the partisan war, the "middlemen" between the Red Army and the partisan field command; that was why they could not be permitted to remain alive in partisan-threatened areas. The Jews were the saboteurs and assassins; that was why the army chose them as hostages in Russia, Serbia, and France. The Jews were plotting the destruction of Germany; and that was why they had to be destroyed. In Himmler's words: "We had the moral right vis-à-vis our people to annihilate this people which wanted to annihilate us." In the minds of the perpetrators, therefore, this theory could turn the destruction process into a kind of preventive war.[32]

It is a straightforward matter to dismiss this as fantasy, as demonstrated by the fact that the supposedly omnipotent Jews proved utterly unable to resist the Nazis' genocidal designs against them. We contend in this volume that subaltern status can usually be demonstrated *objectively*. It may be evident in some or all of the following: a longstanding and generally recognized history of political subordination and material under privilege; explicit measures of political and economic discrimination imposed upon subaltern populations; relative underprivilege with regard to life expectancy, financial wealth, housing, nutritional resources, educational resources, political representation, and other indices; statistical over-representation among incarcerated populations and victims of violence; and victimization by symbolic forms of discrimination and violence, in the form of hate propaganda and pervasive cultural stereotyping.

Reference to these measures helps us to navigate and better understand complex cases of genocide, for example those in Cambodia and Rwanda. In the first, we have seen that the most vociferous expressions of subaltern ideology were made by members of an educated elite (the Khmer Rouge leadership). However, the masses mobilized by such ideologies to participate in the genocide and serve as its foot soldiers—Cambodian peasants—*were* demonstrably underprivileged in the Cambodian social equation (not least, in this case, by the massive bombing campaign directed against their lives and livelihoods). Likewise, and somewhat more ambiguously, Hutu Power in Rwanda arose in a context in which Hutu ethnic dominance had been officially entrenched since 1959. Nonetheless, the post-1959 era unfolded against a backdrop of historical Tutsi dominance, which persisted in the form of cultural stereotypes of Tutsi physical, cultural, and material superiority, held by Hutus and Tutsis alike. Moreover, the crisis of 1993–94 arose in a context in which Tutsi soldiers and politicians were to be granted, under the Arusha peace accords, a place in the political and military order that far exceeded their statistical representation in the Rwandan population. Regardless of the merits of the peace agreement, there was clearly pro-Tutsi discrimination; widespread feelings of impending Hutu dispossession, even mass extermination, were not purely fantasy.

The issues become more clouded when we shift from the national to the local level. How, for example, do we view violence against "market-dominant minorities" (Amy Chua's term) in ethnically divided states? Groups as diverse as European Jews, ethnic Chinese in Southeast Asia, Indians in East Africa, Arabs in Latin America, and Koreans in U.S. inner cities have pursued entrepreneurial occupations that have won them a degree of economic privilege, but also increased their social vulnerability as visible minorities. Are the populations who act in a hostile fashion toward these minorities, and inflict violence in the form of pogroms or race-riots, actually subaltern agents lashing out against real oppressors? We suggest that while the agents of violence may well and rightly claim subaltern status, their vision of market-dominant minorities as oppressive elites is usually drastically misguided. In reality, such violence generally has two distinct sets of roots. First, it derives from feelings of envy mingled with fear at those who have achieved greater success—here, entrepreneurial success—than oneself. The sociologist Donald L. Horowitz, in his book *The Deadly Ethnic Riot*, has referred to subaltern populations' "recurrent fear of being swallowed by those who are more adept at manipulating the external environment," something that "points to the utter helplessness underpinning the violence of those who feel backward."[33] It does not, however, point to any objective relationship of exploitation or oppression between the two sets of actors. Such a relationship lies elsewhere, suggesting that such subaltern violence also has roots in "false consciousness," according to which vulnerable minorities who happen to be nearby, easily recognizable, and vulnerable are targeted as scapegoats. It is hardly surprising that the true agents of oppression may actively encourage subaltern populations to lash out against these scapegoats, as ruling authorities in Eastern Europe long promoted anti-Jewish pogroms and as Uganda's Idi Amin did against East Indians, as a means of deflecting the violent frustrations of the masses.

In some cases, the victims of such subaltern violence may share an ethnic identification with actors who *do* hold a disproportionate amount of economic or political power—as most of the big-business magnates under the Suharto regime of Indonesia, for example, were drawn from the ethnic Chinese minority. This serves as a further reminder that many victims of subaltern genocide are subsumed, by perpetrators' imputation, into a wider group identity—usually ethnically or religiously defined and stereotyped. Thus, for example, the representatives of previously Nazi-occupied populations who from 1945 to 1947 inflicted large-scale violence and dispossession on ethnic Germans selected their victims because of the ethnic attributes they shared with their former oppressors. No attempt was made to ascertain whether particular members of those populations had collaborated with the Nazi occupation forces; the collectivity was simply targeted en masse. Likewise, Tutsis in Rwanda were depicted as the fifth-column agents of the powerful Tutsi-led rebel forces based in Uganda. There is no evidence that Rwandan Tutsis were involved on a significant or even measurable scale with the rebel movement; but this was irrelevant to the purveyors of Hutu Power, and the subaltern masses who imbibed their hateful message.

Outline of This Volume

Despite the often memorable treatments referenced earlier in this chapter, the literature of genocide studies still lacks a broad-based comparative framing of subaltern genocide. The intention of *Genocides by the Oppressed* is to explore more deeply and systematically the nature and dynamics of subaltern genocide; to draw together a range of materials from the early modern, modern, and contemporary periods; to evaluate subaltern genocide as a psychological phenomenon, both in the context of humiliation studies and from an evolutionary-psychological perspective; and to explore the subaltern strain of the "genocidal continuum," Nancy Scheper-Hughes's term for more quotidian and institutionalized expressions of the genocidal impulse.

A recurring theme of the volume is symbolic expressions of subaltern violence. These are explored by Nicholas Robins in "Symbolism and Subalternity: The 1680 Pueblo Revolt of New Mexico and the 1780–82 Andean Great Rebellion." In the case of the Pueblo Revolt, the Indians of what is today New Mexico had experienced a demographic implosion of up to 90 percent between 1580 and 1680. While disease was a major cause, its effects were amplified by Hispanic exploitation, population dislocation, and a concerted and consistent effort by the colonizers to destroy the religious and cultural fabric of native society. After several abortive attempts, a long-planned and highly coordinated genocidal uprising in 1680 was successful in expelling the colonists from the region, and led to the return of native rule in the region for the next twelve years. One hundred years later, the Great Rebellion in the Andes had similar objectives, and although it was ultimately defeated, its regional scope, exterminatory objectives, and massive scale provided the largest single challenge to Spanish rule in the Americas prior to the wars of independence.

These insurgents left little in terms of a written record, save confessions extracted under force, and occasionally correspondence, drafted by scribes who were often rebel captives. It was in their actions, both physical and symbolic, that the rebels spoke both loudly and clearly. On the physical level, they systematically exterminated their enemies, both military and civilian, identifying them not only on the basis of race, but also of ethnicity. One's skin color, occupation, primary language, and religion served to identify victims as Hispanics, as did more mundane habits such as their style of dress and the foods they ate. Indeed, the manner of choosing victims in these and similar uprisings casts indigenous concepts of identity in sharp relief. The systematic nature of the killings, the deliberate targeting of noncombatants, and the selection of victims on racial and ethnic grounds underscore the genocidal nature of these insurgencies.

The symbolic discourse of the rebels corroborates the exterminatory nature of their enterprise, and underscores that it was as much of a physical, terrestrial conflict as one between perceived supernatural powers. Such expression was chosen from many alternatives, and was often directed at figures and symbols of colonial authority, both secular and religious. Generally, symbolic discourse involved the ridicule and humiliation of colonial officials prior to their execution, the inversion of colonial relationships, the systematic destruction of liturgical articles, and occasionally the superimposition of symbols. For example, in the Great Rebellion, the rebels often executed colonial officials at the *rollo,* a stone column which symbolized Spanish authority and also often served as a whipping post. To kill a colonial official there not only inverted previous relationships, but also underscored the "death" of colonial authority generally. Similarly, gathering the Hispanic victims of the rebellion and depositing them at the *rollo,* or placing decapitated heads upon the *rollo,* conveyed the same message. By examining the symbolic nature of rebel expression in these insurgencies, we can better fathom the depth of their objectives and corroborate the genocidal nature of these insurgencies. In so doing, it becomes clear that far from being inarticulate, many insurgents spoke clearly and cogently through their actions.

Chapter 2, "On the Genocidal Aspect of Certain Subaltern Uprisings: A Research Note," builds on Robins's analysis of subaltern genocide in the Andean and North American contexts, as well as the discussion of the Haitian, Cambodian, and Rwandan cases in this introduction. Adam Jones offers an illustrative, though hardly exhaustive, overview of subaltern-genocidal tendencies in slave rebellions such as Nat Turner's in the United States in 1831; anti-colonial uprisings, such as other Native revolts in the Americas, the Algerian uprising against French rule, and contemporary events in Tibet; and peasant rebellions and social revolutions in France, England, Algeria, and elsewhere. The aim is to supplement the empirical data presented elsewhere in the volume, further demonstrating that subaltern-genocidal ideologies and practices are evident at numerous and diverse points in the historical record.

The book then moves decisively to the record of the bloody twentieth century. Although distinct from genocide, ethnic cleansing is often its handmaiden. In "Ethical Cleansing? The Expulsion of Germans from Central and Eastern Europe," Eric Langenbacher examines the controversial case of the forced removal of ethnic Germans from Nazi-occupied European territories in the aftermath of World War II. In this process, Polish and Central European groups which had been relegated to subaltern status during the war engaged in a concerted and comprehensive effort to rid their territories of Germans and individuals of Germanic origin, most of whom were civilians.

Langenbacher begins by tracing the origins of Germanic people in Central and Eastern Europe, demonstrating that this group was both well established and for the most part integrated into their respective societies long before the twentieth century. Underscoring this is the fact that the Poland of 1919 had over 2 million Germans within its borders, although hundreds of thousands would subsequently emigrate as a result of the Polonization polices during the inter-war years. With the rise of Nazi Germany, however, Hitler sought to reverse this process by increasing the German population in Poland and elsewhere, at the expense of Poles and Czechs generally and Jews in particular. Indeed, by the early 1940s, over 1 million Poles had been displaced as a result of such policies.

With Germany's defeat, and the Red Army, looming on the horizon in 1944, the pendulum yet again began to swing the other way, and the "largest example of ethnic cleansing in world history" occurred, targeting some 12 to 15 million Germans and costing up to 2 million of them their lives. As most of the men in the region had long since joined the war effort, women, children, and the elderly bore the brunt. Although part of this exodus was undertaken to avoid the approaching Soviet army, the communists sought to spur the process through rapes and massacres, as depopulated areas were both easier to control and to retain. The Soviets were not the only ones pursuing ethnic cleansing, and numerous exile governments had longstanding plans to implement such policies. Even after the war, between 1946 and 1950, the exodus continued, although in a more orderly manner. Langenbacher emphasizes that the process was aimed not only at the expulsion of Germanic people, but at the "erasure" of German culture and its symbols in the region; both goals were achieved.

Having detailed the processes of expulsion, Langenbacher explores the ways in which postwar governments have viewed these events. Generally, the communist governments and intellectuals presented the issue as one of collective guilt borne by the German people: as a necessary and inevitable consequence of the war, or as a "settling of accounts," to be expected in such situations. This attitude began to change in the 1960s, led by churches in Poland and Germany, which sought to recognize the two-sided nature of the injustices committed. In communist Czechoslovakia, opposition groups in the 1970s saw the expulsion as a means of undermining the legitimacy of the communist government. Although the postcommunist era has witnessed a greater willingness to confront the realities of history, this process has not been without conflict, and empathy for the displaced Germans is often equated with minimizing Nazi horrors. Langenbacher concludes that the continued emphasis on collective guilt as a justification for the expulsions and the rejection of the idea of victimhood for those displaced civilians form the intellectual basis for this "ultimate example of ethical cleansing."

The important role of retribution in motivating and perpetrating subaltern genocide in Central Europe is also central to Alexander Laban Hinton's study of the Khmer Rouge in "Oppression and Vengeance in the Cambodian Genocide," drawn from his book *Why Did They Kill?* Framing his study with quotations by both victims and perpetrators, Hinton details how the Khmer Rouge harnessed rural resentment of more prosperous urban areas, and skillfully transformed it into a "burning rage" which could only be sated by disproportionate revenge against this group. Urbanites were not only seen as exploiters of the peasantry, but were further discredited by their embrace of foreign, Western, values. This is ironic, given that Pol Pot and much of the Khmer leadership were educated in Paris and their communist ideology was a European creation.

The "burning rage" against class enemies did not simply stem from economic exploitation, but was exacerbated by harking back to the era of the Angkor empire's splendor and regional dominance. This glorious history was set against the Cambodia of the 1970s, one that was under overwhelming foreign influence— a fact that was painfully brought home to many rural inhabitants by the massive bombings to which the United States subjected the country during the Vietnam War. A final ingredient was the millennial vision proffered by the Khmer Rouge, promising almost instant development and industrial progress through strict autarky, science, and social engineering. The future they were creating would, in their view, inevitably exceed even the glories of the past.

The road to this future was paved with disproportionate revenge. As Hinton notes, the goal was not "an eye for an eye," but rather "a head for an eye." Once ignited, this anger among the population could be directed at various targets, such as class enemies, political enemies, urbanites, and the international community. All of these factors intersected, as political power, wealth, and a foreign presence all converged in Phnom Penh, which was seen as a lair of corruption, decadence, and exploitation.

Having attained power, the Khmer Rouge initially focused their violence upon members and sympathizers of the Lon Nol regime, up to 200,000 of whom were systematically executed. The root-and-branch approach to social transformation did not stop there, however. By 1977, it had extended to the educated, professional, bureaucratic, and urban classes in general. Dispatched to the countryside, they became "new people," dehumanized slaves of the former underclass. Many who did not die as a result of their living conditions were later executed. As we saw in the Great Rebellion in the Andes, social inversion was often a prelude to death.

Hinton also explores the use of symbolism by the Khmer Rouge to advance their goals and reinforce their power. The red of their flag, to which the national anthem referred, was not so much communist in nature as symbolizing the blood red of violence and revenge. Images of blood informed many cultural expressions, such as songs and dances, and these merged "a number of powerful themes: existential threat, bodily and social disequilibrium, anger and rage, sorrow and loss, and violence against the enemy." Decapitation of one's enemies also had symbolic value, beyond that of "a head for an eye." In Cambodian culture, the head reflects both status, intelligence, and the ability to communicate. Decapitation, physically and symbolically, eliminated these attributes.

Just as the Khmer Rouge utilized the past to frame their concept of the future, the power of memory provided a strong impetus for the Serbian genocide in the Balkans. In "From Jasenovac to Srebrenica: Subaltern Genocide and the Serbs," David B. MacDonald traces the origins of Serb perceptions of victimhood and the role these played in fomenting and implementing the genocide against Croats and Moslems in the 1990s. This sense of victimhood, and the desire for revenge and legitimization of violence which it engendered, has its origins in the Battle of Kosovo in 1389, which resulted in Serbian defeat and ushered in nearly a half-millennium of Ottoman control. The enduring humiliation this produced was reinforced by significant losses in World War I.

The Second World War, however, provided a modern and incendiary referent for Serbian perceptions of oppression by non-Serbs, with the Jasenovac concentration camp complex serving as a real, and symbolic, ground zero for Serbian victimization. Here, between 1941 and 1945, under the Croatian fascist regime, thousands of Serbs, along with Gypsies, Jews, communists, and others deemed undesirable, were executed or died as a result of torture and atrocious conditions. MacDonald notes that a collective, multigenerational feeling of victimization resulted, providing important fodder for ultranationalist propaganda and calls for revenge. This ultimately exploded in the early 1990s, as Serbian forces sought to dominate Bosnia and Croatia through ethnic cleansing, gender-selective mass killing of males, sexual violence against females, and the widespread destruction of cultural symbols such as houses of worship.

In 1995, Serbian forces attacked the U.N. safe haven of Srebrenica. They first isolated it, then prohibited the delivery of supplies, and later attacked it directly. Upon entering the city, in the face of only tepid opposition by U.N. peacekeepers, the Serbs began systematically to round up and remove civilians. In this process, men of fighting age were separated and escapees were hunted down in surrounding hills. Ultimately, thousands of Bosnian Muslim men were executed and buried in mass graves. MacDonald notes that while Srebrenica was important from a military perspective, its capture also had an important symbolic value, as it was intended to be a Bosnian Moslem area under the Dayton Accords. Its fall to the Serbs would send a clear message to the Bosnian Muslims that their presence there, and in the region, was untenable. In the genocide trials that followed, the symbolic importance of the city to the Bosnian Muslims was recognized, raising the issue of people being killed not only because of their religion and ethnicity, but also their physical location—presenting something of a conundrum for students of genocide and international law.

MacDonald closes by examining Serbian scholarly perceptions of their history, and concludes that the pervasive lack of self-criticism bodes ill for the future. He notes a tendency to exaggerate the Serbian deaths at Jasenovac, a conspiratorial view that Croats and the Vatican are in league to destroy the Eastern Orthodox church, a general sense that other nations are anti-Serb, and the continuing resistance of many Serbs to recognize the scale of atrocities in Srebrenica. As a result, MacDonald concludes that it "is doubtful that Serbian nationalists will thus learn anything from history, save for those selective lessons they choose to interpret through a decidedly narrow nationalist lens."

Such selective perception is also evident in "Visions of the 'Oppressor' in Rwanda's Pre-Genocidal Media," in which Christopher Taylor explores the relationship between idealized, often colonially derived portrayals of Tutsi, and deeply rooted Hutu feelings of inferiority. Without minimizing the political and ethnic basis of the genocide, he emphasizes the often-overlooked role of words and images in spawning the genocide, and—most important—what they reveal about contradictions and ambiguities in Hutu identity, especially with regard to Tutsi women.

As free media emerged in Rwanda in the context of increasing democratization in the 1990s, political parties, and even factions within parties, began to publish their own newspapers and magazines. Not only did many publications espouse radical and racist ideologies, but they were affordably priced and often employed cartoons to engage less literate audiences. Such images dehumanized their Tutsi adversaries and revealed a Hutu identity that was significantly shaped by insecurity and envy as a result of prior Tutsi dominance. Despite their being the majority of the population and the post-1959 rulers of Rwanda, Taylor argues, the Hutu retained a distinctly subaltern identification, based on perceptions of oppression by Tutsi and inferiority toward them. This psychic oppression, he suggests, facilitated the genocide.

Taylor examines these dynamics with special attention to what they show about fears and desires concerning gender and sexuality. Such expressions became highly politicized—both describing widely held feelings among a group, and tacitly or otherwise calling for action to purge fears and achieve pragmatic ends and desires. Within this context, Taylor probes the symbolic significance of such actions as impaling, castration, and sexual violence. It is in this last category that the ambiguities of Hutu identity were most strikingly exemplified. Hutu propaganda urging fellow Hutu to shun Tutsi women reflected not only issues of racial purity, but socially ingrained perceptions dating from the colonial era that held Tutsi women to be more beautiful and desirable. Hutu propaganda consistently presented Tutsi women as harlots, prone to sexual deviance and to collaborating with foreigners as well as with the rebel Rwandan Patriotic Front. At another level, however, such propaganda sought to dissuade Hutu men from succumbing to the charms of Tutsi females. Taylor underscores this by pointing out that the first three injunctions of the "Hutu Ten Commandments" centered on this issue, with the emphasis on Hutu women's beauty serving precisely to reveal Hutu doubts on this score. As Taylor notes, "Such evidence of a lingering inferiority complex may partly account for the degree of sadism unleashed by Hutu death squads against Tutsi."

Feelings of inferiority and their manifestations are central to "Genocide, Humiliation, and Inferiority: An Interdisciplinary Perspective," in which physician and psychologist Evelin G. Lindner examines the complex and often paradoxical dynamics which link genocide and the humiliation of its victims. Humiliation, or "the enforced lowering of a person or group, a process of subjugation that damages or strips away their pride, honor or dignity," is not just about power. Rather, it often prompts perpetrators to seek revenge for past humiliations, perceived or otherwise. It may also represent an effort to cleanse fears of future subjection, or purge feelings of admiration for their victims.

Humiliation by its nature is multifaceted, incorporating both actions and emotions. People react differently to this process, although depression, anger, and a thirst for revenge are the principal responses. So strong are these feelings, and the fear of them, Lindner argues, that humiliation is "the nuclear bomb of the emotions," and one that can be readily exploited by leaders with genocidal objectives. From this perspective, Lindner explores the "dynamic of humiliation" and asks if "genocide is more about humiliation than about killing," suggesting that "perhaps killing is rather part of humiliation than vice versa." Lindner also challenges the idea of genocide as advancing the "rational self-interest of the perpetrators," noting that in most cases, the perpetrators' goals are not achieved and that those who sought to be the beneficiaries of genocide end up in a worse situation than before. The result could be termed a dialectic of humiliation, for while humiliation sets the stage and enables the genocidal dynamic, in the end it is often reasserted by the defeat of the genocidal enterprise.

Lindner situates her approach in the larger context of an emerging transition from traditional hierarchal societies, "grounded in ranked honor," to a global society which respects the equal and inherent dignity of each individual. As more people become aware of human rights, a process of conversion occurs, and a sense of relative deprivation sets in. As a result, established and exploitative hierarchies lose their legitimacy, and a gap emerges between people's actual station in life and the one they feel is due them. With this conversion, people may grow ashamed of their subservience. If it is left unmediated by leaders who espouse nonviolent methods, and is instead carried to a genocidal level by followers and leaders alike, subaltern groups do not simply eliminate their enemies; they also seek to purge their own feelings of humiliation by exterminating their oppressors, whether perceived or real. On this basis, Lindner suggests that ethnic cleansing designates more than the removal of another ethnic group: it reflects the perpetrator's desire to purge his or her own feelings of inferiority, even admiration, toward the victims. Within this context, Lindner emphasizes that leadership is a fulcrum in dealing with feelings of humiliation. Where a Nelson Mandela can constructively lead his people to a better life, an Adolf Hitler can perpetrate a holocaust.

The role of hierarchy is also a central theme of "Evolution, Primates, and Subaltern Genocide," where E. O. Smith places subaltern genocide within the larger context of evolutionary biology through probing the relationship between evolution, genocide from below, and primate behavior. Not only does such an approach broaden our understanding of the nature of intraspecific aggression, but it also has implications in terms of preventing genocidal events, subaltern and otherwise.

Smith establishes the context for his analysis by offering a review of evolutionary theory, beginning with a critique of the Standard Social Science Model and subsequently discussing natural selection, intraspecific competition, direct and indirect genetic fitness, and the various forces which alter genotypes over time. On this basis, he compares intraspecific killing among mammals, discussing infanticide as well as intra- and intergroup killing, and the role of coalition-building in these processes. In the case of intergroup killings among chimpanzees, such events are usually marked by coalitions among the perpetrators, who tend to attack when the risk to themselves is minimal. Further, while females may be among the aggressors, the coalitions are usually predominantly male, as are the victims. The extermination of entire groups, however, is very rare among chimpanzees, as attacks are not usually coordinated at a large group level, and violence tends to be more opportunistic than strategic. Furthermore, although there is evidence of retributive violence among chimpanzees, it is rare. Also relevant in this regard is the scale of violence, as humans, unlike chimpanzees, use weapons which increase the destructive impact.

Despite these differences, Smith emphasizes that environmental factors, especially constrained resources, are key in precipitating violence among primates in general, and as a result does not preclude the possibility of subaltern genocide among primates. Nevertheless, he concludes that "subaltern genocide among humans is an elaboration on a theme rather than something that is fundamentally distinct from chimpanzee behavior" and it appears that "humans *are* the only animal species in which oppressed groups seek to gain revenge and liberation by lethal aggression against their oppressors."

The volume closes with Adam Jones's chapter, "'When the Rabbit's Got the Gun': Subaltern Genocide and the Genocidal Continuum," which builds on Nancy Scheper-Hughes's concept of the "genocidal continuum" as a profusion of "small wars and invisible genocides" carried out in "normative, ordinary social spaces," especially institutional ones like nursing homes and jails. Scheper-Hughes considers her task "to draw connections, to make predictions, to sensitize people to *genocidal-like* practices and sentiments hidden within the perfectly acceptable and normative behavior of ordinary, good-enough citizens." These practices reflect the broader "genocidal *capacity*" of human beings to be swayed by "social sentiments of exclusion, dehumanization, depersonalization, pseudo-speciation, and reification which normalize and routinize behavior toward another or a class of others that would otherwise be seen as atrocious and unthinkable."[34]

Jones's chapter adopts a parallel rather than identical approach. It identifies a "continuum" of subaltern genocide ranging from more symbolic/performative expressions of subaltern anger and frustration, through situations where subaltern actors inflict atrocity in a context of localized and/or short-term hegemony, to fully fledged campaigns of subaltern genocide. Among the symbolic expressions held to be part of this "continuum" are carnival in its various forms and the "androcidal" tendency in some feminist manifestos and literary fantasies. Among the instances of atrocity examined, meanwhile, are the Jewish-led campaign of vengeance against Germans at the end and in the wake of World War II, whether in prison camp settings, vigilante killings, or conspiracies of massive retribution; the alleged genocide of Afrikaner farmers in the post-Apartheid era; and other expressions of localized subaltern hegemony, such as hate crimes and other violence against members of an "oppressor" class. It is considered that other chapters in the volume, together with this introduction, provide sufficient examples of fully fledged subaltern genocides to justify excluding these from the concluding chapter.

Jones closes with a consideration of the analytical and theoretical implications of the continuum of subaltern genocide. This section also serves as something of a conclusion for the volume as a whole. It emphasizes the broader relevance of the subaltern-genocide framework for comparative genocide studies, with regard to such subjects as millennialism and utopianism as genocidal ideologies, points of crossover between terrorism and genocide, and gender as a factor in genocidal outbreaks. As with the volume overall, the intent is partly to engage in a "plausibility probe" of the subaltern-genocide framework, and to encourage its further scholarly integration and exploration.

Notes

1. "Actuaciones anteriores ala formación de esta causa de Oruro," 6; "El Corregor. Dela Villa de Cochabamba sobre los destrozos que executaron los indios en Tapacari," 1, 3, 5–9.

2. "Relación de los hechos más notables," 170–71; "Actuaciones anteriores," 23; "Confesión de Josef Daga," 12; "Carta de Estiban Lidosa a Gerónimo Manuel de Ruedas," 24; "Confesión de Lázaro Mamani," 25; "Confesión de Sebastiana Mamani," 25.

3. On the messianic aspect of the Great Rebellion, see Valle de Siles, *Historia de la rebelión de Túpac Katari, 1781–82*; Valle de Siles, "Túpac Katari y la rebelión de 1781: Radiografía de un caudillo aymará," 633–64; Stern, *Resistance, Rebellion and Consciousness in the Andean Peasant World*; Szeminski, *La utopía Tupamarista*; Szeminski, "Why Kill a Spaniard?"; Juan Ossio, *Ideologia mesianica del mundo andino*.

By contrast with the Haitian slave rebellion and other instances of subaltern revolt, such as the Caste War in Mexico in 1846–47, the Spanish did not respond to the Great Rebellion with a no-holds-barred, genocidal race war. Instead, they used a multifaceted approach to quell the uprising. They offered a general amnesty in early 1781 to all participants who would turn in ringleaders and return to their homes. They also worked to establish alliances, often using the god-parentage ties with other Indian leaders, urging them to remain loyal to the government. As many of the leaders were direct beneficiaries of the colonial system, these strategies had considerable success. Overall, the colonial authorities recognized that the mass of participants needed to be kept alive, so that after a Spanish victory they could return to their traditional role as a labor force for the colonial authority.

This was followed, however—as it had been preceded—by the Spaniards' campaign of *ethnocide* (cultural genocide). The victors attempted to expunge all remnants of Inca heritage and consciousness. The position of *curaca*, or a local Indian chief, was eliminated, and all Incaic symbols were banned, such as royal clothing, paintings, and flags. While efforts to eliminate native languages had begun as early as 1774, they were now expanded and reinvigorated with the banning of Quechua. In addition, books and plays associated with the Inca past were proscribed, and Indian communities came under the more direct control of Spaniards.

4. Hochschild, *Bury the Chains*, 257.

5. Ibid., 293.

6. Dubois, *Avengers of the New World*, 298.

7. Girard, "Caribbean Genocide: Racial War in Haiti, 1802-4," 140.

8. For an overview of the Genocide Convention and scholarly definitions, see "The Origins of Genocide," chap. 1 in Jones, *Genocide: A Comprehensive Introduction*, 3–38.

9. Horowitz, *Taking Lives*, 21.

10. Porter, "Introduction: What Is Genocide," 14; Wallimann and Dobkowski, "Introduction," xvii–xxiv.

11. Dadrian, "A Typology of Genocide," 202. Emphasis added.

12. Chalk and Jonassohn, *The History and Sociology of Genocide*, 23.

13. Charny, "Toward a Generic Definition of Genocide," 91.

14. Dadrian, "A Typology of Genocide," 207; Fein, comments on "Genocide and Other State Murders in the Twentieth Century."

15. Harff and Gurr, "Toward Empirical Theory of Genocides and Politicides," 360.

16. John L. Thompson and Gail A. Quets, cited in Fein, "Defining Genocide as a Sociological Concept," 406.

17. Utilizing U.S. Strategic Bombing Survey data, Oxford University scholar Taylor Owen has shown that 2,756,941 tons of bombs were dropped on 115,262 targets in Cambodia, in 230,516 sorties between 1965 and 1973. This is "five times greater than believed and half of all that was dropped during the entire Indochinese campaign," which was in turn "the most intense episode of aerial bombardment in history." See Owen and Kiernan, "Bombs Over Cambodia."

18. Refugee testimony cited in Kiernan and Boua, *Peasants and Politics in Kampuchea, 1942–81*, 345–46.

19. Ngor, *A Cambodian Odyssey*, 202.

20. Vickery, *Cambodia 1975-1982*, 66, 286–87; Vickery himself echoes the depiction of Cambodia's urban population as "spoiled, pretentious, contentious, status-conscious at worst, or at best simply soft, intriguing, addicted to city comforts and despising peasant life" (26).

21. Becker, *When the War Was Over: Cambodia and the Khmer Rouge Revolution*, 137.

22. As Mahmood Mamdani points out, "Hutu Power" itself "had undertones of a subaltern ideology, similar to Black Power in the United States, Black Consciousness in South Africa, or Dalit Power in India." Mamdani, *When Victims Become Killers*, 269.

23. Ibid., 8, 185.

24. Prunier, *The Rwanda Crisis*, 231–32.

25. On the ritual dimension of the killing, see Taylor, *Sacrifice as Terror*. On the participation of Hutu women, see African Rights, *Rwanda: Not So Innocent*; Jones, "Gender and Genocide in Rwanda," 123.

26. Robins, *Native Insurgencies and the Genocidal Impulse in the Americas*.

27. Sack, *An Eye for an Eye.*
28. De Zayas, *A Terrible Revenge.*
29. Ayoob, "Subaltern Realism," 45.
30. Wolf, *Peasant Wars of the Twentieth Century*, 245–46.
31. Jean-Paul Sartre, preface to Fanon, *The Wretched of the Earth*, 21–22.
32. Hilberg, *The Destruction of the European Jews*, 3:1095. Emphasis added. Jeffrey Herf's recent book *The Jewish Enemy* leaves little doubt about the extent of Nazi belief in this chimera, which avoided the obvious logical counter: "If international Jewry had organized an effective anti-German political conspiracy, why had it been incapable of placing any effective deterrent in the way of Hitler's plans?" See Herf, *The Jewish Enemy*, 50.
33. Horowitz, *The Deadly Ethnic Riot*, 182.
34. Scheper-Hughes, "The Genocidal Continuum: Peace-Time Crimes," 32–34.

Works Cited

"Actuaciones anteriores ala formación de esta causa de Oruro." La Plata, February 22, 1781. Archivo General de Indias, Charcas 599.

African Rights. *Rwanda: Not So Innocent: When Women Become Killers.* London: African Rights, 1995.

Ayoob, Mohammed. "Subaltern Realism: International Relations Theory Meets the Third World." In *International Relations Theory and the Third World,* ed. Stephanie G. Neuman. New York: St. Martin's Press, 1998.

Becker, Elizabeth. *When the War Was Over: Cambodia and the Khmer Rouge Revolution.* New York: Public Affairs, 1998.

"Carta de Estiban Lidosa a Gerónimo Manuel de Ruedas." La Plata, April 9, 1781. AGI, Charcas 603.

Chalk, Frank, and Kurt Jonassohn. *The History and Sociology of Genocide.* New Haven: Yale University Press, 1991.

Charny, Israel. "Toward a Generic Definition of Genocide." In *Genocide: Conceptual and Historical Dimensions.* Ed. George Andreopoulos. Philadelphia: University of Pennsylvania Press, 1994.

"Confesión de Josef Daga." La Plata, April 25, 1781. In "Criminales contra Nicolás Catari y otros indios." AGI, Charcas 603.

"Confesión de Lázaro Mamani." La Plata, April 18, 1781. AGI, Charcas 603, p. 25.

"Confesión de Sebastiana Mamani." La Plata, April 18, 1781. AGI, Charcas 603.

Dadrian, Vahakn. "A Typology of Genocide." *International Review of Sociology* 5 (1975): 201–12.

Dubois, Lauren. *Avengers of the New World: The Story of the Haitian Revolution.* Cambridge, Mass.: Belknap Press of Harvard University Press, 2004.

"El Corregor. Dela Villa de Cochabamba sobre los destrozos que executaron los indios en Tapacari." Oropesa, March 7, 1781, Archivo y Biblioteca Nacionales de Bolivia, SGI.1781.62

Fein, Helen. "Defining Genocide as a Sociological Concept." In *The Holocaust: A Reader.* Ed. Simone Gigliotti and Berel Lang. London: Blackwell, 2005.

———. "Genocide and Other State Murders in the Twentieth Century." United States Holocaust Memorial Museum, October 24, 1995, http://www.ushmm.org/conscience/analysis/details.php?content=1995-10-24-02.

Girard, Philippe R. "Caribbean Genocide: Racial War in Haiti, 1802–4." *Patterns of Prejudice* 39, no. 2 (2005): 138–61.

Harff, Barbara, and Ted Gurr. "Toward an Empirical Theory of Genocides and Politicides: Identification and Measurement of Cases since 1945." *International Studies Quarterly* 32, no. 3 (1988): 139–64.

Herf, Jeffrey. *The Jewish Enemy: Nazi Propaganda during World War II and the Holocaust.* Cambridge, Mass.: Belknap Press of Harvard University Press, 2006.

Hilberg, Raul. *The Destruction of the European Jews.* 3rd ed. Vol. 3. New Haven: Yale University Press, 2003.

Hinton, Alexander Laban. *Why Did They Kill? Cambodia in the Shadow of Genocide.* Berkeley: University of California Press, 2005.

Hochschild, Adam. *Bury the Chains: Prophets and Rebels in the Fight to Free an Empire's Slaves.* Boston: Houghton Mifflin, 2005.

Horowitz, Donald L. *The Deadly Ethnic Riot.* Berkeley: University of California Press, 2001.

Horowitz, Irving Louis. *Taking Lives: Genocide and State Power.* New Brunswick, N.J.: Transaction Books, 1997.

Jones, Adam. "Gender and Genocide in Rwanda." In *Gendercide and Genocide,* ed. Adam Jones. Nashville: Vanderbilt University Press, 2004, 98–137.

———. *Genocide: A Comprehensive Introduction.* London: Routledge, 2006.

Juan Ossio. *Ideologia mesianica del mundo andino.* Lima: I. Prado Pastor, 1973.

Kiernan, Ben, and Chantal Boua. *Peasants and Politics in Kampuchea, 1942–81.* London: Zed Press, 1982.

Mamdani, Mahmood. *When Victims Become Killers: Colonialism, Nativism, and the Genocide in Rwanda.* Princeton: Princeton University Press, 2001.

Ngor, Haing, with Roger Warner, *A Cambodian Odyssey.* New York: Macmillan, 1987.

Owen, Taylor, and Ben Kiernan. "Bombs Over Cambodia." *The Walrus,* October 2006. http://www.walrusmagazine.com/articles/2006.10-history-bombing-cambodia.

Porter, Jack N. "Introduction: What Is Genocide: Notes Toward a Definition." In *Genocide and Human Rights: A Global Anthology,* ed. Jack N. Porter. Washington, D.C.: University Press of America, 1982.

Prunier, Gérard. *The Rwanda Crisis: History of a Genocide.* New York: Columbia University Press, 1997.

"Relación de los hechos más notables acaecidos en la sublevación general fraguada en los reynos del Perú, por el indio José Gabriel Túpac Amaru, gobr. del pueblo de Tungasuca en la Provincia de Tinta, que asociado de otros sequaces, causó horrosos estragos desde el año 1780, hasta el de 1782 en que se reprimo el orgullo de la conjuración." In *Revista de archivos y bibliotecas nacionales* 3, vol. 5. Lima, September 30, 1900, 141–298.

Robins, Nicholas A. *Native Insurgencies and the Genocidal Impulse in the Americas.* Bloomington: Indiana University Press, 2005.

Sack, John. *An Eye for an Eye: The Story of Jews Who Sought Revenge for the Holocaust.* 4th rev. ed. N.p., 2000.

Sartre, Jean-Paul. "Preface." In Frantz Fanon, *The Wretched of the Earth.* New York: Grove Press, 1967.

Scheper-Hughes, Nancy. "The Genocidal Continuum: Peace-Time Crimes." In Jeannette Mageo, ed., *Power and the Self.* Cambridge: Cambridge University Press, 2002.

Stern, Steve, ed. *Resistance, Rebellion and Consciousness in the Andean Peasant World, Eighteenth to Twentieth Centuries.* Madison: University of Wisconsin Press, 1987.

Szeminski, Jan. *La utopía Tupamarista.* Lima: Pontífica Universidad Católica del Perú, 1984.

———. "Why Kill A Spaniard? New Perspectives on Andean Insurrectionary Ideology in the 18th Century." In *Resistance, Rebellion and Consciousness in the Andean Peasant*

World, Eighteenth to Twentieth Centuries, ed. Steve Stern. Madison: University of Wisconsin Press, 1987.

Taylor, Christopher C. *Sacrifice as Terror: The Rwandan Genocide of 1994.* Oxford: Berg, 1999.

Valle de Siles, María Eugenia. *Historia de la rebelión de Túpac Katari, 1781–82.* La Paz: Editorial Don Bosco, 1990.

———. "Túpac Katari y la rebelión de 1781: Radiografía de un caudillo aymará." *Anuario de Estudios Americanos* 34 (1977): 633–64.

Vickery, Michael. *Cambodia 1975–1982.* Boston: South End Press, 1984.

Wallimann, Isidor, and Michael N. Dobkowski. "Introduction." In *Genocide and the Modern Age: Etiology and Case Studies of Mass Death,* ed. Isidor Wallimann and Michael N. Dobkowski. New York: Greenwood Press, 1987.

Wolf, Eric R. *Peasant Wars of the Twentieth Century.* New York: Harper Colophon, 1973.

Zayas, Alfred-Maurice de. *A Terrible Revenge: The Ethnic Cleansing of the East European Germans.* 2nd ed. London: Palgrave Macmillan, 2006.

1

Symbolism and Subalternity

The 1680 Pueblo Revolt of New Mexico and the 1780–82 Andean Great Rebellion

Nicholas A. Robins

The study of subaltern genocides in history poses special challenges. Sources are often quite limited and contra-dictory, especially in cases where the dominant group is successful in reestablishing authority. Nevertheless, primary sources may indicate that subaltern perpetrators of genocide speak not only directly through their actions, but also on a symbolic level. While such expression is not limited to subaltern groups, in these cases it reflects to some degree the relative importance of symbolic actions in the context of widespread illiteracy. As a result, symbolic expression provides a valuable window to an understanding of subaltern concepts of race, as well as the objectives and hopes which underpin them. Such expression in and of itself does not prove that genocide took place, but it is often valuable on a corroborative level. This essay examines two anti-colonial subaltern genocides that sought the elimination of Hispanics from the areas of present-day New Mexico in 1680 and Peru and Bolivia in 1780–1782.[1]

Understanding subaltern concepts of race and ethnicity is important, as these rebellions were complicated by the extensive participation of individuals of mixed parentage on both sides of the conflict. These include *Mestizos*[2] and, especially in New Mexico, *Lobos*[3] and *Coyotes*.[4] While ethnicity primarily reflects self-identification and expression, it can also be imputed by others. Apart from skin color, it was one's occupation, social status, place of residence, religious orientation, primary language, style of dress, and even eating habits that rebels often considered to determine whether a person was Indian or Hispanic. As a result, ethnicity and its associated cultural orientations resolved some of the ambiguities of mixed parentage. Among the leaders of the Pueblo Revolt were the *Coyotes* Francisco "El Ollita" and Nicolás Jonva of San Ildefonso, Alonso Catiti from Santo Domingo, and the Mulatto Domingo Naranjo from the pueblo of Santa Clara.[5] In the Great Rebellion, the Peruvian leader Túpac Amaru was a *Mestizo,* and in Upper Peru Túpac Catari was light-skinned by Indian standards.[6] Nevertheless, ethnically all these individuals, and large numbers of those whom they led, were Indians, and they fought for the rebirth of native ways. Reflecting the high degree of miscegenation (especially in the Andes) and the relatively few peninsular Spaniards in both regions, this chapter refers to Hispanics as an ethnic category subsuming those who maintained an Iberian cultural orientation, including Spaniards, Creoles, and often *Mestizos* and others of diverse descent.

The 1680 Revolt of the Pueblos in New Mexico

Having endured decades of disease, exploitation, and death at Hispanic hands, the inhabitants of the Pueblo region rebelled during the nighttime hours of August 10, 1680.[7] In a long-planned and highly coordinated assault, they sought to exterminate the Hispanic colonists in the region in a single blow. Most victims were killed on sight, although some women were taken as captives. Those able to escape fled to Santa Fe, the district seat, where they joined others who had fortified themselves in the governor's compound. They quickly found themselves besieged by seemingly endless multitudes of Indians, and they grew more desperate as the rebels diverted their water supply and set most of the town ablaze. Running out of options and time, Governor Antonio Otermín led a surprise attack on the Indians, which inflicted sufficient damage to provide them with an opportunity to escape southward toward the Rio Grande. There they joined up with other refugees from the region and were able to determine that, of about 2,000 settlers in the region, 401 had perished. Of these, 306 were women and children. Beyond the human toll, the insurgents had razed thirty-four villages, as well as numerous ranches and agricultural estates. It would be twelve years before the Spanish would reassert control in the area, and during this time the Indians would rule themselves.

One hundred years later, a much larger uprising would sweep through the Andes before ultimately being suffocated by the Hispanics and their allies. Due to its scale, severity, and location in silver-producing areas, the Great Rebellion of Peru and Upper Peru (present-day Bolivia) in 1780–82 constituted the most serious threat to Spanish rule in the Americas prior to the wars of independence. The rebellion first broke out in the Upper Peruvian province of Chayanta and was led by Tomás Catari, a hereditary chief who had been prevented from taking office. After his death, his brothers Dámaso and Nicolás presided over the increasing radicalization of the insurgency. Targeting those of lighter skin and Hispanic orientation, they sought an end to colonial rule and the abolition of forced labor and purchases, religious fees, and civil taxes. In the region of Cuzco in present-day Peru, the insurgency was headed by José Gabriel Túpac Amaru, the hereditary leader of the town of Tungasuca. Throughout the region, towns were attacked and looted and non-Indians systematically killed. Following a short and unsuccessful siege of Cuzco, the former Inca capital, in January 1781, Túpac Amaru and his allies were unable to regain the initiative and were ultimately defeated. The city of La Paz suffered a much more severe siege between March and October 1781, led by Túpac Catari. About one-third of the city's population, or 10,000 people, died before the uprising was finally suppressed in early 1782.[9]

The Pueblo Revolt and the Great Rebellion as Subaltern Genocides

The Pueblo Revolt

Both the Pueblo Revolt and the Great Rebellion were exterminatory efforts to escape Hispanic oppression and reclaim native culture, governance, religion, and lands. As well, both were themselves responses to genocides. Not only did the Spanish conquest result in a demographic collapse exceeding ninety percent in many places, but groups that resisted Spanish dominion were subject to genocidal attacks, with any survivors enslaved. Further, the imposition of Catholicism was based on forced conversions and deliberate and systematic extirpation campaigns against native rites. These resulted in the mass destruction of religious shrines and artifacts, and the torture and death of native religious leaders. Beyond this, miscegenation and forced marriages affected native abilities to procreate, and various forms of forced labor and land seizures deprived natives of their livelihoods and often their lives as well.[10]

The effects of the demographic collapse were catastrophic in the Pueblo region. The population plummeted from about 130,000 in 1581 to approximately 15,000 in 1678.[11] Most Indians there and elsewhere perished from diseases brought by the Spanish to which they had no immunity, and also from overwork and suicide. The campaign of subaltern genocide such conditions precipitated was carefully planned and intended as the means to achieve a nativistic, millennial, and utopian social vision.[12]

While perpetrators and victims of genocide generally offer divergent views concerning the objectives of a conflict, this was not the case with either the Pueblo Revolt or the Great Rebellion. A few days before the Pueblo uprising, the Pecos chief Juan Ye reported to the Hispanics that a conspiracy was well underway to "to kill all the Spaniards and religious."[13] When it erupted, a native messenger from the town of Tesuque arrived on August 10 in San Diego de Jemez, convoking the inhabitants to "kill the Spaniards and friars who are here," and insisting that as a result of the rebellion "none of the Spaniards will remain alive" there or elsewhere in the area.[14]

Just before the rebels arrived at the outskirts of Santa Fe, two loyal Indians whom the governor had sent to reconnoiter the Keres and Tano regions hastened back to report that scores of Indians were "on the way to attack it and destroy the governor and all the Spaniards," adding that they planned to "sack the said villa all together and kill within it the señor governor and captain-general, the religious, and all the citizens."[15] An Indian captured during the Hispanic exodus south testified that rebels from Tesuque had told those in San Cristóbal that the "Indians want to kill the Custodian, the Fathers and the Spaniards, and have said that whoever kills a Spaniard shall have an Indian woman as wife, and whoever kills four shall have as many wives, and those killing ten or more shall have as many wives. They have said that they will kill all the servants of the Spaniards and those who talk Castilian, and have ordered everyone to burn their rosaries."[16]

During an armed foray, or entrada, back to the region in 1681, the Hispanics interrogated several Indians concerning the revolt. One, a Tano, stated that the leader of the rebellion, Popé, had "given them to understand that the father of all the Indians, their great captain . . . had ordered the said Popé to tell all the pueblos to rebel and . . . that no religious or no Spanish person must remain."[17] Similarly, the elderly Indian Pedro Ganboa stated that he "has heard . . . that the Indians do not want religious or Spaniards" and in attacking Santa Fe they sought to "destroy the governor . . . and all the people who were with him."[18]

Twelve years later, in September 1692, when Governor Vargas arrived in Santa Fe, the Indians from Galisteo who had taken over the town assured him that "they were ready to fight for five days, [and that] they had to kill us all, we must not flee as we had the first time, and they had to take everybody's life."[19] As he continued in his efforts to pacify the area in 1693, the natives at Ciéneguilla defiantly told Vargas that they "would fight . . . until they left us all dead, once and for all."[20]

The Great Rebellion

Much like the Pueblo Revolt, the objectives of the Great Rebellion—Indian independence and freedom from Hispanic oppression—were in the eyes of many rebels incompatible with the continued presence of most Hispanics in the region. At the time of the outbreak of the rebellion in Chayanta and the surrounding provinces in August 1780, much of the violence was initially directed at local village leaders. Quite often these individuals were *Mestizos* whom the Spanish authorities had appointed on the basis of pliability. Often they had no organic connection to the communities they held sway over, and, in concert with the district governor, systematically exploited their subjects.[21] Why some curacas were killed and others not appears related to the degree to which they were assimilated into the Hispanic system of exploitation and society, and conversely, the degree to which they represented community interests.

Ethnicity and its attributes were often as important as race in determining who became a target of the rebels. Similarly, occupations and social status were associated with Hispanic identity, and people were targeted if they dressed in the Hispanic style or could not speak Aymará or Quechua. Likewise, Túpac Catari in La Paz and Tomás Callisaya in Tiquina decreed death to anyone who ate bread, used fountains for water, did not speak Aymará, or did not wear native clothes.[22] During the rebel siege of Oruro, largely led by the Indian Santos Mamani, the insurgents expressed their intention to kill all non-Indians there, including women, the young, and priests.[23] Throughout Peru and Upper Peru, thousands of Hispanic noncombatants were killed.[24] Rampant conscription led to many Mestizos and Indians involuntarily becoming involved in both sides of the rebellion, and in the case of the former, many probably joined out of fear of being considered Hispanic by other rebels.[25]

In Upper Peru, by September 1781, rebel aggression increasingly targeted Spaniards, Creoles, and others of light skin color, in addition to Mestizos. One contemporary was of the belief that Túpac Amaru had ordered the rebels in Upper Peru and elsewhere to kill "as many Spaniards and Mestizos as they could get their hands on."[26] In October 1780, in the town of Paria, the governor Manuel de Bodega, who would become a victim of rebel wrath a couple of months later, wrote that the insurgents were killing "any Spaniard and *cholo*[27] that they find in the towns . . . so that there will be no person to subject them."[28]

Following the death of Tomás Catari and the ensuing radicalization of the rebellion, some insurgents stated that Dámaso and Nicolás Catari ordered the rebels to "finish off with all those who were not Indians and with those who opposed" them.[29] In Arque, unaware of the breakdown of Creole-Indian relations in Oruro, a Creole desperately wrote to the Creole rebel Jacinto Rodríguez inquiring if "it was true that he had given orders that the Indians kill all whites without distinction" between Creoles and Spaniards.[30] In the village of Tolapampa, in the province of Porco, an order attributed to Nicolás Catari ordered rebels to "kill all the *corregidors*,[31] priests, miners, Spaniards, and *Mestizos*."[32]

The views of Sebastián de Segurola, who headed the defense of besieged La Paz, evolved as the insurgency progressed. He stated his belief that Túpac Catari wanted "not just to kill the corregidors and Europeans, as I thought at the beginning, but rather all those who were not legitimately Indians."[33] The cleric Matías de la Borda, who was held prisoner by Túpac Catari, believed that the Aymará rebel sought the "total extermination of the Spanish people, both patrician and European, and of the[ir] life, customs and Religion."[34] Similarly, Father Josef de Uriate, who was held prisoner by the insurgents in the region of Sicasica, wrote that they intended to "pass under the knife the Spaniards and *Mestizos* without sparing the priests, women nor children, and [to] extinguish the cattle and seeds of Spain."[35]

Apart from their actions, the confessions and statements of captive rebels indicate that the preceding cannot simply be attributed to Hispanic hyperbole. During the siege of La Paz, Túpac Catari called upon the defenders to surrender "all of the corregidors . . . Europeans . . . priests and their assistants, the royal officials, the customs tax collectors, hacendados and firearms."[36] In another letter he commanded "that all the Creoles die," and stated that he intended to "finish off everyone with the objective that there will not be *Mestizos*."[37] His sister Gregoria Apasa, who was also a rebel, stated in her confession that the insurgents would "take the lives of the whites whenever they had the opportunity."[38] The rebel Josefa Anaya also confessed that the insurgents initially planned to "kill the corregidors, the Europeans and bad Creoles, although in reality they always killed everyone they found" who was Hispanic.[39]

Similarly, the insurgent Diego Quispe stated that rebels sought to "kill absolutely all the whites without distinction" between Spaniard and Creole.[40] Also in the region of La Paz, Diego Estaca confessed that "the principal objective of the uprising was to get rid of all of the white people," while not far away in Tiquina, Tomás Callisaya ordered "that all corregidors, their ministers, caciques, collectors, and other dependents be passed by the knife, as well as all the chapetones,[41] Creoles, women, and children, without exception of sex or age, and all persons who are or look Spanish, or at the least is dressed in the imitation of such Spanish."[42] Many of the insurgents who prosecuted the siege of La Paz had earlier rebelled in the southern provinces, and consequently the events there are indicative of the goals of rebels from diverse regions.[43] Likewise, the rebel Ascensio Taquichiro testified that in Challacollo he hoped to "burn the town and kill the inhabitants without leaving one alive who was not an Indian."[44]

Symbolism and Subaltern Genocide

Apart from confessions, usually extracted under force, and occasionally some correspondence, most insurgents in these conflicts left no written record concerning their inspiration and objectives. Although most were illiterate, many were also quite articulate and expressed themselves cogently through the symbolic content of their actions. These serve to corroborate the exterminatory nature of their endeavor. Claude Levi-Strauss argued that people "communicate by means of symbols and signs. For anthropology . . . all things are symbol and sign which act as intermediaries between two subjects," and that symbols are chosen from many alternatives of expression.[45] The deliberate choosing of one form of expression over another is key to understanding the relationship between rebel actions and symbolic expression. The symbolic content of these actions was often pronounced in the manner in which they selected, treated, and killed their victims, and in what they did with their property.

In both rebellions, we find a tendency among the rebels to invert the previous order, often humiliating their victims in the process, and to superimpose symbols, especially religious ones. As Evelin G. Lindner notes in her chapter in this volume, the humiliation of enemies is often a means for perpetrators to purge themselves of their own feelings of inferiority. This can happen both at a personal and physical level, and also at a supernatural level, where the contest, and focus of humiliation, revolves around perceived supernatural powers. Not only had the indigenes been humiliated and oppressed by their overlords, but so had their deities. Within this context, attacks on religious symbols reveal not only objectives, but causes.

In Peru and Upper Peru, rebel symbolic discourse could have a simple eloquence, such as when Andrés Túpac Amaru mandated that when rebels found medallions adorned with an image of Charles III, given to loyal village leaders, the medals should be hanged from a gallows.[46] The message was clear: the period of Spanish rule had ended, and the lives of those who defended it would shortly end too. Symbolic expression could be even more direct. For example, when the rebels attacked district governor Joaquín Alós and his escort in August 1780, they cut off the hand of his scribe, Mateo Tellez, and chopped out the tongue of Alós's advisor, Josef Benavides, before killing both men.[47] A priest suffered a similar fate in the village of Colcha. After capturing but before executing him, the rebels cut out his tongue, physically and symbolically preventing him from preaching.[48]

All these victims were physically and symbolically denied the ability to perform their colonial role.

The manner in which people were usually executed in the Great Rebellion, through beheading, also highlighted the genocidal element of the uprising. By decapitating their enemies, the insurgents communicated a conviction that these victims would never be reincarnated.[49] In their view, to kill by other means, or to bury victims prematurely, ran the risk that their enemies could one day return. Beheading had other uses as well, as very often victim's heads were taken to Túpac Amaru and other leaders, thereby symbolically demonstrating their fealty to the leader.[50] In Palca, Upper Peru, the insurgents executed over four hundred men, women, and children, leaving "some on top of the others . . . [and] many in a shameless position."[51] This again suggests a symbolic content to the manner of execution and its aftermath. Mutilation appears to have been widespread in both of the rebellions under study here, and while it has inherent symbolic content, it is not always clear how it was done or what the roles of the victims were in colonial society.[52]

Symbolic expressions of Indian power in both regions under study were often but not exclusively related to Catholicism and involved the inversion of traditional relationships and the humiliation or ridicule of clerics. The attacks on churches often were the result of people taking refuge in what was generally the strongest buildings in town, and hence best suited to withstand a rebel assault. The tactical considerations which led to its use as a shield, both literally and figuratively, also led to churches becoming a rich backdrop for symbolic theater. The assaults on Catholic symbols in both New Mexico and in the Andes also reflected the fact that many rebels saw the conflict as a contest between humiliated yet reascendant native gods and the alien deity which had oppressed them.

In New Mexico, even before the 1680 rebellion, attacks on clerics often had a symbolic element. When the inhabitants of Zuni rebelled in 1632, they not only killed Friar Francisco Letrado but highlighted their newfound power by scalping him.[53] In the early 1670s, when Apaches attacked the pueblo of Abó, they burned the monastery and killed Friar Pedro de Ayala after "stripping him of his clothing, putting a rope around his neck, flogging him most cruelly, and finally killing him with blows of the macana;[54] after he was dead they surrounded the body with dead white lambs, and covered the privy parts, leaving him in this way."[55] The burning of the mission was a rather blunt symbolic act: by stripping the friars, the Indians were stripping them of their power, and by placing dead lambs around his body the Apaches may have been issuing a warning that a similar fate awaited his flock. In the 1680 revolt, the rebels also used physical abuse and humiliation to express both their hatred of and dominance over their enemies. For example, in Jemez, after capturing Friar Jesus Morador in his bed, the rebels stripped him of his clothes, bound him on the back of a pig, and paraded him through the pueblo as he was attacked by the natives. Later, at least one rebel rode and spurred him like a horse before finally killing him.[56]

The rebels in New Mexico attacked not only priests, but symbols of Catholicism generally. During the entrada into the Pueblo region in 1681, as the Hispanics entered Senecú in early November, they encountered "the holy temple and convent burned," and in the sacristy they found the "hair and crown from a crucifix, thrown on the ground," along with a broken altar. In the cemetery, they found a bell with its clapper removed, in addition to a bronze cannon and a cross which had earlier been in the plaza.[57] Governor Otermín was of the belief that the town had been attacked by Apaches. Whether the assailants were Apache or Pueblo, by scalping an image of Christ and breaking an altar, they were communicating the destruction of Hispanic and Catholic power and demonstrating the resurgence of native power.

During the same *entrada,* on December 17, 1681, as Governor Otermín led his forces into Sandía, he found the symbols of Catholic authority literally in pieces. "The church and convent [were] entirely . . . demolished"; there were "two broken bells, in five pieces," in addition to a "small broken crown." In one building, they encountered "the image of the Immaculate Conception of Our Lady with a dragon at her feet, which work had served as an altar piece for the main altar of the said church, . . . the divine eyes and mouth of the figure were ruined, and . . . there were signs on the other parts of the body of it having been stoned, while the accursed figure at her feet was whole and unspoiled." These were clearly deliberate actions, symbolically muting, blinding, and humiliating Catholic power.

The desire to invert previous relationships was also demonstrated in December 1693, as Governor Vargas was preparing to assault Santa Fe and finalize the Hispanic reconquest of the region. The Indians occupying the town defiantly asserted that they were going to kill all the Hispanics, except for some friars. They shouted that "the friars will for a short time be our servants; we will make them carry firewood and bring it from the woods, and after they have served us, we will kill all of them."[58] They sought to further invert the colonial social order when they asserted that they were "going to kill . . . [the Hispanics] and make slaves of their women and children."[59] This was probably no bluff, as they had done precisely this with numerous Hispanic women captured in 1680.[60]

In the Andean case, two-and-a-half centuries of colonialism produced greater diversity among the rebels concerning their views of Christianity. While it does appear that many insurgents were apostates or never believed in the first place, others appear to have sought to reformulate Catholicism to serve rather than exploit them. Whatever their position, most appear to have believed, as in New Mexico, that the Christian god possessed power; the question was how much and for whose benefit it was expressed. In rebel eyes, the rebellion itself showed the faltering power of the Spanish god to defend the Hispanics, and as the insurgency became radicalized in early 1781, the rebels increasingly ignored the tradition of church sanctuary. Time and again, in the Pueblo Revolts and the Great Rebellion, the rebels overran churches if those inside did not surrender and come out to face an almost certain death.[61] In the Great Rebellion, many clerics died in Tapacari, San Pedro de Buenavista, Oruro, Poopó, Aymaia, Songo, Chucuito, El Alto, and other towns in Peru and Upper Peru.[62]

The humiliation and killing of clerics was a means of inverting relationships and of expressing physical and perceived supernatural powers. During the Great

Rebellion, in Pintatora, the insurgents "made fun" of the assistant priest when he tried to pacify the rebels by displaying a crucifix, while in Sacaca the rebels abused the assistant priest and made him wear a crown of thorns.[63] In Oruro one rebel called out that the Christ of Burgos was "only a piece of" wood, and in Palca another shouted that the host was nothing more than bread.[64] Dancing over corpses, such as was done in Oruro and Tapacari, was another means of ridicule.[65]

Stripping victims of the Great Rebellion was a common method of humiliation which also served to highlight the inversion of traditional power and social relationships. In Challapata, after killing the corregidor, the rebels acceded to the pleas of the village priest to spare the armed escort which had accompanied him, but only after they had been stripped of both their clothing and valuables. In February 1781, in Yura and Anasayas, the rebels stripped clerics of their vestments.[66] When the Indians took Oruro, they stripped a colonial official of his clothing in the Convent of Santo Domingo.[67] Humiliation and inversion were not the only reasons for stripping people, as the Andean Indians equated poverty and nakedness. Stripping their victims brought them to the level of poverty that the Indians knew all too well. In Aymaia, as a band of rebels beat Father Dionicio Cortés to death, one Indian shouted "Priest! Thief! It is because of you that we are naked."[68]

As the insurgency swept through Upper Peru, to underscore native dominance the rebels consistently demanded that all people use native clothing exclusively, speak native languages, and otherwise adopt indigenous customs such as chewing coca leaves.[69] This was quite dramatic in Oruro as the Creole-Indian alliance quickly evaporated, and the insurgents commanded that everyone dress in the native manner, chew coca, and speak Aymara.[70] In Tapacari and Sorata, the rebels spared Hispanic women and made them dress in the Indian manner.[71] The value of adopting native ways was demonstrated by many who failed to do so.[72] In the village of Sicasica the rebels executed "those of their nation who used shirts and were not immediately moving to their dress."[73] Just to the north in the La Paz region and in Tiquina, Túpac Catari and Tomás Callisaya, respectively, ordered the execution of anyone who did not speak Aymará or dress in the native fashion.[74]

The Andean rebels expressed their desire to invert social relationships by other means. For example, when the rebel leader Simón Castillo briefly occupied San Pedro de Buenavista on Christmas Day in 1780, he commanded that all Spaniards leave the town within eight days or "be sent to the mines of Potosí."[75] When the insurgents overran Carangas, they pilloried a treasury official before executing him, while in Chocaya the rebels imprisoned the Spaniard Gerónimo Alquisalete before his execution.[76]

As in New Mexico, sparing Hispanic women so that they could be slaves to the rebels was another way of inverting previous relationships. Not only were women enslaved, but because they were considered chattel in Hispanic society, the insurgents were further stripping Hispanic men of what was considered their property by claiming it as their own. The documents offer few details concerning the experiences of these captives, but we do know that in Upper Peru such servitude was brief for many Hispanic women; often they were soon executed, as happened or was planned in Tapacari, San Pedro de Buenavista, Palca, Lipes, Sicasica, and La Paz.[77] In Chocaya, under the threat of death, the widowed Hispanic women left their hiding places and knelt and kissed the feet and hands of the rebel leaders prior to their rescue by Hispanic forces.[78] Many contemporaries were loath to mention sexual assault, instead noting that many women were victims of "outrages which the pen is horrified to repeat," or an act that "scandalizes the ears" or "horrifies the tongue to" hear or say.[79]

Inversion and assimilation are further shown by the frequency with which insurgents in the Great Rebellion sought the silver of their victims. By taking it and other useful items, the insurgents highlighted the inversion of what they believed would soon be the old order. In El Alto, San Pedro de Buenavista, and elsewhere, Indians drank chicha, a native fermented corn drink, from silver chalices, and adorned monstrances with coca leaves, inverting spiritual relationships while seeking to appropriate whatever vestigial power the Christian god retained.[80]

As in New Mexico, the rebels would often simply destroy items associated with the Catholic church. During the Indian occupation of Oruro, they destroyed numerous statues and other items as they sacked churches and hunted down Hispanics. Subsequently, when they laid siege to the town, they stated their intent to cut "off the head of the image of Our Lady of Rosario" upon their hoped-for victory, thus helping to ensure the permanent demise of Catholic power.[81] In San Pedro de Buenavista, having looted the jewels and silver from the church, they stripped the clothes off the images of Mary and Jesus before destroying them and the monstrance.[82] After the slaughter in Tapacari, the insurgents cast off the crowns from the statues of Mary and Jesus before flames consumed these and other images in the plaza.[83] All such actions symbolically communicated that the long-awaited demise of both the Hispanics and the supernatural powers that had supported them was at hand.

Symbolic Superimposition

The insurgents in these rebellions not only used symbols for expression, but sought to superimpose them. For example, during the Pueblo Revolt in Santo Domingo the friars Juan de Talaban, Antonio de Lorenzana, and Joseph Montes de Oca were taken to the church, where they were killed and their bodies heaped upon the altar.[84] Placing the corpses there communicated the death of Hispanic spiritual and temporal dominance, and the rebels superimposed the offering of Hispanic and religious blood in the place where the symbolic blood of Christ was ritually offered. A similar event occurred in the village of Tapacari in Upper Peru, where people were also executed and deposited on the altar.[85]

In Senecú, in New Mexico, when the Hispanics returned during the 1681 *entrada,* they found a bell separated from its clapper in a cemetery. The bell had for decades summoned the natives for worship or work at the mission, and by severing the clapper the rebels symbolically castrated Spanish authority. Placing the bell in the cemetery, along with a cross and cannon, underscored their belief that Catholicism, and Spanish military power, were finished. During the same *entrada,* the Hispanics also found bells with the clappers removed in Socorro and Alamillo, as did Governor Vargas in November 1692 in the Zuni region.[86]

Symbolic implosion, sometimes involving superimposition, was a recurring theme among the rebels in the Great Rebellion. For example, in January 1781, when the rebels attacked and then killed Corregidor Bodega in Challapata, the rebels did not kill their quarry on sight, but instead caught and shuffled him to the rollo.[87] There, the insurgents ordered his slave, whom they had already captured, to behead him.[88] In Juli, on the shores of Lake Titicaca, the rebels also tied the curaca Fermín Llagua to the rollo and decapitated him, subsequently placing his head at his feet. His colleague, the curaca Rafael Paca, met a similar fate, with his head placed on the top of the rollo.[89]

The corregidor, curaca, and rollo all symbolized Spanish authority and oppression, and symbolically all were easily superimposed. Deliberately decapitating a Hispanic official at the rollo communicated the decapitation of Spanish power. In Bodega's case, not only was Hispanic power destroyed, figuratively and literally, but the rebels choreographed the event so that Bodega was killed literally by his own property, a slave. On both the symbolic and literal levels, Spanish authority was being destroyed by Hispanic property. None of these acts was arbitrary; all were crafted amidst what must have been some degree of turmoil.

The Pueblo Revolt and the Great Rebellion are cases of subaltern genocide in which oppressed people and victims of genocide sought the extermination of their overlords and almost the entirety of the dominant culture in their respective regions. Ethnicity played a central role in determining who was targeted. In addition to skin tone, people were often marked for death for their language, dress, occupation, or religion. Apart from the actions of the insurgents in the field, which were consistently directed toward killing those seen as Hispanic or allied with them, rebel statements underscored the genocidal nature of these insurgencies. The depth of the changes envisioned by the rebels, involving the excising of Hispanic blood and heritage, is further corroborated by the symbolic language of many rebels. Such actions as killing people on the altar, executing people at or dragging bodies to the rollo, hammering away to separate clappers from bells, abusing Catholic images, and forcing slaves to kill their masters all indicate that such actions were not random but well crafted and deliberate. The common people may not have left much in the way of a written record, but they were highly articulate and have left a rich record of their views and objectives.

Abbreviations

ABNB	Archivo y Biblioteca Nacionales de Bolivia, Sucre, Bolivia, Sublevación General de Indios
AGI	Archivo General de Indias, Seville, Spain. Buenos Aires 320 Charcas 437-b, 444, 594, 595, 596, 599, 601, 603.

Notes

1. For a discussion of sources on these rebellions, see Robins, *Native Insurgencies*, 9–10.
2. A person of Indian and Iberian descent.
3. A person of Indian and Negro descent.
4. A person of Indian and Mestizo descent.
5. Hackett, "The Revolt of the Pueblo Indians of New Mexico in 1680," 142–43; Knault, *The Pueblo Revolt of 1680*, 117, 168–69; Bancroft, *The Works of Hubert Howe Bancroft*, vol. 17, *History of Arizona and New Mexico*, 175–76.
6. "Copias de documentos citados en el diario," no. 18, 23; Fisher, *The Last Inca Revolt*, 25; O'Phelan, *Rebellions and Revolts in Eighteenth Century Peru and Upper Peru*, 253; Rowe, "El movimiento nacional Inca del siglo XVIII," 32, 38.
7. For detailed treatments of the course of these rebellions, see Robins, *Native Insurgencies*, 23–50.
8. Ibid., 30–34.
9. Ibid., 38–50.
10. Cook, *Born to Die*, 206; Smith, "Depopulation of the Central Andes in the 16th Century," 459; Cook and Borah, *Essays in Population History: Mexico and California*, vol. 3, 1; Pierre Duviols, *La destrucción de las religiones andinas (Conquista y colonia)* (Mexico City: UNAM, 1977), 9, 249–59, 373–77, 423–24; Robins, *Priest-Indian Conflict in Upper Peru*), 48.
11. Knault, *The Pueblo Revolt of 1680*, 153–55.
12. "Testimony of Juan Lorenzo and Francisco Lorenzo," 65–66; "Testimony of José," 53, 57; "Carta del Padre Fray Silvestre Velez de Escalante, escrita en 2 de Abril de 1778," 311; "Auto of Antonio de Otermín," 219; "Opinion of fray Francisco de Ayeta," 310; "Declaration of Jerónimo, a Tigua Indian," 361; "Reply of the Fiscal, Don Martin de Solís Miranda," 382; "Testimony of Juan of Tesuque," 53; "Testimony of Lucas, a Piro Indian," 60; "Carta del Padre Fray Silvestre Velez de Escalante," 311; "Testimony of Pedro Naranjo," 63–64; "Declaration of Sargento Mayor Sebastian de Herrera," 269; Simmons, "History of Pueblo-Indian Relations to 1821," 184. See also "Auto of Antonio de Otermín," 219; Bancroft, *History of Arizona and New Mexico*, 184–85; Knault, *The Pueblo Revolt of 1680*, 174–75; and Silverberg, *The Pueblo Revolt*, 131.
13. "Tercer cuaderno [of Fray Salvador de San Antonio]," 350.
14. Hackett, "The Revolt of the Pueblo Indians," 125.
15. "Auto of Antonio de Otermín," 13.
16. "Salida para el Paso del Norte, 23 de augusto, hasta 5 de Octubre," 17.
17. "Declaration of Diego López Sambrano," 295.
18. "Declaration of one of the rebellious Christian Indians who was captured on the road," 61.
19. "Diego de Vargas, campaign journal," 389.
20. "Diego de Vargas to the King," 186.
21. Serulnikov, "Revindicaciones indígenas y legalidad colonial," 7–8, 16; O'Phelan, *Rebellions and Revolts*, 118–19, 153.
22. "Carta de Fray Matías de la Borda a Sebastían de Segurola," 1–2; "Copias de documentos citados en el diario," no. 18, 21; "Diario de Sebastían Segurola," 6; Diez de Medina, *Diario del alzamiento del indios conjurados contra la ciudad de Nuestra Señora de La Paz*, 30.
23. "Actuaciones anteriores ala formación de esta causa de Oruro," 21, 83, 84–85, 89, 90, 123; "Testimonio de Santos Mamani," 73; "Declaración de Francisco Xavier Condori," 24; "Testimonio de Martín Lopes," 26.

24. "Carta que refiere a los estragos hechos," 508–509; "Carta de Arequipa con fecha 2 de Mayo de 1781 que refiere los estragos executados," 693–94; "Relación de sucesos de la Provincia de Cochabamba," 4–5, 6–7; "Actuaciones anteriores," 5, 6, 21, 23, 87, 99, 144; "Relación de los hechos más notables acaecidos," 162, 170–73; "Carta del Cabildo de Cochabamba al Rey," 1; "El Regente Presidente," 1; "Confesión de Josef Daga," 1; "Confesión de Augustín Ventura," 12; "Confesión de Sebastiana Mamani," 25; "Carta de Luís Palacio y Santelices a Gerónimo de Ruedas," 22; "Causa de Augustín Solís," 21; "Dn. Pedro Antonio Zernudas," 5; "Informe de Josef Atanacio Baspineyro," 1; "Parte de D. José de Reseguín al Virey de Buenos Aires," 348.

25. "Carta de Félix Villalobos a Gerónimo Manuel de Ruedas," 6–7; "Actuaciones anteriores," 5, 87, 99, 144; "Relación de los hechos más notables," 206; "Representación de Félix Josef de Villalobos a Gerónimo Manuel de Ruedas," 7; "Relación de los sucesos de la Provincia de Cochabamba año de 1781," 4; "Declaración de Fray Josef Serbantes," 18.

26. "Carta de Gerónimo Manuel de Ruedas a Juan José Vertíz," 1; "Carta de Gerónimo Manuel de Ruedas a Josef de Galvez," 1.

27. A Hispanicized Indian, also known as a Ladino.

28. "Informe del Corregidor de Paria Manuel de Bodega," 92.

29. "Oficio de Francisco Javier Beltrán," 1.

30. "Carta que refiere los estragos," 508; "Relación de los sucesos de la provincia de Cochabamba," 4.

31. A district governor.

32. "Oficio de Francisco Javier Beltrán," 1.

33. "Diario del cerco de La Paz en 1781, por Sebastían de Segurola," 2.

34. "Copias de documentos citados en el diario," no. 18, 21.

35. "Declaración de Padre Fr. Josef de Uriarte," 1.

36. "Diario del cerco de La Paz en 1781, por Sebastían de Segurola," 8.

37. "Carta de Túpac Catari a José de Ayarza," 230; "Copias de documentos citados en el diario," no. 10, 19.

38. "Confesión de Gregoria Apasa," 1.

39. "Confesión de Josefa Anaya," 5–6.

40. "Confesión de Diego Quispe," 8.

41. A derogatory name for a Spaniard.

42. "Copias de documentos citados en el diario," no. 18, 21; "Carta de Borda a Segurola," 1; "Confesión de Diego Estaca," 20–21; O´Phelan, *Rebellions and Revolts,* 252–54.

43. "Relación verdadera de los lástimos sucesos ocuridos," 98; "Diario de Sebastían de Segurola," 17; "Confesión de Julián Apasa o Túpac Catari," 24; "Carta de Ignacio Florez a Josef de Galvez," 2.

44. Cajías de la Vega, "Los Objectivos de la revolución indigena de 1781: El Caso de Oruro," 421.

45. Claude Levi-Strauss, *Structural Anthopology,* vol. 2, pp. 9, 11.

46. "Confesión de Gregoria Apasa," 3; "Confesión de Ascencia Flores," 23.

47. "Levantamiento de la Provincia de Chayanta o Charcas," 239–41.

48. "Carta que refiere los estragos," 81; "Carta de Arequipa," 694.

49. "Carta de Joseph Antonio de Areche," 2; "Diario fabuloso del cura de Oruro Doctor Don Patricio Gabriel Menéndez," 289; "Relación verdadera," 77; "Actuaciones anteriores," 176; "Causas de Oruro," 141; "Informe del Consejo de Indias al Rey," 106; "Causa de Augustín Solis," 21; Jan Szeminski, "Why Kill the Spaniard?," 170.

50. "Testimonio de Ventura Balencia," 24; "Sobre los alboratos y sublevación de indios en Cochabamba," 24; "Carta de Capellán Theodoro Gutiérrez de Seballos a Ramón Urrutía y las Casas," 5; "Actuaciones anteriores," 11, 42–43, 45, 48, 62; "Testimonio de

Santos Mamani," 37; "Declaración de Francisco Xavier Condori," 12; "Testimonio de Martín Lopes," 13; "Declaración de Luís de Palacio y Santelises," 11; "Causa de Augustín Solís," 11; "Fragment of Informe," 3.

51. "Relación de los sucesos de Cochabamba," 24–25.

52. "Relación verdadera," 78; "Diario fabuloso," 288; "De los sucesos más principales acaecidos en la villa de Oruro entre europeos y criollos," 294; "Relación de los horribles estragos," 299; "Relación traxica de los funestros y ruinosos acaecemientos de la villa de Oruro," 3; "Relación de los sucesos de la Provincia de Cochabamba," 14; "Auto of Antonio de Otermín," 194.

53. Simmons, "History of Pueblo-Indian Relations to 1821," 184.

54. A club.

55. Knault, *The Pueblo Revolt of 1680*, 163.

56. Bancroft, *The Works of Hubert Howe Bancroft*, vol. 17, *History of Arizona and New Mexico*, 182.

57. "March of the army from El Paso to La Isleta," 203–4.

58. "El Proveido de D. Diego de Vargas Sobre la peticion espresada del Padre Custodio y demas religiosos misioneros dice," 355.

59. "The Cabildo of Santa Fe to the Conde de Galve," 561.

60. "Letter from the Governor and Captain-General," 329–30; "Auto of Antonio de Otermín," 17; Carlos de Siguenza y Gongora, "Mercurio Volante con la noticias de la recuperacion de las Provincias del Nuevo Mexico," 100–111; Hackett, "The Revolt of the Pueblo Indians of New Mexico in 1680," 119.

61. "Bando de coronación de Túpac Amaru," 206; "Actuaciones anteriores," 13, 45; "Carta de Capellan Augustin Flores Urito a Jorge Escobedo," 49; "Declaración de Roque Argote," 18–20; "Relación histórica," 24–27; "Diario fabuloso," 289–90; "Relación de los hechos más notables," 170–71; "Confesión de Josef Daga," 23; "Carta que refiere a los estragos," 508, 694; "Relación de sucesos de la Provincia de Cochabamba," 9, 14, 17–18; Jan Szeminski, *La utopía Tupamarista*, 246, 277; Szeminski, "Why Kill the Spaniard," 176, 178; Leon Campbell, "Banditry and the Túpac Amaru Rebellion in Cuzco, Perú, 1780–1784," 152–53.

62. "Diaro fabuloso," 289; "Actuaciones anteriores," 351, 354; "Relación traxica," 5; "Carta que refiere a los estragos," 509, 694; "Relación de los hechos más notables," 170–71, 206; "Representación de Domingo Angeles a Gerónimo Manuel de Ruedas," 23; "Carta de Arequipa," 693–94; "Relación de los sucesos de Cochabamba," 14; "Carta de Oruro," 158; Diez de Medina, 66; "Carta de Borda a Segurola," 155; "Carta de Ramón de Moya y Villareal a Juan José Vertíz," 13.

63. "Relación de los hechos más notables," 163; "Declaración de Alvento Arze," 134.

64. "Relación de los horribles," 343; "Diario fabuloso," 289; "Relación histórica," 25; "Relación traxica," 4; "Relación de los hechos más notables," 162.

65. "Relación verdadera," 78; "Diario fabuloso," 288; "De los sucesos más principales," 299; "Relación traxica," 3.

66. "Oficio de Capellán de Challapata, Juan Antonio Beltrán," 3; "Carta de Capellán Theodoro Gutiérrez de Seballos a Ramón Urrutía y las Casas," 10; "Testimonio formado sobre la sublevación de los Indios del pueblo de Challapata," 3.

67. "Actuaciones anteriores," 24.

68. "Confesión de Espiritu Alonso," 24; "Confesión de Bartolome Vello," 67.

69. "Carta de Felíx Villalobos a Gerónimo Manuel de Ruedas," 13–14; "Actuaciones anteriores," 10, 173, 198, 288; "Relación de los hechos más notables," 206; "Representación de Felíx Josef Villalobos a Gerónimo Manuel de Ruedas," 14; "Relación de los sucesos de la

Provincia de Cochabamba," 7; "Declaración de Fray Josef Serbantes," 36; "Anexo al diario y relación prolija jurada," 1; "Declaración de Alvento Arze," 135; "Sumaria información recibida de varios indios de Chocaya," 45, 47.

70. Relación traxica," 4; "Relación histórica," 29; "Carta del Cabildo de Cochabamba al Rey," 2.

71. "Relación de los sucesos de la Provincia de Cochabamba," 6; "Declaración de Da. María Crespo," 5; "Declaración de Dn. Salvador Conde," 10.

72. "Relación traxica," 2; "Relación verdadera," 85; "Relación histórica," 29; "Confesión de Mariano Quispe," 45; "Carta de Félix Villalobos a Gerónimo Manuel de Ruedas," 7; "Actuaciones anteriores," 5, 87, 99, 144; "Relación de los hechos más notables," 206; "Representación de Félix Josef de Villalobos," 7; "Relación de los sucesos de la provincia de Cochabamba," 4; "Declaración de Fray Josef Serbantes," 18; "Confesión de Alvento Arze," 68.

73. "Carta de Arequipa," 694; "Copias de documentos citados en el diario," no. 18, 21; "Carta de Borda a Segurola," 1; "Confesión de Diego Estaca," 20–21; O´Phelan, *Rebellions and Revolts*, 252–254.

74. "Carta de Borda a Segurola," 1–2; "Copias de documentos citados en el diario," no. 18, 21; "Diario de Sebastían de Segurola," 6; Diez de Medina, 30.

75. "Informe de Pedro Yavira Ylario Caguasiri," 101; "Confesión de Simón Castillo," 64.

76. "Oficio del oficial real de Carangas a la Audiencia de Charcas, en el que avisa haber muerto los indios a su corregidor D. Mateo Ibañez Arco," 340; "Sumaria información recibida de varios indios de Chocaya," 44.

77. "Diario que formo yo Esteban Losa," 4; "Relación de los sucesos de la Provincia de Cochabamba," 11.

78. "Sumaria información recibida de varios indios de Chocaya," 28, 32.

79. "Carta de Arequipa," 692; "Carta de Cabildo de Cochabamba al Rey," 2.

80. "Relación de los sucesos de Cochabamba," 8; "Actuaciones anteriores," 12; "Declaración de Roque Argote," 19–20; "Confesión de Lázaro Mamani," 47; "Carta de Estiban Lidosa a Gerónimo Manuel de Ruedas," 48; "Confesión de Sebastiana Mamani," 50; "Confesión de Francisco Gonzalo," 50; "Confesión de Pasqual Tola," 53; "Confesión de Thomas Molina," 60; "Carta de Arequipa," 693; "Sumaria información recibida de varios indios de Chocaya," 2, 7.

81. "Actuaciones anteriores," 168; "Relación traxica," 4.

82. "El Regente de la Rl. Audiencia de Charcas,"1; "Relación de los hechos más notables," 171–72; "El corregidor de la villa de Cochabamba sobre los destrozos," 10.

83. "Carta que refiere los estragos," 509; Valentín Abecia Baldivieso, "La insurreción india de Tapacari en 1781," 41.

84. Hackett, "The Revolt of the Pueblo Indians," 123.

85. "El corregidor de la villa de Cochabamba sobre los destrozos que executaron los indios en Tapacari," 2.

86. "March of the army from El Paso to La Isleta," 205–6; "El provedio de D. Diego de Vargas sobre la petición espresada del Padre Custorio y demas religiosos misioneros dice," 355.

87. A cross symbolizing Spanish authority and often used as a whipping post.

88. "Oficio de capellán de Challapata, Juan Antonio Beltrán," 3; "Carta de Capellán Theodoro Gutiérrez de Seballos a Ramón Urrutía y las Casas," 10.

89. "Carta de Ramón de Moya y Villarroel a Juan José Vertíz," 4; "Oficio de capellán de Challapata, Juan Antonio Beltrán," 3; "Carta de Capellán Theodoro Gutiérrez de Seballos a Ramón Urrutía y las Casas," 10.

Works Cited

Primary Sources

"Actuaciones anteriores ala formación de esta causa de Oruro." La Plata, February 22, 1781. AGI, Charcas 599.

"Anexo al diario y relación prolija jurada que yo el general Don Juan Gelly hago de todos los pasajes y sucesos acaecidos en varios distritos y lugares." La Plata, September 9, 1780. AGI, Charcas, 594.

"Auto of Antonio de Otermín." N.p., n.d. In vol. 2 of *The Spanish Archives of New Mexico,* ed. Ralph Emerson Twitchell. Cedar Rapids, Ia.: Torch Press, 1914, 16.

"Auto of Antonio de Otermín." Santa Fe, August 13, 1680. In vol. 8 of *Revolt of the Pueblo Indians of New Mexico and Otermín's Attempted Reconquest 1680–1682,* ed. Charles Wilson Hackett. Translations of original documents by Charmion Clair Shelby. Albuquerque: University of New Mexico Press, 1942, 11.

"Auto of Antonio de Otermín." Paraje del Rio del Norte, October 9, 1680. In vol. 8 of *Revolt of the Pueblo Indians of New Mexico and Otermín's Attempted Reconquest 1680–1682,* ed. Charles Wilson Hackett. Translations of original documents by Charmion Clair Shelby. Albuquerque: University of New Mexico Press, 1942, 194.

"Auto of Antonio de Otermín." La Isleta, December 9, 1681. In vol. 9 of *Revolt of the Pueblo Indians of New Mexico and Otermín's Attempted Reconquest 1680–1682,* ed. Charles Wilson Hackett. Translations of original documents by Charmion Clair Shelby. Albuquerque: University of New Mexico Press, 1942, 218.

"Bando de coronación de Túpac Amaru." N.p., n.d. In *Documentos históricos del Perú en las épocas del coloniaje despúes de la conquista y de la independencia hasta la presente,* ed. Manuel de Odriozola. Lima: Tipografia de Aurelio Alfaro, 1863, 206.

"The Cabildo of Santa Fe to the Conde de Galve." Santa Fe, January 1694. In *To The Royal Crown Restored: The Journals of Don Diego de Vargas, New Mexico, 1692–1694,* ed. John L. Kessell, Rick Hendricks, and Meredith Dodge. Albuquerque: University of New Mexico Press, 1995, 561.

"Carta de Arequipa con fecha 2 de Mayo de 1781 que refiere los estragos executados por los indios alzados en varios pueblos de las provincias de ambos virreyenatos." Arequipa, May 2, 1781. In book 2, vol. 1, *Colección Documental de la independencia del Perú,* ed. Cárlos Daniel Válcarcel. Lima: Comisión Nacional del Sesquicentenario de la Independencia del Perú, 1971, 692–695.

"Carta del Cabildo de Cochabamba al Rey." Cochabamba, January 31, 1782. AGI, Charcas 595.

"Carta de Capellán Augustin Flores Urito a Jorge Escobedo." Porco, February 21,1781. AGI, Charcas 437-b.

"Carta de Capellán Theodoro Gutíerrez de Seballos a Ramón Urrutía y las Casas." Poopó, January 18, 1781. AGI, Charcas 437-b.

"Carta de Capitán General y Gobernador Andrés Mestre a Josef de Galvez." Salta, June 24, 1781. AGI, Charcas 595.

"Carta de Estiban Lidosa a Gerónimo Manuel de Ruedas." La Plata, April 9, 1781. AGI, Charcas 603.

"Carta de Félix Villalobos a Gerónimo Manuel de Ruedas." February 24, 1781. Cochabamba, February 24, 1781. AGI, Charcas 596.

"Carta de Fray Matías de la Borda a Sebastían de Segurola." La Paz, May 30, 1781. AGI, Charcas 595.

"Carta de Gerónimo Manuel de Ruedas a Juan José Vertíz." La Plata, May 15, 1781. AGI, Charcas 595.

"Carta de Ignacio Florez a Josef de Galvez." La Plata, December 10, 1782. AGI, Charcas 595, also Charcas 444.

"Carta de Joseph Antonio de Areche, Visitador de Tribunales y Superintendente de la Real Hacienda en Perú al Superior Consejo de Indians," Cuzco, May 23, 1781. AGI, Charcas 595.

"Carta de Luís Palacio y Santelices a Gerónimo de Ruedas." Santiago de Cotagaita, March 9, 1781. AGI, Charcas 596.

"Carta del Padre Fray Silvestre Velez de Escalante, escrita en 2 de Abril de 1778." Santa Fe, April 2, 1778. In *Documentos para servir a la historia del Nuevo Mexico, 1538–1778*, Madrid: Ediciones José Porrua Turanzas, 1962, 305.

"Carta de Ramón de Moya y Villareal a Juan José Vertíz." Arequipa, May 25, 1781. AGI, Charcas 596.

"Carta de Túpac Catari." La Paz, April 7, 1781. In "Relación de los hechos más notables acaecidos en la sublevación general fraguada en los reynos del Perú, por el indio José Gabriel Túpac Amaru, gobr. del pueblo de Tungasuca en la Provincia de Tinta, que asociado de otros sequaces, causó horrosos estragos desde el año 1780, hasta el de 1782 en que se reprimo el orgullo de la conjuración." In *Revista de archivos y bibliotecas nacionales* 3, vol. 5. Lima, September 30, 1900, 263.

"Carta que refiere a los estragos hechos por los Yndios alzados en Suchesmineral de la Provincia de Larecaja del Obispado de La Paz; y en los pueblos de Arque, Tapacari, y Colcha en la Provincia de Cochabamba, perteneciente al Arzobispado de la Plata." Cochabamba, February 26, 1781. In book 2, vol. 1, *Colección Documental de la independencia del Perú*, ed. Carlos Daniel Válcarcel. Lima: Comisión Nacional del Sesquicentenario de la Independencia del Perú, 1971, 508.

"Causa de Augustín Solis." La Plata, March 11, 1781. AGI, Charcas 594.

"Causas de Oruro. Testimonio de la acusación del Señor Fiscal de S.M. contra los reos de la sublevación de la villa de Oruro y otras acusaciones" (1784). In vol. 2, *Noticia y Proceso de la muy noble y leal villa de San Felipe de Austria de Oruro*, ed. Adolfo Mier. N.p., 1906, 127.

"Confesión de Ascencia Flores." Santuario de Nuestra Señora de las Peñas, October 18, 1781. AGI, Charcas 595.

"Confesión de Augustín Ventura." La Plata, April 25, 1781. In "Criminales contra Nicolás Catari y otros indios." AGI, Charcas 603.

"Confesión de Bartolome Vello." La Plata, April 21, 1781. AGI, Charcas 603.

"Confesión de Diego Estaca." Santuario de Nuestra Señora de las Peñas, October 18, 1781.

"Confesión de Diego Quispe." Santuario de Nuestra Señora de las Peñas, October 18, 1781. AGI, Charcas 595.

"Confesión de Espiritu Alonso." La Plata, April 25, 1781. AGI, Charcas 603.

"Confesión de Francisco Gonzalo." La Plata, April 20, 1781. AGI, Charcas 603.

"Confesión de Gregoria Apasa." Santuario de Nuestra Señora de Peñas, October 18, 1781. AGI, Charcas 595.

"Confesión de Josef Daga." La Plata, April 25, 1781. In "Criminales contra Nicolás Catari y otros indios." AGI, Charcas 603.

"Confesión de Josefa Anaya." Santuario de Nuestra Señora de las Peñas, October 18, 1781. AGI, Charcas 595.

"Confesión de Julián Apasa o Túpac Catari." Santuario de NuestraSeñora de Peñas, November 11 and 13, 1781. AGI, Buenos Aires 320.

"Confesión de Lázaro Mamani." La Plata, April 9, 1781. AGI, Charcas 603.

"Confesión de Mariano Quispe." Chichas, November 23, 1781. In "Sumaria información recibida de varios indios de Chocaya como sindicados en la sublevación." ABNB, SGI.1781.10.

"Confesión de Pasqual Tola." La Plata, April 20, 1781. AGI, Charcas 603.

"Confesión de Sebastiana Mamani." La Plata, April 18, 1781. AGI, Charcas 603.

"Confesión de Simón Castillo." La Plata, April 25, 1781. AGI, Charcas 603.

"Confesión de Thomas Molina." La Plata, April 21, 1781. AGI, Charcas 603.

"Copias de documentos citados en el diario," no. 10. La Paz, May 30, 1781. In "Diario del cerco de La Paz en 1781, por Sebastían de Segurola." ABNB, SGI.1781.s.n.

"Copias de documentos citados en el diario," no. 18. La Paz, May 30, 1781. In "Diario del cerco de La Paz en 1781, por Sebastían de Segurola." ABNB, SGI.1781.s.n.

"De los sucesos más principales acaecidos en la villa de Oruro entre europeos y criollos" (1781). In *Capítulos de la historia colonial de Oruro,* ed. Marcos Beltrán Avila. La Paz: La República, 1925, 294.

"Declaración de Alvento Arze." Oropesa, Cochabamba, October 2, 1780. AGI, Charcas 596.

"Declaration of Diego López Sambrano." Hacienda of Luis de Carbajal, December 22, 1681. In vol. 9 of *Revolt of the Pueblo Indians of New Mexico and Otermín's Attempted Reconquest 1680–1682,* ed. Charles Wilson Hackett. Translations of original documents by Charmion Clair Shelby. Albuquerque: University of New Mexico Press, 1942, 292.

"Declaración de Francisco Xavier Condori." Oruro, April 10, 1781. AGI, Charcas 601.

"Declaración de Fray Josef Serbantes." Oruro, April 9, 1781. In "Testimonio del expedientes y diligencias practicadas para averiguar los tumultos meditadas contra Oruro." AGI, Charcas 601.

"Declaración de Padre Fr. Josef de Uriarte." El Alto, April 17, 1782. In "Diversas declaraciones hechas por varios sujectos sobre las disposiciones y sacriligios de los rebeldes de varias provincias ante Dr. Esteban de Loza." ABNB, SGI,1782.97.

"Declaración de Luís de Palacio y Santelises." La Plata, March 12, 1781. AGI, Charcas 594.

"Declaración de Da. María Crespo." Oropesa, March 7, 1781. In "El Corregor. dela Villa de Cochabamba sobre los destrozos que executaron los indios en Tapacari." ABNB, SGI.1781.62.

"Declaración de Roque Argote." Potosi, March 7, 1781. AGI, Charcas 596.

"Declaración de Dn. Salvador Conde." Oropesa, March 7, 1781. In "El Corregor. dela Villa de Cochabamba sobre los destrozos que executaron los indios en Tapacari." ABNB, SGI.1781.62, 10.

"Declaration of Jerónimo, a Tigua Indian." Opposite La Isleta, January 1, 1682. In vol. 9 of *Revolt of the Pueblo Indians of New Mexico and Otermín's Attempted Reconquest 1680–1682,* ed. Charles Wilson Hackett. Translations of original documents by Charmion Clair Shelby. Albuquerque: University of New Mexico Press, 1942, 359.

"Declaration of one of the rebellious Christian Indians who was captured on the road." Alamillo, September 6, 1680, 61. In vol. 8 of *Revolt of the Pueblo Indians of New Mexico and Otermín's Attempted Reconquest 1680–1682,* ed. Charles Wilson Hackett. Translations of original documents by Charmion Clair Shelby. Albuquerque: University of New Mexico Press, 1942, 61.

"Declaration of Sargento Mayor Sebastian de Herrera." Rio del Norte, December 21, 1681. In vol. 9 of *Revolt of the Pueblo Indians of New Mexico and Otermín's Attempted Reconquest 1680–1682,* ed. Charles Wilson Hackett. Translations of original documents by Charmion Clair Shelby. Albuquerque: University of New Mexico Press, 1942, 267.

"Dn. Pedro Antonio Cernudas y Dn. Lorenzo Blanco Ciceron oydores en la Rl. Audiencia de Charcas continuan el informe de los sucesos de las provincias cuios naturales incurrieron en el delito de rebelión." La Plata, May 15, 1781. AGI, Charcas 594.

"Dn. Pedro Antonio Zernudas oidor dela Rl Audiencia de la Plata informa a V.M. haber echo la prisión de Dr. Gregorio de Merlo cura dela Doctrina de Macha." La Plata, March 13, 1781. AGI, Charcas 594.

"Diario de Sebastían Segurola." La Paz, July 1, 1781. AGI, Charcas, 595.

"Diario fabuloso del cura de Oruro Doctor Don Patricio Gabriel Menéndez-Relación trajica de los funestros y ruinosos aconticimientos de Oruro." In *Capítulos de la historia colonial de Oruro,* Marcos Beltrán Avila, 282.

"Diario que formo yo Esteban Losa escribano de S. Magd. y de guerra de la presente expedición a cargo del Señor Dn. Josef Reseguín Theniente Coronel de Dragones, y Comandante gral della con destino al socorro de la ciudad de La Paz." Oruro, December 22, 1781. AGI, Charcas 595.

"Diego de Vargas, campaign journal." New Mexico, August 9 -October 15, 1692. In *By Force of Arms: The Journals of Don Diego de Vargas, 1691–1693,* ed. John L. Kressell, Rick Hendricks, and Meredith Dodge. Albuquerque: University of New Mexico Press, 1992, 359.

"Diego de Vargas to the King." Zacatecas, May 16, 1693. In *To The Royal Crown Restored: The Journals of Don Diego de Vargas, New Mexico, 1692–1694,* ed. John L. Kessell, Rick Hendricks, and Meredith Dodge. Albuquerque: University of New Mexico Press, 1995, 186.

Diez de Medina, Francisco Tadeo. *Diario del alzamiento del indios conjurados contra la ciudad de Nuestra Señora de La Paz.* Transcribed with an introduction by María Eugenia del Valle de Siles. La Paz: Banco Boliviano Americano, 1981.

"El Proveido de D. Diego de Vargas Sobre la peticion espresada del Padre Custodio y demas religiosos misioneros dice." In *Documentos para servir a la historia del Nuevo Mexico, 1538–1778.* Madrid: Ediciones José Porrua Turanzas, 1962, 351.

"El Regente Presidente de la Rl. Audiencia de Charcas informa del cuidadoso estado de la rebelión de Indios." La Plata, April 15, 1781. AGI, Charcas 594.

"Fragmento de Informe." N.p., n.d. AGI, Charcas, 594.

"Informe de Josef Atanacio Baspineyro." Potosi, March 14, 1781. AGI, Charcas 437-b.

"Informe de Pedro Yavira Ylario Caguasiri." San Pedro de Buenavista, December 28, 1780. AGI, Charcas 596.

"Informe del Consejo de Indias al Rey, sublevación de Oruro." 1800. In vol. 2, *Noticia y proceso de la muy noble y muy leal Villa de San Felipe de Austria de Oruro,* ed. Adolfo Mier. N.p., 1906, 101.

"Letter from the Governor and Captain-General, Don Antonio de Otermín, from New Mexico." September 8, 1680. In vol. 4, *Historical Documents Relating to New Mexico, Nueva Vizcaya, and Approaches Thereto, to 1773,* ed. Charles Wilson Hackett. Washington, D.C.: Carnegie Institution, 1937, 327.

"Levantamiento de la Provincia de Chayanta o Charcas . . . y lo acaecido en el pueblo de Pocoata de dha provincia a su corregidor Dn. Joaquín Alós." La Plata, September 29, 1780. In book 2, vol. 1, *Colección Documental de la independencia del Perú,* ed. Cárlos Daniel Válcarcel. Lima: Comisión Nacional del Sesquicentenario de la Independencia del Perú, 1971, 235.

"March of the army from El Paso to La Isleta." November 5–December 8, 1681. In vol. 9 of *Revolt of the Pueblo Indians of New Mexico and Otermín's Attempted Reconquest*

1680–1682, ed. Charles Wilson Hackett. Translations of original documents by Charmion Clair Shelby. Albuquerque: University of New Mexico Press, 1942, 191.

"Oficio de Capellán de Challapata, Juan Antonio Beltrán." Challapata, January 18, 1781. AGI, Charcas 595.

"Oficio de Francisco Javier Beltrán." Potosi, Mar. 14, 1781. AGI, Charcas 437-b.

"Oficio del oficial real de Carangas [Pablo Gregorio de Castilla] a la Audiencia de Charcas, en el que avisa haber muerto los indios a su corregidor D. Mateo Ibañez Arco." Carangas, February 6, 1781. In vol. 1, *Documentos históricos del Perú en las épocas del coloniaje despúes de la conquista y de la independencia hasta la presente,* ed. Manuel de Odriozola. Lima: Tipografia de Aurelio Alfaro, 1863, 340.

"Opinion of Fray Francisco de Ayeta." Hacienda of Luis de Carbajal, December 23, 1681. In vol. 9 of *Revolt of the Pueblo Indians of New Mexico and Otermín's Attempted Reconquest 1680–1682,* ed. Charles Wilson Hackett. Translations of original documents by Charmion Clair Shelby. Albuquerque: University of New Mexico Press, 1942, 305.

"Parte de D. José de Reseguín al Virey de Buenos Aires, sobre la sublevación de la Provincia de Tupiza." Tupiza, March 18, 1781. In vol. 1, *Documentos históricos del Perú en las épocas del coloniaje despúes de la conquista y de la independencia hasta la presente,* ed. Manuel de Odriozola. Lima: Tipografia de Aurelio Alfaro, 1863, 347.

"Relación de los hechos más notables acaecidos en la sublevación general fraguada en los reynos del Perú, por el indio José Gabriel Túpac Amaru, gobr. del pueblo de Tungasuca en la Provincia de Tinta, que asociado de otros sequaces, causó horrosos estragos desde el año 1780, hasta el de 1782 en que se reprimo el orgullo de la conjuración." In *Revista de archivos y bibliotecas nacionales* 3, vol. 5 (Lima, September 30, 1900): 141–298.

"Relación de los horribles estragos que en el día 10 de febrero de 1781 hicieron los Cholos e Yndios patricios en Oruro." 1781. In vol. 1, *Guerra Separatista-Rebeliones de indios en sur america-La sublevación de Túpac Amaru,* ed. L. Eguriguren. Lima: Imprenta Torres Aguirre, 1952, 342.

"Relación de los sucesos de la Provincia de Cochabamba año de 1781." Written by the cabildo de Cochabamba. Cochabamba, December 17, 1781. AGI, Charcas 595.

"Relación traxica de los funestros y ruinosos acaecemientos de la villa de Oruro." Potosi, April 13, 1781. AGI, Charcas 437-b.

"Relación verdadera de los lástimos sucesos ocuridos en la villa de Oruro con motivo de haber los mestizos y cholos de ella, procidido inicuamente a quitar la vida a los españoles europeos, que la habitaban." 1781. In vol. 2, *Noticia y proceso de la muy noble y muy leal Villa de San Felipe de Austria de Oruro,* ed. Adolfo Mier. N.p., 1906, 56.

"Reply of the Fiscal, Don Martín de Solís Miranda." Mexico, June 25, 1682. In vol. 9 of *Revolt of the Pueblo Indians of New Mexico and Otermín's Attempted Reconquest 1680–1682,* ed. Charles Wilson Hackett. Translations of original documents by Charmion Clair Shelby. Albuquerque: University of New Mexico Press, 1942, 375.

"Representación de Domingo Angeles a Gerónimo Manuel de Ruedas." La Plata, October 17, 1780. AGI, Charcas 596.

"Representación de Félix Josef de Villalobos a Gerónimo Manuel de Ruedas." La Plata, March 7, 1781. AGI, Charcas, 594.

"Salida para el Paso del Norte, 23 de Agosto, hasta 5 de Octubre de 1680." Antonio de Otermín, Arroyo de San Marcos. In vol. 2, *The Spanish Archives of New Mexico,* ed. Ralph Emerson Twitchell. Cedar Rapids, Ia.: Torch Press, 1914, 13.

Siguenza y Gongora, Carlos de. "Mercurio Volante con la noticias de la recuperacion de las Provincias del Nuevo Mexico," 1693. In *Documentos para servir a la historia del Nuevo Mexico, 1538–1778.* Madrid: Ediciones José Porrua Turanzas, 1962, 84–111.

"Sobre los alboratos y sublevación de indios en Cochabamba." Quillacollo, May 26, 1781. ABNB, SGI.1781.210.

"Sumaria información recibida de varios indios de Chocaya como a sindicados en la sublevacion." La Plata, November 23, 1781. ABNB.SGI.1781.10.

"Tercer cuaderno [of Fray Salvador de San Antonio]" Santa Fe, December 18, 1693. In *Documentos para servir a la historia del Nuevo Mexico, 1538–1778*. Madrid: Ediciones José Porrua Turanzas, 1962, 342.

"Testimonio de Josef Manuel de Santander." La Plata, n.d. In "Causa contra los cabezas de la rebelión de Oruro." AGI, Charcas 599.

"Testimonio de Martín Lopes." Oruro, April 7, 1781. AGI, Charcas 601.

"Testimonio de Santos Mamani." Oruro, May 25, 1781. AGI, Charcas 601.

"Testimonio de Ventura Balencia." Oruro, April 10, 1781. AGI, Charcas 601.

"Testimonio formado sobre la sublevación de los Indios del pueblo de Challapata y muerte que dieron a su corregidor Dn. Manuel de la Bodega y Llano." La Plata, January 26, 1781. AGI, Charcas 596.

"Testimony of José." Rio del Norte, December 19, 1681. In "Interrogatories and Depositions of Three Indians of the Tehua Nation, Taken by the Order of Don Antonio Otermín." Rio del Norte, December 28, 1681. In vol. 2, *The Spanish Archives of New Mexico*, ed. Ralph Emerson Twitchell. Cedar Rapids, Ia.: Torch Press, 1914, 56.

"Testimony of Juan Lorenzo and Francisco Lorenzo." Paso del norte, December 20, 1681. In "Interrogatories and Depositions of Three Indians of the Tehua Nation, Taken by the Order of Don Antonio Otermín." Rio del Norte, December 28, 1681. In vol. 2, *The Spanish Archives of New Mexico*, ed. Ralph Emerson Twitchell. Cedar Rapids, Ia.: Torch Press, 1914, 65.

"Testimony of Juan of Tesuque." Rio del Norte, December 28, 1681. In "Interrogatories and Depositions of Three Indians of the Tehua Nation, Taken by the Order of Don Antonio Otermín." Rio del Norte, December 28, 1681. In vol. 2, *The Spanish Archives of New Mexico*, ed. Ralph Emerson Twitchell. Cedar Rapids, Ia.: Torch Press, 1914, 51.

"Testimony of Lucas, a Piro Indian." Rio del Norte, December 18, 1681. In "Interrogatories and Depositions of Three Indians of the Tehua Nation, Taken by the Order of Don Antonio Otermín." Rio del Norte, December 28, 1681. In vol. 2, *The Spanish Archives of New Mexico*, ed. Ralph Emerson Twitchell. Cedar Rapids, Ia.: Torch Press, 1914, 60.

Secondary Sources

Abecia Baldivieso, Valentín. "La insurreción india de Tapacari en 1781." In *Actas de coloquio Internacional: "Túpac Amaru y su tiempo,"* ed. Cárlos Daniel Válcarcel. Lima: Comisión Nacional del Bicentenario de la Revolución Emancipadora de Túpac Amaru, 1982.

Bancroft, Hubert H. *The Works of Hubert Howe Bancroft*, vol. 17, *History of Arizona and New Mexico, 1530–1888*. San Francisco: History Company, 1889.

Cajías de la Vega, Fernando. "Los Objetivos de la revolución indigena de 1781: El Caso de Oruro." *Revisita Andina* 1, no. 2 (December 1983): 407-28.

Campbell, Leon. "Banditry and the Túpac Amaru Rebellion in Cuzco, Perú, 1780–1784." *Bibliotheca Americana* 1, no. 2 (November 1982): 131–62.

Cook, Noble David. *Born to Die: Disease and New World Conquest, 1492–1650*. Cambridge: Cambridge University Press, 1998.

Cook, Sherburne F., and Woodrow Borah, *Essays in Population History: Mexico and California*, vol. 3. Berkeley: University of California Press, 1979.

Duviols, Pierre. *La destrucción de las religiones andinas (Conquista y colonia)*. Mexico City: Universidad Nacional Autónomade México, 1977.

Fisher, Lillian Estelle. *The Last Inca Revolt: 1780–1783*. Norman: University of Oklahoma Press, 1966.

Hackett, Charles W. "The Revolt of the Pueblo Indians of New Mexico in 1680." *Texas State Historical Association Quarterly* 15 (October 1911): 93–147.

Knault, Andrew L. *The Pueblo Revolt of 1680: Conquest and Resistance in Seventeenth-Century New Mexico*. Norman: University of Oklahoma Press, 1995.

Levi-Strauss, Claude. *Structural Anthropology*, vol. 2. Trans. Monique Layton. New York: Basic Books, 1976.

O'Phelan Godoy, Scarlett. *Rebellions and Revolts in Eighteenth Century Peru and Upper Peru*. Cologne: Bohlau Verlag, 1985.

Robins, Nicholas. *Native Insurgencies and the Genocidal Impulse in the Americas*. Bloomington: Indiana University Press, 2005.

————. *Priest-Indian Conflict in Upper Peru: The Generation of Rebellion, 1750–1780*. Syracuse: Syracuse University Press, 2007.

Rowe, John H. "El movimiento nacional Inca del siglo XVIII." *Revista Universitaria* 43, no. 107 (1954): 17–40.

Serulnikov, Sergio. "Revindicaciones indígenas y legalidad colonial. La rebelión de Chayanta (1777–1781)." Buenos Aires: Centro de Estudios de Estado y Sociedad, 1989.

Silverberg, Robert. *The Pueblo Revolt*. New York: Weybright and Talley, 1970.

Simmons, Marc. "History of Pueblo-Indian Relations to 1821." *Handbook of North American Indians*, vol. 9, *The Southwest*, ed. Alfonso Ortíz. Washington, D.C.: Smithsonian Institution, 1979, 178–223.

Smith, C. T. "Depopulation of the Central Andes in the 16th Century." *Current Anthropology* 11, nos. 4–5 (1970): 453–64.

Szeminski, Jan. *La utopía Tupamarista*. Lima: Pontífica Universidad Católica del Perú, 1984.

————. "Why Kill The Spaniard? New Perspectives on Andean Insurrectionary Ideology in the 18th Century." In *Resistance, Rebellion, and Consciousness in the Andean Peasant World, Eighteenth to Twentieth Centuries*, ed. Steve Stern. Madison: University of Wisconsin Press, 1987.

2

On the Genocidal Aspect of Certain Subaltern Uprisings

A Research Note

ADAM JONES

This short chapter builds on those preceding by examining the genocidal strategies and motifs deployed in di-verse genres of subaltern mass violence. I examine slave rebellions, indigenous uprisings, peasant revolts (*jacqueries*), and modern anti-colonial revolts. It should be acknowledged at the outset that individual events are not easily slotted into particular, mutually exclusive categories. For example, the Caste War of Yucatán (1847–49), considered below, can be viewed as a war of national liberation, a peasant uprising, a native (indigenous) uprising, and a social revolution—even as a quasi-slave rebellion, given the hyper-exploitative labor conditions that prevailed on the plantations of the Yucatán peninsula. For a given event, therefore, I adopt the framing that seems most appropriate.

Slave Uprisings

I was never so glad to hear anything in my life. . . . I could slay the white people like sheep.

—King, an American slave, on learning of an impending rebellion, Virginia, 1800, quoted in Egerton, *Gabriel's Rebellion*

The epic slave uprising in Haiti that began in 1791 and culminated in Haitian independence in 1804 (see Introduction) may be the slave rebellion best suited to a genocide studies perspective. It is to my knowledge the only one to have received a sustained scholarly treatment in this context.[1]

As with the peasant uprisings discussed below, it is hardly surprising that, despite their oppressive conditions, slaves rarely rose up against their masters. Like serfs and other populations whose labor is highly coerced, they were usually unarmed and tightly constrained in their contacts with potential confederates (and were, moreover, overwhelmingly illiterate). Only in exceptional circumstances did conditions support widespread eruptions, and even these were highly unlikely to succeed against the massed repressive forces of the state or other constituted authority. In the Haitian case, these circumstances included the heavy concentration and demographic preponderance of slaves on the Northern Plain of Saint-Domingue, as well as the high proportion of slaves born in Africa. Tens of thousands of slaves shared memories of African freedom, along with cultural and linguistic bonds that greatly facilitated conspiracy. A dialectic thus emerged in which the genocidal institution of slavery in Saint-Domingue, by importing so many new slaves unaccustomed to bondage to replace those rapidly worked to death, sowed the seeds of its own genocidal destruction.

Given the constraints described, most slave rebellions containing a genocidal kernel were brief and localized (or regional) outbreaks. Usually, they were rapidly suppressed, at mortal cost to their planners and participants. An early nineteenth-century example, directly inspired by the Haitian rebellion, was the Aponte Rebellion in Cuba (1812). It killed relatively few whites (fewer than a dozen), but was so palpably a reflection of subaltern frustrations and hatreds and elite fears that, according to Matt Childs, it galvanized Cuban culture at both popular and elite levels for decades—at least through to the final abolition of slavery in 1886. Reflecting the overlap between performative and atrocious aspects of subaltern genocide (see chapter 9), Childs notes the influence of revolutionary "songs and chants" on the Aponte rebels. These "played an important role in organizing the rebellion," and included such classic subaltern articulations of a "world turned upside down" as the following (sung in Spanish, language of the oppressor):

Donde come mi amo,	Where my master eats,
como yo;	I eat;
donde duerme mi amo,	Where my master sleeps,
duermo yo;	I sleep;
donde jode mi amo,	Where my master fucks,
jodo yo.	I fuck.[2]

David Brion Davis's magisterial summary of a lifetime's research on Atlantic slavery, *Inhuman Bondage,* cites diverse examples from the United States of a genocidal strand manifested in violent slave insurrections. In the 1822 Denmark Vesey conspiracy in South Carolina, for example, witnesses stated that slave leader Vesey "exhorted his followers 'not to spare one white skin alive, as this was the plan they pursued in Santo Domingo'"—that is, during the Haitian revolution. Vesey also cited biblical verses such as Deuteronomy 20:10–18, which he presented, in another witness's recollection, as God's command "that all should be cut off, both men, women, and children." (Rolla Bennett, another slave leader, supplied a different interpretation of the passages from Deuteronomy. Women, he argued, should be preserved alive after white males were killed, because "we know what to do with the wenches." According to Davis, he "even boasted that the governor's daughter would be his future 'wench.'")[3]

The best-known American slave rebellion was Nat Turner's revolt in Virginia in 1831, immortalized by William Styron in a Pulitzer Prize-winning novel.[4] This campaign "was primarily aimed at killing whites," and, according to Davis, it did so on a substantial scale:

> Turner's revolt began in the dark early hours of August 22, 1831, in Southampton County, Virginia, a somewhat isolated rural region in which most whites owned only a few slaves and many owned none at all. Starting with Turner's "own" white family (he was legally owned by the nine-year-old Putnam Moore), Turner and his followers killed all the whites in one farmhouse after another as they moved by horse through the countryside. While there is no evidence of rape, plunder, or burning houses, the blacks—eventually but briefly including some fifty to sixty mounted insurgents—murdered nearly sixty whites, most of them women and children.[5]

Other examples can be cited from the history of slave rebellions in North America, the Caribbean, and Brazil—and doubtless from other parts of the world. It should be emphasized, however, that such genocidally tinged campaigns are rather rare in the historical record, and not only because of the logistical and military challenges of coordinating a widespread violent campaign against colonizers and racial oppressors. We should reckon, in addition, with a regular and surprising propensity of subaltern populations, when they gain the upper hand, to extend mercy to their oppressors. In the great Jamaican uprising of 1831, for instance, Davis, citing eyewitness accounts, notes that "despite the destruction of these sugar estates, the causes and scenes of their life-long trials and degradation, tears, and blood," rebellious slaves took notable care to avoid violating the physical integrity of their tormentors: "amid the wild excitement of the night, not one freeman's life was taken, not one freewoman molested by the insurgent slaves." Incitement to restraint rather than vengeance by the movement's leaders appears to have been key. Samuel 'Daddy' Sharpe "urge[d] his followers 'to drive the whites off the estates but not to harm them except in self-defense.'"[6]

In other cases, subaltern populations—like other conquerors—may choose to preserve former hegemons alive, consigning them to subordinate roles that doubtless afford considerable psychological gratification to the formerly oppressed. For example, the period of "low-intensity conflict" in Yucatán following the Caste War of 1847–49 was marked by sporadic but substantial massacres of Ladino (Hispanic-identified) populations. But it also featured the widespread enslavement, rather than outright extermination, of captured whites. Nelson Reed reports:

> And there were the white slaves. The wasteful slaughter of Bacalar would not be repeated by a more confident Cruzob [the mobilized Mayan population]. By Ladino count, 500 prisoners were taken in 1859 but only 200 of them killed. Women were kept in thatched barracks in the church compound and used as domestic servants by the Tatich [Mayan leader] and commandants, the more attractive ones also serving in the higher-ranking hammocks. Men were parceled out to work in the fields, to cut wood, burn lime, and haul stone for the new buildings, and to serve as teachers of music, Spanish, reading, and writing. It was a very complete reversal of roles: the master had become a slave and the slave a master, with whip and gun in his hand.[7]

Surely the "mercy" extended under such circumstances was strictly limited. But these instances suggest that subaltern rage may be bounded in its exterminatory expression—especially, perhaps, at later stages of revolt. In chapter 9 I return to this subject and inquire whether attention to it may assist in constructing a "phase model" of subaltern genocidal outbreaks.

Native Rebellions

The example of our actions has made the
savages nearly as bad as ourselves.

—Voltaire, writing to Jean-Jacques Rousseau on the North American
"Indian wars," 1755, quoted in Vidal, *Palimpsest: A Memoir*

Nicholas Robins's trailblazing research on native uprisings in the Americas, sampled in chapter 1 and explored at greater length in both *Genocide and Millennialism in Upper Peru* and *Native Insurgencies and the Genocidal Impulse in the Americas,* provides a rich portrait of key revolts in which a millenarian vision was paired with a genocidal strategy. In addition to the Andean and New Mexican revolts examined in the preceding chapter, Robins has incorporated in his investigations the Caste War of Yucatán (usually dated as 1847–49, although residual conflict stretched to the dawn of the twentieth century). This ferocious race war featured genocidal atrocities on both sides, with up to 200,000 killed. Against a backdrop of hyper-exploitation of Indian labor on the henequen plantations that dominated the Yucatecan economy, the precipitating event was a genocidal massacre of Maya by Hispanics/Ladinos/whites[8] at Tepich in July 1847. In the most intense phase of the violence, lasting to 1849, Robins finds the "genocidal tendency" to have been "quite pronounced":

> The clearest indication of the exterminatory aims of the rebels was expressed in their actions and sometimes in their words. Civilians and those identified as Hispanics were clearly rebel targets. In January 1847, when the Indians nominally led by Antonio Trujeque stormed Valladolid, some shouted, "Kill those who have shirts!" Six months later, an Indian spy for the Hispanics reported that the natives gathering at Jacinto Pat's hacienda at Culumpich were organizing "a great conspiracy against the white race." At the outbreak of the rebellion, on July 30, 1847, the rebels screamed, "Perish the Whites!" as they attacked Tepich. During this time they were also "announcing their war of extermination." Indian prisoners from the siege of Peto in January 1948 acknowledged "the existence of a conspiracy" to exterminate the Hispanics. In town after town, such as Kancaboonot, Santa María, Valladolid, Sitilpech, and others, the rebels killed people on the basis of race or perceived racial affinity.[9]

Native atrocities likewise figure prominently in the history of native-white interaction in North and South America. The tit-for-tat character of much frontier violence is evident in detailed accounts like John Ellis's *The First Way of War* and William Osborn's *The Wild Frontier.*[10] Large-scale uprisings like the Andean and Pueblo revolts were aimed at a genocidal "final solution" to white settlement through root-and-branch extermination of the colonizer population, usually wedded to a millennial vision of native resurrection. An example is the Red Sticks uprising among Creeks in 1813. The rallying cry of the Red Sticks (so named because of the color of their war clubs) is one of the more chilling calls to arms in recent centuries: "War now. War forever. War upon the living. War upon the dead; dig up their corpses from the grave; our country must give no rest to a white man's bones."[11]

As such injunctions attest, native insurgents—like subaltern actors the world over—attached great significance to symbolic and ritualistic forms of rebellion. What was rhetorical in the Red Sticks' battle cry was actualized in earlier conflicts like King Philip's War of 1675–76, in what would become the northeast United States. In her study of the war and its role in forming American identity, Jill Lepore describes intricately coded tortures, mutilations, and other atrocities inflicted by members of the Algonquian nation upon the European settlers, with whom they were much more evenly matched militarily than would be true in subsequent centuries. "New England's Algonquians were attempting, in small, physical dramas, to turn the English world inside out and upside down"; they "sought to cultivate chaos" and to "disorder . . . English society." Lepore cites the Algonquian practice of "burying English captives alive and taunting them, 'You English since you came into this Countrey [*sic*] have grown exceedingly above the Ground, let us now see how you will grow when Planted into the Ground.'"[12]

Even today, one does not have to dig very deep into the discourse of indigenism to find echoes—fortunately distant—of such motifs. Bolivia has witnessed a profound resurgence of the expression of indigenous identity and culture. The first indigenous president, Evo Morales, is a moderate figure, but there are many more radical voices that have fomented the blockades and resistance to resource exploitation in recent years. Perhaps the best known is Felipe Quispe, the Aymara Indian whose "bitterness and venom" shocked the country's pigmentocratic elite, according to Amy Chua. Quispe's comments exhibited a finely tuned sense of past humiliations and their power to mobilize subaltern populations in the present. "After negotiations between protesting Amerindian farmers and the cabinet broke down, Quispe shouted at the (white) minister: 'The whites should leave the country. We cannot negotiate the blood of my brothers. Kill me if you are men!' Years before, when asked by a journalist why he was engaging in terrorist activity, Quispe lashed back, 'So that my daughter will not have to be your maid.'"[13]

Peasant *Jacqueries*

"I am horrified!" wrote Mexican intellectual Francisco Bulnes in 1910, decrying the agrarian radicalism preached by Otilio Montaño, a schoolteacher who strongly influenced peasant leader Emiliano Zapata. For Bulnes, Zapata and his legions of "illiterate, darkskinned and crooked peasants" had "raised the holy banner of the war of the poor against the rich":

> Everything now belongs to the poor; the haciendas, with all their land and waters, cattle and brush pasture; the women, the honor and the life of those who are not

Indians. Crime is being preached like a new Gospel, the landowners are to be killed like vipers, smashing their heads with a stone. Their wives and children belong to the people, in revenge for the wantonness of untrammelled hacienda owners, violators of the virgins of the people.[14]

Bulnes's vision of class annihilation is typical of the nightmares of hegemonic actors throughout history. In these fevered imaginings, the resentful poor are always on the verge of rising up to slaughter their overlords. But the terror at the heart of these dreams is hardly baseless. The greatest uprisings in human history have been peasant revolts—the nineteenth-century Taiping Rebellion in China alone mobilized tens of millions of peasants, and its suppression may have claimed upward of *20 million* lives.[15] Instances of peasant revolt (*jacquerie*) on a greater or lesser scale are scattered throughout the history of nearly every European country.

The motives for such uprisings are not difficult to discern: material deprivation combined with a consuming sense of oppression, injustice, and exploitation. The Croquant rebels who rose in Périgord, France, between 1637 and 1641, repeatedly declared their unwillingness to bow before "oppression"—"the word recurs four times" in their "Declaration of the Assembled Communities," as Yves-Marie Bercé notes. And so "the rebels . . . cried death to their oppressors, and vowed to exterminate them." Such subaltern revolts are depicted as "act[s] of justice and cleansing."[16] The cry for *justice* almost always features. The world is to be turned upside down; the mighty will be brought low; a just order will prevail. English radicals of the mid-seventeenth century cheered proclamations like that of Quaker leader George Fox, in 1653: "O ye great men and rich men of the earth! Weep and howl for your misery that is coming. . . . The fire is kindled, the day of the Lord is appearing, a day of howling. . . . All the loftiness of men must be laid low."[17] From the other side of the world, a Vietnamese folk song expressed a similar vision, minus the fire and brimstone:

> The son of the king becomes king
> The son of the pagoda caretaker knows only how to sweep
>   with the leaves of the banyan tree.
> When the people rise up,
> The son of the king, defeated, will go sweep the pagoda.[18]

Such peasant revolts, like native uprisings, regularly display a millenarian dimension.[19] Yves-Marie Bercé describes the peasant rebels of early modern France as "looking back to a golden age of freedom . . . the return of a mythical past. They located this past in the reign of a king with a legendary reputation for justice."[20] Eric Wolf's survey *Peasant Wars of the Twentieth Century* likewise notes that it is "peasant anarchism [rejection of state authority]" combined with "an apocalyptic vision of the world" that "together, provide the ideological fuel that drives the rebellious peasantry."[21]

Millenarian revolts by subaltern masses are frequently, by disposition or direction, anti-modern and primitivist in their orientation. Ben Kiernan, in his recent book *Blood and Soil*, has examined the atavistic element in genocidal ideology, extending back millennia. The elements of "pastoral romance, agrarian ideals, or historical myth," Kiernan writes, were combined with "striking" frequency in genocidal outbreaks. All "share a basis in the utopian, the intangible, the irrational." In their most extreme form, they generate the "violent racism" and "aggression" that underpin genocide and other forms of mass violence.[22]

Modern Anti-Colonial Rebellions

Violence by natives against their overlords, wrote Frantz Fanon in *The Wretched of the Earth*, is "a cleansing force. It frees the native from his inferiority complex and from his despair and inaction; it makes him fearless and restores his self-respect." It exposes the settler to vengeful victimization according to the same binary racial categories that colonialism had constructed: "To the saying 'All natives are the same' the colonized person replies, 'All settlers are the same.'" And violence melds the native masses, driving them irresistibly forward. It "binds them together as a whole, since each individual forms a violent link in the great chain, a part of the great organism of violence which has surged upward in reaction to the settler's violence in the beginning." *"The native,"* Fanon asserts, *"is an oppressed person whose permanent dream is to become the persecutor."*[23]

Fanon is viewed as the oracle of the Algerian revolution of 1954–62, and in this, one of the bloodiest anti-colonial wars of the twentieth century, many militants proved willing to inflict indiscriminate "retributive" violence against the colonizer. Sometimes this took the form of terrorist attacks on civilians, of the type evoked unforgettably in the café-bombing scene of Gillo Pontecorvo's 1966 film *The Battle of Algiers*. Massacres of French civilians were also accomplished by more traditional means. Provoked by the vicious *ratissages* (rat-hunts) conducted by French forces against guerrillas and their supporters, the National Liberation Front (FLN) "launch[ed], for the first time, a policy of total war on all French civilians, regardless of age and sex." In terms echoing those of Fanon, FLN Youssef Zighout declared: "To colonialism's policy of collective repression we must reply with collective reprisals against the Europeans, military and civil, who are all united behind the crimes committed upon our people. For them, no pity, no quarter!" The most notorious massacre occurred in and around Philippeville in August 1954, when the FLN mobilized mobs and death squads to kill over a hundred civilians across a wide area. At El-Halia, the killers, led by mineworkers,

> went from house to house, mercilessly slaughtering all the occupants regardless of sex or age, and egged on by Muslim women with their eerie *you-you* chanting. . . . In houses literally awash with blood, European mothers were found with their throats slit and their bellies slashed open by bill-hooks. Children had suffered the same fate, and infants in arms had had their brains dashed out against the wall. Four families had been wiped out down to the last member. . . . Men returning home from the mine had been ambushed in their cars and hacked to pieces. Altogether thirty-seven Europeans had died, including ten children under fifteen, and another thirteen had been left for dead.[24]

The Algerian war was a cataclysmic eruption, by comparison with most processes of decolonization and national liberation in the post–World War II period.

It was also a particularly vicious and murderous one. Parallels can be found in the subaltern atrocities against whites during the "Mau-Mau" uprising in British-ruled Kenya in the 1950s.[25] More common in the contemporary era, however, have been anti-colonial and anti-neocolonial riots stopping short of systematic massacre, let alone full-scale genocide. Consider this news dispatch from Ivory Coast in 2004:

> French troops clashed with soldiers and angry mobs Saturday after Ivory Coast warplanes killed eight French peacekeepers and an American civilian in an air-strike—mayhem that threatened to draw foreign troops deeper into the West African nation's escalating civil war. After France retaliated for the airstrike, thousands of pro-government youths, some armed with machetes, axes or chunks of wood, took to the streets of the country's commercial capital, Abidjan. Crowds went door to door looking for French citizens and set fire to a French school, sending a pall of smoke over the city. 'Everybody get your Frenchman!' young men in the mob shouted to each other.[26]

Or this, from Tibet at the time of writing (March 2008):

> Tibetans randomly beat and killed Chinese solely on the basis of their ethnic-ity. . . . A young Chinese motorcyclist is struck by stones. Witmore utters a silent scream to the man, "Keep moving!" but the motorcyclist stops, as if to reason with the mob. Soon his flashy gold helmet is off and the mob is pound-ing his head with stones and pipes. . . . Police flee, and by early afternoon the mobs have the run of the city. They go after Chinese shopkeepers, who these days dominate the commercial life of Lhasa. "They thought we Han Chinese people were coming to steal from their rice bowls," says the manager of Top of the World Hotel on Ramoche Street, near the temple. She cowers in her courtyard as the crowd sets fire to many of her neighbors' businesses. . . . Riots spread to the Muslim quarter, targeting the Hui, Chinese Muslims who have been opening businesses in Tibet. Rioters smash holes through metal shop gates and pour in gasoline. A Muslim family later describes to Chinese jour-nalists how they hid in a bathroom as flames spread around them. The main gate of the mosque is set on fire, but the mob doesn't get inside.[27]

Such atrocities—pogroms, riots, and vigilante killings, as well as murders where an element of subaltern hatred may accompany motives of material gain—are not usually of a sufficient scale and systematic character to qualify as fully realized genocide. They are better placed elsewhere on a continuum of subaltern genocidal actions, among phenomena that likewise exude a "proto-genocidal quality," serving as "an augury of extermination."[28] I explore the continuum of subaltern genocide in the closing chapter of this volume.

Notes

1. See Girard, "Caribbean Genocide," 138–61.
2. Childs, *The 1812 Aponte Rebellion in Cuba and the Struggle against Atlantic Slavery*, 129.
3. Davis, *Inhuman Bondage*, 224.
4. Styron, *The Confessions of Nat Turner*.

5. Davis, *Inhuman Bondage*, 208.

6. Ibid., 219–20.

7. Reed, *The Caste War of Yucatan*, 175.

8. Robins notes that "although the Hispanics were referred to as whites, as elsewhere ethnicity was intimately linked with racial orientation, language, clothing, and occupation. At the beginning of the national period [in the 1820s] over half of the rural Hispanics were part Indian. . . . The insurgents . . . also killed Indians who, due to their support of the Hispanics, were considered 'spiritual Spaniards' and were often relatively well-off compared with the mass of rebels." Robins, *Native Insurgencies and the Genocidal Impulse in the Americas*, 88. James C. Scott describes the continuum of "*kulturkampf*" (cultural war) that prevails in many subaltern communities. "Subordinate groups do their own patrolling . . . singling out anyone who puts on airs, who denies his origins, who seems aloof, who attempts to hobnob with elites. These sanctions brought against them may run the gamut from small gestures of disapproval to a complete shunning and, of course, to physical intimidation and violence." Scott, *Domination and the Arts of Resistance*, 130.

9. Robins, *Native Insurgencies*, 89. The devastation of the Caste War is still strikingly evident in some towns and villages of the Yucatán. See my photo galleries at http://www.genocidetext.net/gaci_yucatan.htm.

10. Grenier, *The First Way of War: American War Making on the Frontier, 1607–1814*; Osborn, *The Wild Frontier*.

11. Quoted in Wilson, *The Earth Shall Weep*, 156. Emphasis added.

12. Lepore, *The Name of War*, 118–19.

13. Chua, *World on Fire*, 50.

14. Wolf, *Peasant Wars of the Twentieth Century*, 30–31.

15. See the estimates compiled by Matthew White in "Statistics of Wars, Oppressions and Atrocities of the Nineteenth Century," http://users.erols.com/mwhite28/wars19c.htm.

16. Bercé, *History of Peasant Revolts*, 120, 238, 272.

17. Hill, *The World Turned Upside Down*, 234.

18. Quoted in Scott, *Domination and the Arts of Resistance*, 81.

19. Eric Van Young defines "a millenarian/messianic belief system" as a common feature of "subaltern groups." Such belief systems "encompass a number of ideas: that the end of the world is nigh and/or can be precipitated by the action of the chosen, that a divinely annointed [sic] (or divine) figure will lead the faithful to a better world through a period of travail and the settling of old accounts, that renewal will thus be spiritual as well as material, that the last shall be first, and so on." Young, *The Other Rebellion*, 25, 27.

20. Bercé, *History of Peasant Revolts*, 276. Reynald Secher writes that for the Vendean rebels of the 1790s, the "'old days'" likewise were perceived "as a kind of golden age that was regretted, idealized, not forgotten, and that had been violated." Secher, *A French Genocide*, 13.

21. Wolf, *Peasant Wars*, 295.

22. Kiernan, *Blood and Soil*, 23, 27.

23. Fanon, *The Wretched of the Earth*, 53, 93–94. Emphasis added.

24. Horne, *A Savage War of Peace*, 120–22.

25. See Anderson, "Killing Bwana" [i.e., the white person], in Anderson, *Histories of the Hanged*, 86–111.

26. "French, Ivory Coast Forces Battle."

27. Demick, "Witnesses to Tibet Violence Describe Scenes of Horror." According to "a 27-year-old migrant worker from Sichuan province," "The Tibetans were looking

for Han Chinese to kill, adults and children. Somebody told me they suspended these Chinese schoolboys from the beams inside the Jokhang Temple, to protest, I guess. . . . It's normal for the Tibetans to hate the Chinese. You are on their turf, of course they hate you." Quoted in Ching-Ching Ni, "Tibet Witnesses Describe 'Mayhem Everywhere.'"

28. Horowitz, *The Deadly Ethnic Riot*, 459, 465.

Works Cited

Anderson, David. *Histories of the Hanged: The Dirty War in Kenya and the End of Empire.* New York: W. W. Norton, 2005.

Bercé, Yves-Marie. *History of Peasant Revolts: The Social Origins of Rebellion in Early Modern France.* Ithaca: Cornell University Press, 1990.

Childs, Matt D. *The 1812 Aponte Rebellion in Cuba and the Struggle against Atlantic Slavery.* Chapel Hill: University of North Carolina Press, 2006.

Chua, Amy. *World on Fire: How Exporting Free Market Democracy Breeds Ethnic Hatred and Global Instability.* New York: Anchor Books, 2004.

Davis, David Brion. *Inhuman Bondage: The Rise and Fall of Slavery in the New World.* Oxford: Oxford University Press, 2006.

Demick, Barbara. "Witnesses to Tibet Violence Describe Scenes of Horror." *Los Angeles Times,* March 22, 2008.

Egerton, Douglas R. *Gabriel's Rebellion: The Virginia Slave Conspiracies of 1800 & 1802.* Chapel Hill: University of North Carolina Press, 1994.

Fanon, Frantz. *The Wretched of the Earth.* New York: Grove Press, 1963.

"French, Ivory Coast Forces Battle." Associated Press dispatch, November 6, 2004.

Girard, Philippe. "Caribbean Genocide: Racial War in Haiti, 1802–04." *Patterns of Prejudice* 39, no. 2 (2005): 138–61.

Grenier, John. *The First Way of War: American War Making on the Frontier, 1607–1814.* Cambridge: Cambridge University Press, 2005.

Hill, Christopher. *The World Turned Upside Down: Radical Ideas during the English Revolution.* London: Penguin, 1991.

Horne, Alistair. *A Savage War of Peace: Algeria, 1954–1962.* New York: Viking Press, 1977.

Horowitz, Donald L. *The Deadly Ethnic Riot.* Berkeley: University of California Press, 2001.

Kiernan, Ben. *Blood and Soil: A World History of Genocide and Extermination from Sparta to Darfur.* New Haven: Yale University Press, 2006.

Lepore, Jill. *The Name of War: King Philip's War and the Origins of American Identity.* New York: Vintage, 1998.

Ni, Ching-Ching. "Tibet Witnesses Describe 'Mayhem Everywhere.'" *Los Angeles Times,* March 18, 2008.

Osborn, William M. *The Wild Frontier: Atrocities during the American-Indian War from Jamestown Colony to Wounded Knee.* New York: Random House, 2000.

Reed, Nelson. *The Caste War of Yucatan.* Stanford: Stanford University Press, 1964.

Robins, Nicholas. *Native Insurgencies and the Genocidal Impulse in the Americas.* Bloomington: Indiana University Press, 2005.

Scott, James C. *Domination and the Arts of Resistance.* New Haven: Yale University Press, 1990.

Secher, Reynald. *A French Genocide: The Vendée.* Trans. George Holoch. Notre Dame, Ind.: University of Notre Dame Press, 2003.

Styron, William. *The Confessions of Nat Turner.* New York: Random House, 1967.

Vidal, Gore. *Palimpsest: A Memoir.* New York: Penguin, 1995.

White, Matthew. "Statistics of Wars, Oppressions and Atrocities of the Nineteenth Century." http://users.erols.com/mwhite28/wars19c.htm

Wilson, James. *The Earth Shall Weep: A History of Native America.* New York: Atlantic Monthly Press, 1996.

Wolf, Eric R. *Peasant Wars of the Twentieth Century.* New York: HarperColophon, 1973.

Young, Eric Van. *The Other Rebellion: Popular Violence, Ideology, and the Mexican Struggle for Independence, 1810–1821.* Stanford: Stanford University Press, 2001.

3

Ethical Cleansing?

The Expulsion of Germans from Central and Eastern Europe

ERIC LANGENBACHER

The defining historical event of the twentieth century for Central and Eastern European countries, and for their mutual interaction, remains World War II and the Holocaust. During this period, Nazi Germany waged genocidal total war, killing millions of civilians, including 6 million Jews. Later, as the Red Army advanced into Reich territory in 1944–45, a massive flight and, later, forced deportation of Germans ensued. This ethnic cleansing—known in German as *Vertreibung*, or expulsion—lasted until 1949. It affected millions of Germans from the former Eastern provinces that had been attached to Poland and the Soviet Union, as well as from Czechoslovakia, other areas of Poland, the Baltic lands, Hungary, and the Balkans. Following the removal of the inhabitants, communist authorities almost completely effaced the physical and cultural traces of centuries of German settlement.

This chapter has three parts. The first section reviews the events, decision making, and post-expulsion fate of the expellees. Second, it analyzes postwar and post-communist discourses about the expulsion, focusing especially on the recent debates in response to plans for a museum/memorial devoted to the expellees. Finally, I conclude with some thoughts on international law, norms, and ethics. I do not argue that the expulsion of Germans was a full-blown subaltern genocide. It was, however, an unequivocal case of ethnic cleansing that many in Poland, the Czech Republic, and Germany nonetheless believe to be just—not ethnic cleansing, but ethical cleansing.

This element of "just deserts" attests to the retributory character of the deportations, the subaltern identification of their perpetrators, and the vengeful motivations—born of invasion and oppression—of key actors, including Soviet soldiers and the mostly Slavic populations of the former Nazi-occupied territories. Even though many of the defining characteristics of subaltern genocide were present (one-sided mass killing, defenselessness of the victim, the role of the state), the expulsion of the Germans does not fit unequivocally under the rubric. Nevertheless, an in-depth overview and analysis of precisely such a messy, borderline case can illuminate greatly the more general concepts and classificatory schemes discussed elsewhere in this volume.

Origins of the Ethnic German Populations

Few historical events are as fraught with complexity and controversy as the expulsion of Germans from Central and Eastern Europe at the end and in the aftermath of World War II. Every fact seems contested, and political-intellectual battles over interpretation are fierce. There are even extreme sensitivities over place names—Wrocław vs. Breslau, Szczecin vs. Stettin, Gdansk vs. Danzig, Karlovy Vary vs. Karlsbad—and over terminology: expulsion, transfer, resettlement, relocation, and ethnic cleansing. One would think that chronological distance would allow for a more dispassionate treatment, but this is not so. The events are not distant and abstract history, but very much present as collective memories and emotions.

Much of what I write about here needs to be carefully prefaced and qualified. In this chapter, I do not focus on the fate of Poland and Poles. It is an uncontested fact that the Polish nation suffered immensely at the hands of Nazi Germans—5 million were killed (3 million of them Jewish), often in the atrocious conditions of concentration and death camps.[1] Approximately 17 percent of the prewar population of 35 million died—or 160–170 per 1,000—whereas in Czechoslovakia the toll was 21 per 1,000, and in France 13 per 1,000.[2] Many civilians perished in acts of resistance or in Wehrmacht reprisals; millions more were killed by conscious Nazi/Wehrmacht policies of starvation.[3] Moreover, millions of Poles and Soviet citizens were deported to Germany and forced to perform slave labor in wartime industries—2.5–3 million Poles, many of whom died because of the inhumane conditions. The Nazis murdered the country's political, cultural, and intellectual elite, and willfully decimated its physical and cultural infrastructure—exemplified by the destruction of Warsaw at the very end of the war. It took decades for Poland to recover from this calamity, as Nazi depredations gave way to Soviet communism and nearly half a century of continued dictatorship. The thriving Jewish community, a central component of Polish life for centuries, was utterly destroyed and never recovered.

A second important point is that it was Hitler who began the modern round of population transfers in the 1930s and 1940s—beginning with German Jews. Nazi dreams of an expanded Germany—of *Lebensraum* (living space)—called for large parts of ethnically mixed areas of Poland to be "cleansed" of Poles and repopulated by Germans. The Nazis began to implement this policy in 1939, expelling almost 1 million Poles from regions such as Poznan and the so-called Generalgouvernement (Zamosc), and repopulating them with (often unwilling) ethnic Germans from the Baltic lands, Volhynia, and elsewhere.[4]

I also do not deal explicitly with the tragic fate of the 1.5–2 million Poles who themselves were victims of ethnic cleansing in the former *kresy*—the provinces of eastern Poland that Stalin attached to Soviet Republics (Lithuania, Belorussia, and

Ukraine) after 1939 and again after 1945.[5] Although ethnic settlement patterns were intermingled in these regions, many contiguously Polish areas, including the predominantly Polish cities of Wilno/Vilnius and Lwów/Lviv, were "cleansed." The vast majority of these victims were resettled in lands formerly inhabited by Germans (especially residents of Lwów in Wrocław and of Wilno in Gdansk). The trauma of the loss of these provinces and cities, which had belonged to Polish states for centuries, still festers, and has inhibited a fuller normalization between Poland and Ukraine, Lithuania, Belorussia, and Russia.[6]

I should also clarify the German populations of the regions discussed in this chapter. *Reichsdeutsche* (Imperial Germans) had lived in what were before 1945 the eastern provinces of the German state. Silesia, Pomerania, and East Prussia had been part of a unified Germany since 1871, and before that were included in other German states or empires (the Holy Roman Empire, the German Confederation, the Habsburg Empire, Prussia).[7] In the Middle Ages, most of these provinces formed part of Polish or Bohemian kingdoms, or territories of the Teutonic Knights. All were included in the first Polish Piast kingdom, founded around AD 1000. But despite the historical question of formal "ownership," these areas had German majorities for the entire modern period. Before World War II, Lower Silesia (around Breslau), the Neumark area of Brandenburg, and the area of Pomerania around Stettin were 100 percent German; the rest of Pomerania, 99 percent; Danzig, 92.8 percent; East Prussia, 93.8 percent; and Weimar Upper Silesia, 57 percent.[8]

Volksdeutsche (ethnic Germans) are a more disparate grouping that refers to Germans who did not or never lived in a modern German state, although many had lived during certain periods in a German-dominated empire. The millions of Bohemian and Moravian Germans, later known as Sudeten Germans, had lived in contiguously German regions abutting the borders with Bavaria, Saxony, Austria, and Silesia since the Middle Ages. Many of them constituted a privileged ruling group during most of the Habsburg period until 1918. There were also ethnic Germans in the region of Poznan and West/Royal Prussia/Danzig, who had lived in a German state for much of the modern period.[9]

Indeed, there were 2.1 million Germans in Poland in 1919. Two-thirds lived in regions that had been part of Bismarck's empire (Polish Upper Silesia, West/Royal Prussia, Posen/Poznan)[10]—and Germans constituted two-thirds of the population of West/Royal Prussia and a third of Poznan.[11] Until the mid- to late nineteenth century, many of the cities throughout Central and Eastern Europe were populated predominantly by Germans (and/or Germanized Jews), including Thorn/Torun, Bromberg/ Bydgoszcz, and Posen/Poznan (which was 60 percent German in 1848); Riga (where German was the official language until 1891, and a German aristocracy persisted until the twentieth century); Budapest; Prague (which had a German majority until 1861 and remained an important center of German culture until 1945); and Bratislava (which was called Pressburg until 1919). Finally, there were more scattered German settlements in Yugoslavia (Donauschwaben), Romania (Transylvania and Siebenbürgen), Slovakia (Zips and the Carpathian Germans), Poland proper, Russia/Ukraine (Volhynia and the Volga Germans), and Hungary.

Like *Reichsdeutsche, Volksdeutsche* were not late transplants—most had first settled these territories in the Middle Ages.[12] Josef Korbel, whose influential history of twentieth-century Czechoslovakia is otherwise not very sympathetic to the Sudeten Germans, writes: "One cannot speak of the origins of the German minority in the Sudetenland in any sense that implies a policy of imperialism."[13] It is important to note that some of these "Germans" were actually not ethnically German, but rather Germanized Slavs—who had, voluntarily or not, adopted German language and culture. Mention must also be made of various "indigenous" or autochthon populations—especially the Masurians in East Prussia and so-called Water Poles in Upper Silesia, who were ethnically Slav but with strong Germanic influences.[14]

Scale and Nature of the Expulsions

The populations described in the previous sections were the targets of the largest campaign of "ethnic cleansing" in world history, affecting 12–15 million Germans at the end of World War II and in its aftermath.[15] The expulsions caused as many as 2 million deaths, as well as featuring tens of thousands—perhaps as many as 2 million—rapes of German women by Red Army soldiers.[16] They began with the mass flight of much of the civilian population in late 1944 and early 1945 as the Red Army approached Reich territory. The Nemmersdorf (East Prussia) incident, in which the Red Army massacred an entire village, was heavily propagandized by the Nazi regime as an example of Soviet barbarity, with the intent of fortifying the population's will to resist.[17] Instead, a massive flight ensued—used later in communist propaganda to justify postwar territorial changes (i.e., the Germans' decision to leave "voluntarily" meant that they no longer wanted to live there).

There is substantial evidence that maximum flight was the intent of Soviet policy. Stalin and his communist allies wanted to create depopulated regions—"facts on the ground"—before the end of hostilities and a peace conference. Because the Nazis wanted the population to stay and fight until the bitter end, they did little to plan and prepare for the consequences of defeat. Evacuations took place late and haphazardly, which certainly contributed to the high number of casualties.[18] The especially cold winter of 1944–45 intensified the suffering.

The vast majority of refugees at this time were women, children, and the elderly. Most adult men already had died at the front, or would die later as Soviet captives and slave laborers. Hence the overwhelmingly "feminine" nature of the events: Elizabeth Heineman calls this one of the key "moments of women" during this historical period.[19] The brutality of the Red Army and East European partisans is amply documented.[20]

In addition to the rapes (as many as 100,000 in Berlin alone after it fell) and numerous murders of civilians, the Red Army constantly attacked refugee convoys, sinking many boats trying to evacuate refugees—including the *Wilhelm Gustloff,* often referred to as the biggest maritime disaster of all time, with over

9,000 deaths.[21] Again, this behavior was officially encouraged through policy and propaganda,[22] in what Richard Blanke calls a policy of "ethnic self-cleansing."[23] Approximately 4–5 million Germans fled during these months, taking only what they could carry or retain after pervasive looting.[24] Nevertheless, millions were left in these regions at the end of the war; and millions more returned after the cessation of formal hostilities.

After the war's end, Allied agreements validated the expulsion (which had already begun) of all Germans east of the so-called Oder-Neisse line—proclaimed as the new border between Germany and Poland—and from elsewhere in Central and Eastern Europe. However, early agreement in principle among the Big Three gave way to discord at the Potsdam Conference in August 1945. All present concurred that Poland would be reconstituted, and that Germany would be punished territorially. The Soviets also made it clear that they would not return prewar Polish lands occupied in 1939, so that Poles from the *kresy* would need somewhere to resettle. Although Stalin kept the full extent of planned changes vague, it was agreed early on that East Prussia would be given to Poland, cleansed of its Germans, and repopulated with expelled Poles. The numbers involved were approximately equal: about 2.5 million on either side.[25]

Potsdam was thus a fait accompli.[26] All western leaders could do by that point was seek to mitigate the situation by insisting on "orderly and humane transfers" of population, which probably did reduce the number of deaths. It was left to the British press, Western civilian authorities, and the International Red Cross to raise moral and ethical qualms.[27] The *Economist* wrote in September 1945: "The Germans, no doubt, have deserved punishment—but not by torture of this kind. If the Poles and Czechs wish to be rated higher in civilization than the Nazis, they will stop the expulsions at once."[28] Even Churchill, in his famous "iron curtain" speech of 1946, was highly critical as the numbers of those expelled mounted to three or four times what he had envisioned.

Importantly, the various governments-in-exile had contemplated expelling Germans from a very early point. The London Poles wanted East Prussia, Danzig, and the rest of Upper Silesia, as well as the return of the *kresy*. Churchill had to lobby intensely for them to accept Stalin's plans,[29] which were also supported fully by the so-called Lublin Poles, the pro-Moscow communists who eventually gained power. In the Czech case, territorial issues were less complicated, given that the Sudetenland had not belonged to a modern German state. President Eduard Beneš (forced to flee to London in 1939) already had contemplated ethnic cleansing from the time of the Munich Agreement (intensified in response to Nazi occupation and crimes), but certainly not solely in response to such crimes.[30] As Christopher Kopper puts it: "The expulsion of ethnic Germans from Czechoslovakia was not an act of spontaneous anger and revenge. The Czech plans . . . did not only reflect the brutalization of the German occupation regime. From the very beginning, the concept of mass expulsion was a means to solve the general ethnic conflicts."[31] Beneš noted in 1945: "I declare categorically: we must get rid of our Germans, and they will go in any case."[32] These nationalistic preferences helped pave the way for Western acceptance of such decisions.

The eastern German provinces were quickly placed under Polish and Soviet (northern East Prussia) administration, and the Czechs emptied the Sudetenland of Germans.[33] After the end of formal hostilities, there were at least two phases of expulsion—the *wilde Vertreibungen* (wild expulsions), when many atrocities took place,[34] and a more planned, regulated, orderly, and humane "transfer." After the process was complete in 1949–50, a small German minority still remained— many were actually autochthones who were often discriminated against by newcomers.[35] Ironically, given how important these groups were in nationalist propaganda justifying Polish claims to these regions, the vast majority (1.4 million) declared their Germanness in the postwar period and emigrated to one of the Germanys as *Spätaussiedler* (late resettlers). Today, there are about 300,000 Germans remaining in Poland (concentrated in the Opole region), with official minority status and full political rights.[36]

The Postwar and Postcommunist Era: Poland and the Czech Republic

The scale and systematic character of Germans' erasure from these countries is difficult to convey. In the new western territories of Poland, all German place names were expunged and replaced with Polish alternatives, often created from scratch.[37] Many of the cities and towns destroyed in the war were meticulously rebuilt, but minus their German signs and symbols. Derek Sayer writes of Prague that "the record of the Germans' presence was swiftly wiped from the landscape."[38] Gregor Thum deems this "the deliberate attempt of degermanization which I call the cleansing of memory."[39] In Wrocław, the government had special teams that roved for years painting over and chiseling out German inscriptions. Derelict German cemeteries were converted into parks, and headstones were used to line ditches and sewers. Many ethnically "cleansed" Poles from the *kresy* took up residence in the previous German lands—one of the prime justifications offered for the Germans' "transfer." The majority of newcomers were relocated from overpopulated traditional regions in central Poland.[40]

Intellectually, the history of the German presence was expunged, and a nationalist narrative put in its place. National-communist propaganda created a distorted historical picture—a veritable "expulsion complex."[41] Edmund Dimitrów, quoting Borodziej's influential recent study of Polish historiography, writes of an "arbitrary and tendentious" approach which failed to acknowledge "that expellees were defenseless people, the vast majority of whom were not personally guilty of National Socialism."[42] Vocabulary also reinforced the nationalist right of possession.[43] When geographic monikers were not used, the preferred terms were "recovered territories," "reclaimed lands," or "western provinces."[44] The fact that these areas were under the control of the first Polish Piast dynasty around the year 1000 was emphasized to the exclusion of any other historical facts. Indeed, postwar Poland is frequently referred to as Piast Poland, "which with the incorporation of the Prusso-German eastern provinces, became an integral whole."[45]

Germans were recent, colonial interlopers[46] who had simply been sent back to their rightful and original homeland.[47]

Accompanying this is an imputation of collective guilt to the entire German population. Top cultural official Leon Kruczkowski proclaimed in 1949 that "the Germans are criminals—all Germans, the entire German nation."[48] In 1979, Karel Douděra expressed the official Czech communist view that the expulsion "was not an act of vengeance, but an act of national and state defense."[49] Such perspectives persist in many quarters today. In the postcommunist period, the ruling party until 2007, Law and Justice (PiS), stated in a parliamentary resolution: "Responsibility must be borne by the entire German people, the great majority of which supported Hitlerism and accepted Hitler's rule."[50] According to this vision, as Jerzy Kranz describes it, "reparations have to be paid equally by the guilty and not guilty alike. One does not have to participate personally in a crime to be held historically or politically co-responsible for such an event."[51]

This restricted vision of the past was accompanied by biting attacks on the West German government and expellee groups, whenever the issue of the expulsions would arise. The Polish communists equated expellees with the Nazis, diehard revanchists and incorrigible revisionists (*Ewiggestrige*). They also adeptly stoked fears of a return of German aggression, repeatedly stressing how vulnerable Poland's western borders were.[52] These rhetorical strategies were buttressed by the material distribution of former German properties and goods, creating a core group of supporters for the regime. Indeed, the expropriation of German property paved the way for the nationalization of the entire economy in both Poland and Czechoslovakia, and thus greatly facilitated the imposition and stabilization of communist dictatorship.[53]

Another regular emphasis was that Nazi German destruction was so wanton and atrocious that these lands were both just compensation and a form of retribution—also, given what Poland had lost in the east, a kind of "settling of accounts." Communists also played on what has been called a "martyrological" memory—"Poles' comfortable image of their one-nation state and of themselves as the nation of eternal victims."[54] This subaltern framing of history and identity was central to justifying, on both personal and political levels, the expropriation and expulsion of Germans. Sometimes overall numbers of the ethnically cleansed would be mentioned, without differentiating between ethnic Poles and Germans. Most commonly, silence prevailed—toward the expulsions and toward the entire German histories of these provinces.[55] And Poles could always claim that Poland had no say over the postwar settlement—it was only "following orders," dutifully enforcing decisions that it could not influence.[56]

Despite the consistent deployment of such tropes and propaganda ploys, attempts at reconciliation began in the mid-1960s.[57] Noteworthy were the efforts of churches in Poland and West Germany, including an initial 1965 memorandum drafted by the Evangelical Church in which "it accepts the German guilt for Poland's sufferings prior to and during World War Two, and acknowledges German liability for the crimes committed against the Polish population."[58] Also important was the 1965 "Letter of Reconciliation from Polish Bishops to our

German Colleagues"—influenced heavily by the future Pope John Paul II—in which the bishops famously proclaimed, "We forgive and ask for forgiveness."[59] The implementation of Willy Brandt's new Ostpolitik, his gesture of atonement at the memorial to the Warsaw Ghetto Uprising,[60] and the Warsaw Treaty of 1970 led to a proliferation of official contacts during the détente era—such as the joint history school textbook commission.[61] The tone was different with East Germany, given the (often forced) cordiality of communist brethren and the interactions that slowly improved relations. Yet the expulsion remained a taboo subject everywhere behind the iron curtain. In East Germany, when the expelled were referred to at all, it was as *Aussiedler* (resettlers).

In the 1970s, dissidents in Czechoslovakia seized upon the expulsion of the Sudeten Germans as part of their critical agenda to delegitimize the communist regime and to change the culture of their compatriots.[62] An intense *samizdat* (underground newspaper) debate was unleashed by the publication of Danubius's "Theses on the Deportation of the Czechoslovak Germans," in which he wrote: "Masaryk's nation had no ambition to act using the methods of Hitler's nation; by this act it betrayed its most noble ideals and put the future into danger."[63] These authors criticized Czech nationalism and chauvinism, and highlighted the role the expulsion had played in perpetuating totalitarianism. Most important, for these authors, was the depravity of the actions, and the erosion of values and rights that they represented: they asked if "the moral question of whether it is right to punish inhumane treatment with further inhumane treatment is thereby glossed over by blaming the victims collectively for the earlier behavior of a part of the population."[64] This history was also seized upon in Poland, most notably in Jan Jósef Lipski's "Two Fatherlands–Two Patriotisms: Thoughts on the National Megalomania and Xenophobia of the Poles" (1981), in which he called for an honest confrontation with the dark chapters of Polish history and the necessity of forgiveness and reconciliation with Germans, if Poland's Western and European destiny were to be achieved.[65]

After the Fall

When he became president of Czechoslovakia in 1989, former dissident Vaclav Havel, as one of his first acts in office, recognized and apologized for the expulsion. Welcoming German president Richard von Weizsäcker to Prague in 1990, Havel declared:

> Six years of Nazi rule was enough, for example, for us to allow ourselves be infected with the germ of evil. . . . Instead of giving all those who betrayed this state a proper trial, we drove them out of the country and punished them with the kind of retribution that went beyond the rule of law. This was not punishment. It was revenge. Moreover, we did not expel these people on the basis of demonstrable individual guilt, but simply because they belonged to a certain nation. And thus, on the assumption that we were clearing the way for historical

justice, we hurt many innocent people, most of all women and children. And, as is usually the case in history, we hurt ourselves even more. . . .We have to understand that it was not the German nation that caused our agony, but particular human individuals. . . . In other words, to accept the idea of collective guilt and collective responsibility means directly or unwittingly to weaken the guilt or the responsibility of individuals. And that is very dangerous. . . . To impose the guilt of some Germans upon the entire German nation means absolving those particular individuals of their guilt and, with a pessimistic fatalism, submerging them in an irresponsible anonymity.[66]

Since this time, however, German-Czech relations have been strained, mainly because the Sudeten Germans and their conservative/Bavarian allies have called for the revocation of the Beneš Decrees.[67] Such tensions peaked shortly after the fall of communism, and again in the years leading up to the Czech Republic's ascension to the European Union in 2004.[68] After bilateral negotiations went nowhere, Sudeten Germans filed lawsuits before Czech and European courts, losing each time, most notably in 1995, 1999, and 2002. The 1995 decision of the Czech Constitutional Court, described by the Czech press as a German "Trojan Horse," upheld the legality of the decrees, and, breaking with all other legal precedents (including the Nuremberg tribunal), declared Sudeten Germans' collective guilt.[69] Even Havel, in an apparent change of heart, noted: "We are not prepared to let new storms wreck [sic] havoc in the area of property rights, and thus to resurrect all the evil spirits of the past."[70]

The rhetoric on both sides was bitter. In 1996, Christian-Social Union (CSU) politician Theo Waigel linked Czech membership in the European Union to revocation of the decrees. Czech prime minister Vaclav Klaus declared himself "surprised that anybody should wish us to speak about WWII with regret. I have the feeling it is the German side which should speak about the whole matter very quietly."[71] Another commentator referred later to neighboring Germany, Austria, and Hungary as the "European Axis of Evil" for pushing revocation of the decrees.[72] In 2002, Prime Minister Milos Zeman stated that the Sudeten Germans were "Hitler's 5th column that destroyed Czechoslovakia . . . [they] should be happy that they were only 'transferred.' Can you really demand reconciliation with traitors?"[73] Such statements mirrored mainstream opinion: a "majority of young Czechs believed that the Sudeten Germans came to Czechoslovakia as part of Hitler's occupation and deserved to be sent back."[74]

These issues were the major reason that the German-Czech Declaration was delayed for years until 1997. By contrast, German-Polish bilateral relations were considered exemplary during the 1990s.[75] Toward the expulsion, however, a (national) elite silence persisted, albeit with a new hint of sympathy. Noteworthy was the speech of the Polish foreign minister, Władysław Bartoszewski, to the Bundestag in 1995, widely interpreted in Germany as an apology:

As a people that has been particularly devastated by war, we have gotten to know the tragedy of forced migration, as well as the related acts of violence and crimes. We remember that countless persons of the German population were also affected and that Poles belong to the perpetrators. I would like to say this openly: we lament the individual fate and the sufferings of innocent Germans, who were affected by the consequences of war and who left their homeland.[76]

On the ground, numerous expellees and their descendants traveled to their former homes. Large amounts of financial aid and economic investment have also intensified cross-border interaction, doing much to forge intercultural understanding. Academically and intellectually there was an impressive effort to fill historical and historiographical gaps in knowledge.[77] The old communist/nationalistic narratives were exposed to vociferous criticism; local history was recovered, and some of the German material presence has been restored, in regional centers like Gdansk.

Many of the new findings and perspectives, however, have led to controversy —perhaps none more so than the publication of Jan Gross's books, *Neighbors: The Destruction of the Jewish Community in Jedwabne, Poland* (2001) and *Fear: Anti-Semitism in Poland after Auschwitz: An Essay in Historical Interpretation* (2006), both of which unleashed a heated discussion about Polish antisemitism and collaboration with the Nazis.[78] Continuing debates that dated back at least to President Lech Walesa's awkward comments at the fiftieth anniversary of the liberation of Auschwitz,[79] such trends were partially responsible for the general deterioration of memory discourses after 2000, especially following the right-wing Kaczyński twins' rise to power.[80]

In sum, after the fall of communism, things changed, but not quickly or particularly comprehensively. Communist-era tropes and phraseology remain surprisingly common, as many contemporary travel publications reveal. The Polish National Tourist Office's brochure "Silesia: Main Tourist Attractions," for example, states:

> Silesia is a vast historical land in the south-west of Poland. . . . Silesia, in the past, was owned by different rulers; the Piast duchies were passing to Czech, Austrian, or German hands—all the time it was a melting pot of nations, cultures and religions; and this is the origin of the rich cultural heritage of this land. After 1945 the population of Upper Silesia inhabiting this land for generations, with their habits, folk arts, spiritual culture, was complemented, mainly in lower Silesia by the newcomers—Polish citizens from the former eastern territories of Poland, lost after the [Second] World War.

By such strategies, the German past is marginalized and effaced in public discourse.

Germany

In the postwar Federal Republic of Germany (as well as the German Democratic Republic), about 25 percent of the population consisted of expellees. One of the most overlooked achievements of this period was the integration of this potentially destabilizing and irredentist group.[81] The economic miracle in the West helped, by creating full employment and quickly raising standards of living. Specific state policies and institutions also aided—an entire ministry was devoted to expellee issues until 1969; the *Lastenausgleich* (equalization of burdens) partially compensated the expellees for their losses and helped them to build new homes.[82]

The expellees themselves were quite adept at self-organization. The various *Landsmannschaften* (heritage groups) and the Bund der Vertriebenen (BdV, Federation of Expellees) were founded early, and have been constant and influential forces.[83] The Sudeten Germans deserve special mention; they formed one of the most effective and well-financed organizations, the Sudetendeutsche Landsmannschaft. Moreover, the vast majority settled in Bavaria—leading the Bavarian government to "adopt" the group as the fifth tribe of Bavaria, a close political relationship that persists today. These groups, and especially the BdV, were a constant and effective special interest and substantial voting bloc that no politician could ignore—especially from the 1950s to the 1970s. Importantly, the foundational document, the 1950 Charta der Heimatvertriebene, proclaimed that "the right to the homeland is recognized and carried out as one of the fundamental rights of mankind given by God." Yet it renounced seeking retaliation and revenge for the "infinite wrong" of the expulsion.[84]

Symbolically, a concerted official effort was made in the 1950s to document the culture and society of the lost Eastern regions, focusing especially on the experiences of the expulsion. Every postwar government until the 1970s supported the expellees and their issues, and no West German government recognized the finality of the Potsdam settlement—including recognition of the Oder-Neisse border—until 1990. In society and culture, the expulsion, with the bombing of German cities and prisoners of war becoming a core component of the memory of German suffering, was highly salient, even hegemonic in the early postwar decades.[85] Robert Moeller's (2001) seminal study shows how essential was the memory of German suffering during the 1950s and 1960s, attested to by best-selling novels and memoirs, the so-called *Heimatfilmen* (films about the homeland), and commemorations.[86] Manfred Kittel notes that many West German jurisdictions "adopted" a lost, eastern one, naming streets, schools, and even autobahn rest areas after the lost regions.[87] In East Germany, the expulsion was taboo (as was the Holocaust until the late 1980s), but there was much propaganda about Anglo-American bombings constituting war crimes. Indeed, the commemoration of the destruction of Dresden took on national significance.[88]

Things changed decisively, both materially and discursively, in the Federal Republic in the late 1960s and 1970s. The Social Democrats and Left abandoned and soon demonized expellee groups, the price to be paid for reconciliation and normalization with Eastern Europe—Brandt and Scheel's new *Ostpolitik*. The degree of acrimony that this initial period of détente produced, along with the new partisan politics of memory and expellee issues, was a notable turning point in West German history.[89] The SPD-FDP government disbanded the expellee ministry, cut funding for expellee activities, and refused to publish a report in 1974 on crimes committed against Germans in the course of the expulsion. The SPD newspaper opined that publication "would only help the Nazis here."[90] Henceforth, leftists equated expellees with revanchist, radical-right, neo-Nazis.[91]

From that point on the expellees and their descendants became a core constituency of the conservative CDU/CSU coalition.

Moreover, during this period many leftists came to represent Holocaust memory, asserting that the memory of German crimes must be hegemonic if the postwar transformation of Germany were to continue. Many thought that German public discourse could not accommodate memories of both German crimes and German suffering.[92] The children of the perpetrators (called '68ers) comprehensively questioned the Nazi-era behavior of their parents and the Nazi continuities in Chancellor Konrad Adenauer's "restorationist" republic. By the 1980s, and certainly by the *Historikerstreit* (Historians' Debate) of 1985–86, the Left had predominated; most conservatives also came to represent these positions. Holocaust memory and its associated infrastructure, what David Art calls the "culture of contrition," became hegemonic, as the expellees and their memories were not just outmaneuvered but demonized, and even worse forgotten.[93]

This situation changed slightly after the fall of communist regimes and the unification of the country, but expellee issues never gained mainstream attention. Despite fears that memory of the Holocaust and Nazi German crimes would wane in the face of a reunified and normalized Germany, they actually gained greater prominence, as the seamless series of Holocaust-centered memory events since 1990 attest. The expellee plight was highlighted by the fiftieth anniversary commemorations in 1995[94] and in some literary treatments.[95] These developments were strengthened by contemporary events in Rwanda and the former Yugoslavia. But the issue only really became manifest after 2002, with the publication of Günter Grass's novel *Crabwalk* and Jörg Friedrich's account of the area bombing of German cities, *The Fire*.[96] Judging by the media frenzy, these memories and that of the expellees returned with a vengeance. They did not unequivocally dominate the discourse (Holocaust-related memory events continued), but they gained far greater attention and even intruded on international affairs, above all on German-Polish relations.

The *Zentrum gegen Vertreibungen* Initiative

Controversy over plans for a *Zentrum gegen Vertreibungen* (Center against Expulsions) reveals the state of current discourse surrounding the expulsion. A foundation and fundraising strategy were set up in 2000 under the auspices of the BdV and several national politicians, such as Erika Steinbach (CDU), the BdV chairwoman, and Peter Glotz (SPD). They proposed a commemorative and informational center in Berlin, focusing on the expulsion of Germans, yet also presenting other cases and sensitizing visitors to the continuing potential of such acts.[97] The plans generated little attention until the summer of 2003, when they became a topic of debate, mainly in response to Polish criticism.

Many Poles voiced concerns that the German expellees, as before, were working to achieve compensation, the right of return or a recovery of expropriated property.[98] They felt that the planned Zentrum would give "moral legitimacy" to such demands, calling into question Polish wartime suffering, the memory of Polish expulsion from the *kresy*, and resettlement in the old German areas. More generally, they perceived a will to revise history, bolster German nationalism, and portray Germans as (sole) victims of World War II.[99] One historian noted: "Consciousness is created by symbols . . . and this center would be their symbol, the Germany [*sic*] symbol, that they were victims, too, and that would be a symbol detached from the truth about the past."[100] The discussion heated up when the Polish newsmagazine *wprost* published a cover photograph of Steinbach in an SS uniform, riding and whipping Chancellor Gerhard Schröder, with the title "The German Trojan Horse."

Many prominent individuals spoke out. Adam Krzeminski wrote that "Germans are like bitter football players. With a Valhalla of expellees they belatedly want to reach a moral equalization." He saw a "strengthened interest for one's own past that is leading to a new cult of victims and to a German history of suffering."[101] Marek Edelmann, the last living leader of the Warsaw Uprising, also criticized the initiative, asserting that the ever-arrogant Germans paid for Hitler with the expulsion.[102] Leszek Kolakowski wrote: "A Berlin monument for the expellees would be a mistake. It could relativize the horrors of the Second World War and underpin territorial claims for which there are no justifications."[103] Bartoszewski noted that "an old chapter is being reopened to manipulate people's awareness" and proposed a counter-museum dedicated to the history of Germanization in Poznan.[104]

Criticism of the Zentrum initiative, shared by the entire Polish political spectrum, has been heightened by other memory issues. Claims advanced by the *Preussische Treuhand*—a rogue group of expellees which is suing in various jurisdictions to gain restitution (without governmental or BdV support)— confirmed earlier fears, and motivated many jurisdictions to assert financial counterclaims.[105] Lech Kaczyński, as mayor of Warsaw, cited a figure of US $31.5 billion. In September 2004, the Sejm passed a resolution 328–0, demanding that the government launch "appropriate measures against the government of the Federal Republic" to ensure that Poland received adequate compensation for World War II–era destruction.[106]

Although most recent criticism has emanated from Poland, the Czech Republic has also expressed negative reactions. In a May 2005 speech to the annual meeting of the Sudeten German Association in May 2005, Edmund Stoiber, Bavarian premier until 2007, criticized a statue of Beneš that had just been erected in Prague. Socialist Prime Minister Jiri Paroubek lambasted this as inappropriate "meddling" in the internal affairs of the Czech Republic. A statement from his party went even further: "the Czech people heard similarly bitter assaults on Czechoslovakia and Beneš from the mouths of the representatives of Nazi Germany. . . . [We reject] the tone and words of Stoiber." A major rift surfaced between the prime minister and President Vaclav Klaus, with the former advocating the compensation of anti-Nazi Germans who were expelled. Klaus, who had often criticized his predecessor, Havel, for his sympathetic and reconciliatory statements, deemed Paroubek's perspective "exceptionally dangerous." He reiterated sentiments expressed in

May 2005, lambasting the "rewriting of history" and the inability "to distinguish between culprits and victims."[107]

In Germany, although a few politicians and intellectuals defended the plans for the Zentrum, many voiced opposition. A 2003 manifesto condemned the initiative as "one-sidedly national"; it was signed by Markus Meckel (SPD), as well as Grass, who was having second thoughts regarding points of view unleashed by his novel that highlighted German suffering in the late stages of the war. The SPD-Green government also denounced the idea. Schröder, after meeting with Polish prime minister Leszek Miller at the end of September 2003, declared his fear that the Zentrum would be too one-sided, leading to dangerous historical revisionism and revanchism. A "Europeanized" solution was considered necessary; he proposed Strasbourg (others suggested Wrocław/Breslau) as a more appropriate location. The governing parties quickly followed up with concrete counterproposals, trying to outmaneuver backers of the Berlin initiative. A high-level meeting between Presidents Johannes Rau and Aleksander Kwasniewski in October 2003 resulted in the so-called Gdansk Declaration: "Every nation has the self-evident right to mourn, and it is our common duty to ensure that memory and mourning are not mishandled to divide Europe again. Therefore, there is no room today for claims of compensation, for mutual attributions of guilt and for the reckoning of crimes and losses."[108]

A follow-up meeting of cultural ministers from Poland, the Czech Republic, Hungary, Slovakia, Austria, and Germany in summer 2004 advocated establishing a European network for the "documentation and scientific working-through of forced migration and expulsion in the 20th century," based in Warsaw and (partially) financed by the EU. By 2007, this initiative had been largely forgotten, and most observers concluded that it had been undermined from within, by the Polish and Czech governments.[109] In one of the most forceful and direct statements of the SPD-Green government's attitude, Schröder, the first German chancellor to be invited to the commemorations of the Warsaw Uprising, in August 2004, asserted:

> We Germans know very well who started the war and who its first victims were. Therefore, there may be no more room for restitution claims from Germany that turn history on its head. Property questions associated with the Second World War are not a topic in German-Polish relations for either government. Neither the federal government nor other serious political forces in Germany supports individual claims. . . . The federal government will also take this position in front of all international courts.[110]

Despite all this criticism inside and outside the country, the museum/memorial initiative moved forward, aided by the change in government in 2005 and Chancellor Angela Merkel's (low-key) support. In summer 2006, a temporary exhibition, *Erzwungene Wege* (Forced Paths), was mounted in the heart of Berlin. It was met with bitter protests by German leftists and Polish nationalists. Indicative were the comments of Prime Minister Jarosław Kaczyński: "We wish that everything that is connected with the name of Mrs. Steinbach ends as quickly as possible, because nothing good will come of that for Poland, Germany or Europe. . . . [We must remember] who was the aggressor and who was the victim."[111]

By fall 2007, a resolution had been achieved. The grand coalition agreed to spend 1.2 million euros on the Zentrum in 2008. The SPD did, however, make its support conditional on Steinbach and the Bund not being directly involved.[112] Prominent socialist Wolfgang Thierse stated: "The BdV will not be involved with the project that the federal government is actualizing. We will do everything that we can to make sure that the projects are not mixed up." Merkel, however, noted that "the commemoration of the expulsion is a 'part of our German identity and a part of our culture of memory.' . . . 'We will not mix up causes and consequences when we commemorate the expulsion.'"[113]

This endgame proved much less dramatic than the previous debates. It was rumored that the German government had waited until after the predicted defeat of Kaczyński's PiS in the Sejm elections of October 2007. Indeed, the new Polish government has been more neutral, although Prime Minister Donald Tusk also has launched a counter-initiative, a World War II museum to be located in Gdansk, observing that "we possibly could also end the shameful and endless argument about the commemoration of expellees when we discuss such a project."[114] Nevertheless, the kind of criticisms seen previously did surface. The Central Council of Jews in Germany called for the BdV to forgo its "disastrous tradition of morally paralleling the Holocaust and the expulsion . . . want[ing] to treat the two in the same way." Left Party deputy Ulla Jepke stated that the BdV relativized fascism, presenting perpetrators as victims, and that fifty years of revanchism was enough.[115]

Ethical Cleansing

Space does not allow for a full examination of debates about the status of "ethnic cleansing" in international law. Using the precedent of the Nuremberg Tribunal, some scholars have made the case that ethnic cleansing is a war crime or crime against humanity.[116] Others believe that it is a form of genocide: they cite the 1948 Genocide Convention, which outlaws "acts committed with intent to destroy, in whole or in part, a national, ethnic, racial or religious group." Rather than passing a verdict on this matter, I want to emphasize instead *how rare it is to find a case of ethnic cleansing that most observers do not deplore.* Admittedly, in an application of "realist" thinking, some authors argue that ethnic cleansing can "solve" intractable ethnic conflicts.[117] Others argue that no real legal redress is available, or that certain events happened too far in the past to be actionable. Nevertheless, identification and condemnation of the acts as brutal, criminal, and unjust is typical.

As this chapter has demonstrated, however, this is mostly not true with regard to the expulsion of the Germans. In fact, many will not even classify this as a case of ethnic cleansing or expulsion. Elites in Poland and the Czech Republic still deploy embittered rhetoric from the communist period—evincing no sympathy, vilifying the expellees and their initiatives, barely recognizing centuries of German settlement, and emphasizing solely the victimization of their own nations by the Nazis. These positions are widely supported in Germany as well—although there, a vigorous debate covering all positions has taken place. One can only conclude that political and media elites (but not academics) in Poland and the Czech Republic, along with most of the German Left, believe that the "transfer" of Germans was warranted and eminently just. Notions of collective guilt and punishment are unquestioningly assumed, to ensure that Germans can in no way be construed as "victims." If the Holocaust is for many the quintessential example of genocide, this is a paradigmatic example of *ethical cleansing*.

Interestingly, the publics of Germany, Poland, and the Czech Republic are more nuanced in their attitudes, displaying more empathy than their elites. Despite the rhetorical excesses of the last few years, 80 percent of Poles still think that Polish-German unity is possible, and a plurality believes that Germany is Poland's closest ally in the European Union.[118] Sixty-two percent would look favorably on having a German in-law; 97 percent are favorable toward German tourists; and over 50 percent have no problem with a German becoming a Polish citizen.[119] A 2003 survey found that 57 percent of Poles and 36 percent of Germans thought that Germans were victims of World War II, just like Jews and Poles.[120] In Germany, 31 percent (37 percent of expellees and their descendants) answered that "the Germans certainly committed many crimes in World War II, but that does not justify the expulsion of Germans from the eastern territories. The governments of the Czech Republic, Poland and Russia should apologize for that." By contrast, 44 percent (38 percent of expellees) said that "flight and expulsion would never have happened if Germans had not committed so many crimes in World War II. Therefore, the governments of these countries must not apologize."[121] Nevertheless, as Table 3.1 shows, in Poland and the Czech Republic, the limits of sympathy (and perhaps the effects of elite-level discourses) are apparent.[122]

Overall, however, assessments of this past may be less important than a rather pervasive indifference and a marked lack of knowledge. As Tables 3.2 and 3.3 reveal, mass publics in all three countries greatly underestimate the number of Germans expelled, while Poles simultaneously overestimate the number of Poles expelled from the *kresy*.[123]

TABLE 3.1   Was the Expulsion of Germans Justified? (June 2004)

	Poland				Czech Republic			
Age	16–29	30–44	45–59	60+	16–29	30–44	45–59	60+
Expulsion was justified	66	72	66	73	61	76	71	76
Expulsion was unjust	18	14	15	10	14	10	14	13

TABLE 3.2   UNDERESTIMATION OF THE NUMBER OF EXPELLED GERMANS
(GERMANY, DECEMBER 2002; POLAND AND CZECH REPUBLIC, JUNE 2004)

	Germany	Poland	Czech Republic
Mean Estimate	5.6 M	3.5 M	2.0 M
Actual Number	14.0 M	7.0 M	3.0 M
Degree of Underestimation	60%	50%	33%

TABLE 3.3   OVERESTIMATION OF POLISH REFUGEES AND EXPELLEES (JUNE 2004)

	Total Population	Expellees and Relatives
Mean Estimate	3.9 M	5.1 M
Actual Number	1.5 M	1.5 M
Degree of Overestimation	260%	340%

Distortion of history and forgetting may thus be the ultimate fate of the expellees. The subaltern identification of the Polish inhabitants of lands and settlements from which Germans were expelled, and the broad moral legitimacy this identification commands across Europe (even in Germany), combines with "collective guilt" even to undermine expellee claims for symbolic recognition. In this sense, they are very similar to the murdered Afrikaner farm families in South Africa, discussed by Adam Jones in chapter 9, who were likewise viewed as representatives of an oppressive former order, and to ethnic-Serb refugees expelled from the Krajina region of Croatia during "Operation Storm" in 1995.[124] "The Serbs" were widely viewed as having "gotten what was coming to them" after years of war in which Serbs from Bosnia and Serbia had inflicted the majority of war crimes and other atrocities. Still today, they constitute the largest refugee population in Europe; but stemming from their popular identification as perpetrators and human rights abusers, they are denied the kind of moral legitimacy (and resultant policy initiatives) that Kosovar Albanians, for example, were afforded during the crisis of 1999 and into the present vis-à-vis the independence movement.

Let me leave the reader with a quote, which nicely captures my perspective on current discourses regarding the expulsion of the Germans and other similar cases:

> Of all of Poland's neighbors, however, the Germans have the most reason to query the official version of Polish History. . . . No amount of sophistry can dismiss the fact that the German element was dominant in those parts for the last six or seven hundred years. . . . The list [of famous sons and daughters] is endless. . . . Who is to say that so many distinguished names, and the ancient German communities which produced them, are now to be dissociated from the land of their birth? How, if they are simply struck from the record, can their evil deeds, as well as their noble ones, be remembered?[125]

Notes

1. Polish statistics previously reported 6 million deaths. Postcommunist scholarship has revised that to 5 million, concluding that between 1.8–1.9 million ethnic Poles died. Note the problems of counting given the border shifts of the World War II era. For instance, how should Lithuanians or Ukrainians living in interwar Poland be counted?

2. Urban, *Der Verlust*, 94.

3. Hartmann, Hürter, and Jureit, *Verbrechen der Wehrmacht*.

4. Urban, *Der Verlust*.

5. Also, about 500,000 Ukrainians and Belarussians were deported from post-1945 Poland—most notably in Operation Wisla in 1947.

6. Snyder, "Memory of Sovereignty."

7. Silesia was Prussian since 1741 (and Austrian from 1526–1741), as was most of Pomerania since 1720 and most of East Prussia from 1618 (although attached to the Margravate of Brandenburg and ruled by Hohenzollerns since 1525—and before that by the Teutonic Knights). Unlike Silesia and Pomerania, East Prussia was never a part of the Holy Roman Empire or German Confederation.

8. De Zayas, *Nemesis at Potsdam*, 54–55. Due partially to demographic growth in the more heavily populated western regions, German settlement began in the 1100s—called the *Drang nach Osten* (drive to the East). This process was officially encouraged by Polish kings (and Slavic rulers in Bohemia and Russia), who also called in the Teutonic Knights to fight the non-Slav pagan Prussian tribes on the Baltic coast in 1226. Some Slavs were displaced in these processes, but the vast majority of newcomers settled on previously uninhabited land and founded many towns and cities. Also, Poles had their own *Drang nach Osten* in these centuries, expanding into marchlands like the Wilno and Lwów regions.

9. West/Royal Prussia was attached to Prussia after the First Partition of Poland in 1772, although German inhabitants had been already there for centuries. Danzig had numerous allegiances (Hanseatic League)—usually to a Polish kingdom with a degree of independence—but became Prussian in 1793.

10. Blanke, "The German Minority in Inter-War Poland and German Foreign Policy," 88.

11. Urban, *Der Verlust*, 28. Not all of the older Prussian province was attached to Poland after World War I—indeed, the area that became known as the Polish Corridor had a much lower proportion of Germans.

12. The last appreciable wave of *Volksdeutsche* had been in the eighteenth century, especially to Russia—Volga Germans—Romania, Hungary, and Yugoslavia (part of a repopulation campaign after the Ottoman Turks were pushed out).

13. Korbel, *Twentieth-Century Czechoslovakia*, 112.

14. A plebiscite held after the Treaty of Versailles in eastern West Prussia and southern East Prussia where the Masurians lived resulted in 96.7 percent voting to stay with Germany. In the more contentious Upper Silesian plebiscite, 59.7 percent voted to remain with Germany and 40.3 percent voted to join Poland. In the midst of rather severe violence (the Upper Silesian Uprising), the area was divided between interwar Poland and Weimar Germany.

15. Rummel, *Statistics of Democide*, 133. Some authors assert that the ethnic cleaning of Muslims and Hindus in Pakistan and India as those two countries gained independence in 1947 are comparable—certainly they are close in absolute numbers. Overall, however, there were more Germans affected; there were many more rapes and deaths involved in the German case; and Germans were the only group affected in their case, as opposed to two groups (Hindus and Muslims) in the other situation. See Bell-Fialkoff, *Ethnic Cleansing*.

16. Rummel's most probable figure is 1,863,000 deaths, 138. Many Polish women were also raped as Red Army soldiers did not always differentiate between Germans and Poles.

17. Aust and Burgdorff, *Die Flucht: über die Vertreibung der Deutschen aus dem Osten*.

18. Ibid., 21, 71.

19. Heineman, "The Hour of the Woman." The other two "moments" were the bombing of German cities and the clearing of the rubble during and after hostilities (*Trümmerfrauen*).

20. Schieder, *The Expulsion of the German Population from the Territories East of the Oder-Neisse-Line*; Spieler, *Vertreibung und Vertreibungsverbrechen 1945–1948*.

21. Grass, *Crabwalk*; see also Aust and Burgdorff, *Die Flucht*.

22. De Zayas, *Nemesis at Pottsdam*, 65–66.

23. Blanke, "Polish-Speaking Germans and the Ethnic Cleansing of Germany East of Oder-Neisse," 284.

24. Rummel, *Statistics of Democide*, 133.

25. Later, Danzig and Upper Silesia (contested for decades and divided between Poland and Germany after World War I) were also put into play—as was a small portion of Pomerania.

26. The inopportune timing of Churchill's electoral defeat and Roosevelt's death also greatly reduced the West's ability to negotiate effectively.

27. Brandes, *Der Weg zur Vertreibung 1938–1945*, 449; see also R. C. Raack, "Stalin Fixes the Oder-Neisse Line," 467–88; Frank, "The New Morality," 230–56.

28. De Zayas , *Nemesis at Potsdam*, 99.

29. Ibid., 47–49.

30. Brandes, *Der Weg zur Vertreibung 1938–1945*, 462.

31. Kopper, "The London Czech Government and the Origins of the Expulsion of the Sudeten Germans," 255.

32. Ryback, "Dateline Sudetenland: Hostages to History," 170.

33. This legal situation pertained until German unification in 1990—with the exception of the German Democratic Republic, where the Oder-Neisse "peace" border was recognized already in 1950.

34. Germans were shot/thrown off the bridge at Aussig/ústí nad Labem; the German population of Brünn/Brno was forcibly marched forty kilometers to the Austrian border; Germans were interned in the Lamsdorf camp in Silesia.

35. Linek, "Recent Debates on the Fate of the German Population in Upper Silesia," 384; Blanke, "Polish-Speaking Germans and the Ethnic Cleansing of Germany East of Oder-Neisse."

36. Urban, *Der Verlust*, 141.

37. Linek, "Recent Debates on the Fate of the German Population in Upper Silesia," 372.

38. Sayer, "The Language of Nationality and the Nationality of Language," 20.

39. Thum, "Cleansed Memory," 341.

40. Given wartime deaths and the territory involved, there were not enough Poles or Czechs to sufficiently repopulate these regions—the German population displaced and that of newcomers did not coincide—and it took at least a generation for similar population levels and densities to be achieved.

41. Linek, "Recent Debates on the Fate of the German Population in Upper Silesia," 374.

42. Dimitrów, "Vergangenheitspolitik," 252. The three major tropes utilized have been deemed the "minimalizing," "Potsdam," and "migration."

43. Ibid., 245.

44. Zernack and Friedrich, "Developments in Polish Scholarship on German History," 313.

45. Ibid., 312.

46. Constantly mentioned was also *Ostflucht*, the fact that many Germans from the Prussian/German eastern provinces had emigrated to the cities and industrial regions of the central and western portions of the country during the nineteenth and early twentieth centuries. Such authors use this typical rural-urban, modernizing dynamic to indicate that Germans did not want to be there in the first place.

47. This policy was also applied to "Germans" who were left—assumed to be Germanized Slavs, simply needing re-acculturation.

48. Dimitrów, "Vergangenheitspolitik," 236.

49. Abrams, "Morality, Wisdom and Revision," 238.

50. Urban, "Historische Belastungen," 34–35.

51. Kranz, "Shadows of the Past in Polish-German Relations," 35.

52. Dimitrów, "Vergangenheitspolitik," 248.

53. Wolff, "Can Forced Population Transfers Resolve Self-Determination Conflicts?," 18–19.

54. Linek, "Recent Debates on the Fate of the German Population in Upper Silesia," 395; Ruchniewicz, *Zögernde Annäherung*.

55. Dimitrów, "Vergangenheitspolitik," 251.

56. Urban, "Historische Belastungen," 35; Kranz, "Shadows of the Past in Polish-German Relations," 38.

57. Gardner-Feldman, "The Principle and Practice of 'Reconciliation' in German Foreign Policy," 333–56.

58. Görgey, "New Consensus in Germany's Eastern European Policy," 685.

59. This was a major change from clerical and church behavior during the actual expulsion, where many Polish priests and prelates justified and facilitated the expulsion of Germans—causing considerable friction with the Vatican. See Urban, *Der Verlust*, 132–38. Very early in the communist period, a deep and growing cleavage opened up between the regime and the Church. Indeed, the Church became one of the most important civil societal oppositional forces during this period—and especially after the election of the "Polish pope." This pastoral letter also led to a wave of repression of Polish priests and clerics.

60. Krzeminski, "Der Kniefall."

61. See Ruchniewicz, *Zögernde Annäherung*. Relations improved at the societal and cultural level in the 1980s with the support from West German political and civil societies for Solidarity and the packages sent to Poles oppressed by the imposition of martial law.

62. Hauner, "Czechs and Germans over the Centuries," 127–54.

63. Abrams, "Morality, Wisdom and Revision," 239.

64. Ibid., 241.

65. Available at http://www.europa.clio-online.de

66. Available at http://old.hrad.cz/president/Havel/speeches/1990/1503_uk.html.

67. Kopstein, "The Politics of National Reconciliation," 57–78.

68. Both the Bundestag and the European Parliament declared in 2002 that the decrees would not stand in the way of Czech EU membership, as long as EU law took precedence. Nagengast, "The Beneš Decrees and EU Enlargement," 344–45.

69. Ryback, "Dateline Sudetenland: Hostages to History," 173.

70. Quoted in ibid., 172.

71. Ibid., 163.

72. Nagengast, "The Beneš Decrees and EU Enlargement," 335.

73. Ibid., 340.

74. Ibid., 341.

75. Bingen, "Die deutsch-polnischen Beziehungen nach 1945," 13.

76. Mildenberger, "Funktioniert die 'Interessengemeinschaft'?," 120.

77. See Kamusella, "Ethnic Cleaning in Upper Silesia, 1944–1951"; see also Linek, "Recent Debates on the Fate of the German Population in Upper Silesia" and Zernack and Friedrich, "Developments in Polish Scholarship on German History."

78. The 2001 controversy arguably paved the way for the creation of the Museum of the History of Polish Jews, the building of which commenced in 2007 on a site just across from the famed Warsaw Ghetto Uprising Memorial in Warsaw. Controversy over the second book has led some Polish prosecutors to threaten to charge Gross for "slandering the Polish nation." See Whitlock, "A Scholar's Legal Peril in Poland."

79. Wróbel, "Double Memory: Poles and Jews after the Holocaust," 560–74.

80. Lech Kaczyński became president in 2005 and Jarosław Kaczyński served as prime minister from 2006 to 2007.

81. Schulze, "The Politics of Memory," 367–82; see also Kopstein, "The Politics of National Reconciliation."

82. Harris and Wülker, "The Refugee Problem in Germany," 10–25; Kittel, *Vertreibung der Vertreibenen?*

83. See Nagengast, "The Beneš Decrees and EU Enlargement"; Süssner, "Still Yearning for the Lost Heimat?," 1–26; Wood, "German Expellee Organisations in the Enlarged EU," 487–97.

84. Nagengast, "The German Expellees and European Values."

85. Langenbacher, "Changing Memory Regimes in Contemporary Germany," 46–68.

86. Moeller, *War Stories*; see also Benz, *Die Vertreibung der Deutschen aus dem Osten*; Faulenbach, "Die Vertreibung der Deutschen aus den Gebieten jenseits von Oder und Neisse," 44–54.

87. Kittel, *Vertreibung der Vertreibenen?*

88. Ten Dyke, *Dresden: Paradoxes of Memory in History*; Norbert Frei, *1945 und Wir*, 11. Several authors have pointed out that geopolitical Realpolitik made the expulsion taboo in the East and the bombing of cities by the Western allies rather taboo in the West (although much recent scholarship disagrees that this memory was repressed significantly).

89. Kittel, *Vertreibung der Vertreibenen?*

90. Ibid., 120.

91. Madajczyk, "The Centre against Expulsions vs. Polish-German Relations," 49.

92. Eric Langenbacher, "*Moralpolitik* versus *Moralpolitik*," 106–34.

93. Art, *The Politics of the Nazi Past in Germany and Austria*.

94. Naumann, *Der Krieg als Text*.

95. These include Walter Kempowski's multivolume "collective diary" *Das Echolot* (Munich: Knaus, 1993, 1999); Dieter Forte, *Der Junge mit den blutigen Schuhen* (Frankfurt/ Main: Fischer, 1995); and W. G. Sebald, *On the Natural History of* Destruction (New York: Random House, 2003).

96. Friedrich, *The Fire: The Bombing of Germany, 1940–1945*.

97. The mandate of the Zentrum calls for fighting ethnic cleansing worldwide, the formulation of a European experience in order to build a lasting peace in Europe, and working through history together with neighboring peoples to create a peaceful potential for the future. See the foundation's website: http://www.z-g-v.de.

98. Some compensation estimates are as high as 6 billion euros. See "Handfeste Drohung," *Der Spiegel* (39) 2003.

99. Lutomski, "The Debate about a Center against Expulsions."

100. Bernstein, "Holocaust Legacy: Germans and Jews Debate Redemption."

101. Krzeminski, "Die schwierige deutsch-polnische Vergangenheitspolitik," 3–5.

102. Urban, "Historische Belastungen," 34.

103. Kolakowski , "Noch Einmal."

104. Madajczyk, "The Centre against Expulsions vs. Polish-German Relations," 65–66.

105. Rak and Muszyński, "Recent Claims against Poland," 1300–1304; "Poles Angered by German WWII Compensation Claims," *Spiegel* online, December, 18, 2006.

106. Another festering dispute surrounds possession of the "Berlinka" collection, previously part of Berlin's State Library that was moved to Silesia during World War II for safekeeping, but which has been in Krakow ever since. Negotiations, ongoing since 1992, reached a low point in 2007, after a German newspaper ran an opinion piece that referred to the collection as *Beutekunst* (looted art). According to the Polish official empowered to resolve such issues, Wojciech Kowalski: "The treasures were moved to Poland, which was then German territory. . . . These territories became part of Poland. We found the treasures and saved them. Since it was abandoned property and former German property, the property was nationalized by the Polish state." Dempsey, "Dispute Widens over Nazis' destruction of Polish Art." Foreign Minister Fotyga stated, "Rather, the German cultural treasures in Poland were 'left behind by fleeing Nazis' at the end of the war and according to international law 'they belong to Poland.'" Connolly, "Poles Furious at German War Booty Claims."

107. "Schröder und Tschechen weisen Stoiber zurecht," *Spiegel* online, May 17, 2005; "Who's the Madman?" *Economist*, July 21, 2005.

108. Available at http://www.bundespraesident.de, October 29, 2003.

109. Dietrich, "Protokoll einer Ernücterung."

110. "Rede von Bundeskanzler Schröder zum 60. Jahrestag des Warschauer Aufstandes," August 1, 2004. Available at http://www.bundesregierung.de.

111. "Kaczynski verurteilt Vertriebenen-Ausstellung," *Spiegel* online, August 10, 2006. Mention should also be made of another exhibition that was curated by the House of History (Haus der Geschichte, Bonn), but staged at the German Historical Museum (Deutsches Historisches Museum) in Berlin in 2005. Ironically, this exhibition, intended to compete directly with and preempt Steinbach's initiative (revealing already the success pushing this memory into the mainstream), had a much more exclusive German focus than the vilified exhibition of the Zentrum.

112. They also mandated that the 2005 Haus der Geschichte exhibition (and not the BdV's Erzwungene Wege) will be the substantive basis.

113. "SPD und Union einigen sich auf Vertriebenen-Zentrum," *Spiegel* online, October 23, 2007; "Merkel kündigt Vertriebenen-Mahnmal in Berlin an," *Spiegel* online, October 22, 2007.

114. "Poland's new premier proposes World War II museum in Gdansk," *International Herald Tribune*, December 10, 2007.

115. "Merkel kündigt Vertriebenen-Mahnmal in Berlin an," *Spiegel* online, October 22, 2007.

116. De Zayas, „Ethnic Cleansing 1945 and Today," 789.

117. See Bell Fialkoff, *Ethnic Cleansing*; Wolff, "Can Forced Population Transfers Resolve Self-Determination Conflicts?"

118. Strzeszewski, "Opinions about the Polish Situation in the International Arena and Relations with Germany," 11.

119. Bukalska, "G like German," 57.

120. Madajczyk, "The Centre against Expulsions vs. Polish-German Relations," 63.
121. Petersen, *Zeit Fragen*, 51.
122. Ibid., 88–89.
123. Ibid., 74, 75.
124. See Nagengast, "The Beneš Decrees and EU Enlargement," 339.
125. Davies, *God's Playground*, 525, 530.

Works Cited

Abrams, Bradley F. "Morality, Wisdom and Revision: The Czech Opposition of the 1970s and the Expulsion of the Sudeten Germans." *East European Politics and Society* 9, no. 2 (1993): 234–55.

Art, David. *The Politics of the Nazi Past in Germany and Austria*. Cambridge: Cambridge University Press, 2006.

Aust, Stefan, and Burgdorff, Stephan, eds. *Die Flucht: Über die Vertreibung der Deutschen aus dem Osten*. Munich: Deutscher Taschenbuch Verlag, 2005.

Bell-Fialkoff, Andrew. *Ethnic Cleansing*. New York: St. Martin's Press, 1996.

Benz, Wolfgang, ed. *Die Vertreibung der Deutschen aus dem Osten: Ursachen, Ereignisse, Folgen*. Frankfurt: Fischer Taschenbuch Verlag, 1985.

Bernstein, Richard. "Holocaust Legacy: Germans and Jews Debate Redemption." *New York Times* October 29, 2003.

Bingen, Dieter. "Die deutsch-polnischen Beziehungen nach 1945." *Aus Politik und Zeitgeschichte* 5–6 (2005): 9–17.

Blanke, Richard. "The German Minority in Inter-War Poland and German Foreign Policy —Some Reconsiderations." *Journal of Contemporary History* 25, no. 1 (1990): 87–102.

———. "Polish-speaking Germans and the Ethnic Cleansing of Germany East of Oder-Neisse." In *Ethnic Cleansing in Twentieth-Century Europe*, ed. Steven Várdy and T. Hunt Tooley. Boulder, Colo.: Social Science Monographs, 2003.

Brandes, Detlef. *Der Weg zur Vertreibung 1938–1945: Pläne und Entscheidungen zum "Transfer" der Deutschen aus der Tschechoslowakei und aus Polen*. Munich: Oldenbourg, 2005.

Bukalska, Patrycja. "G like German" (N jak Niemiec). *Więź*, May 2006, 57–62.

Connolly, Kate. "Poles Furious at German War Booty Claims." *The Guardian*, August 29, 2007.

Davies, Norman. *God's Playground: A History of Poland, Vol. 2*. New York: Columbia University Press, 1982.

Dempsey, Judy. "Dispute Widens over Nazis' Destruction of Polish Art." *International Herald Tribune* August 29, 2007.

De Zayas, Alfred. "Ethnic Cleansing 1945 and Today; Observations on Its Illegality and Implications." In *Ethnic Cleansing in Twentieth-Century Europe*, ed. Steven Várdy and T. Hunt Tooley. Boulder, Colo.: Social Science Monographs, 2003.

———. *Nemesis at Potsdam: The Expulsion of Germans from the East*. Lincoln: University of Nebraska Press, 1989.

Dietrich, Stefan. "Protokoll einer Ernücterung; Die Abwehrschacht gegen Erika Steinbachs Zentrumsprojekt." *Frankfurter Allgemeine Zeitung*, May 22, 2007, 11.

Dimitrów, Edmund. "Vergangenheitspolitik in Polen 1945–1989." In *Deutsch-polnische Beziehungen 1939–1945–1949: Eine Einführung*, ed. Włodzimierz Borodziej and Klaus Ziemer. Osnabrück: fibre Verlag, 2000.

Dyke, Elizabeth A. Ten. *Dresden: Paradoxes of Memory in History*. London: Routledge, 2001.

Faulenbach, Bernd. "Die Vertreibung der Deutschen aus den Gebieten jenseits von Oder und Neisse: Zur wissenschaftlichen und öffentlichen Diskussion in Deutschland." *Aus Politik und Zeitgeschichte* (2002): 44–54.

Frank, Matthew. "The New Morality—Victor Gollancz, 'Save Europe Now', and the German Refugee Crisis, 1945–46." *Twentieth Century British History* 17, no. 2 (2006): 230–56.

Frei, Norbert. *1945 und Wir: Das Dritte Reich im Bewußtsein der Deutschen.* Munich: Becl, 2005.

Friedrich, Jörg. *Der Brand: Deutschland im Bombenkrieg 1940–1945.* Berlin: Propyläen, 2002.

Gardner-Feldman, Lily. "The Principle and Practice of 'Reconciliation' in German Foreign Policy; Relations with France, Israel, Poland and the Czech Republic." *International Affairs* 75, no. 2 (1999): 333–56.

Görgey, Laszlo. "New Consensus in Germany's Eastern European Policy." *Western Political Quarterly* 21, no. 4 (1968): 681–97.

Grass, Günter. *Crabwalk.* Orlando: Harcourt, 2002.

Harris, Chancey, and Gabriele Wülker. "The Refugee Problem in Germany." *Economic Geography* 29, no. 1 (1953): 10–25.

Hartmann, Christian, Johannes Hürter, and Ulrike Jureit, eds. *Verbrechen der Wehrmacht: Bilanz einer Debatte.* Munich: Beck, 2005.

Hauner, Milan. "Czechs and Germans over the Centuries: An Historical Review." *East Central Europe* 19, no. 2 (1991): 127–54.

Heineman, Elizabeth. "The Hour of the Woman: Memories of Germany's 'Crisis Years' and West German National Identity." In *The Miracle Years: A Cultural History of West Germany, 1949–1968*, ed. Hanna Schissler. Princeton: Princeton University Press, 2001.

Kamusella, Tomasz. "Ethnic Cleaning in Upper Silesia, 1944–1951." In *Ethnic Cleansing in Twentieth-Century Europe*, ed. Steven Várdy and T. Hunt Tooley. Boulder, Colo.: Social Science Monographs, 2003.

Kittel, Manfred. *Vertreibung der Vertriebenen? Der historische deutsche Osten in der Erinnerungskultur der Bundesrepublik (1961–1982).* Munich, Oldenbourg, 2007.

Kolakowski, Leszek. "Noch einmal: über das Schlimmste." *Die Zeit* (39), September 18, 2003.

Kopper, Christopher. "The London Czech Government and the Origins of the Expulsion of the Sudeten Germans." In *Ethnic Cleansing in Twentieth-Century Europe*, ed. Steven Várdy and T. Hunt Tooley. Boulder, Colo.: Social Science Monographs, 2003.

Kopstein, Jeffrey S. "The Politics of National Reconciliation: Memory and Institutions in German-Czech Relations since 1989." *Nationalism and Ethnic Politics* 3, no. 2 (1997): 57–78.

Korbel, Josef. *Twentieth-Century Czechoslovakia: The Meaning of Its History.* New York: Columbia University Press, 1977.

Kranz, Jerzy. "Shadows of the Past in Polish-German Relations." *Polish Quarterly of International Affairs* 1 (2005): 5–49.

Krzeminski, Adam. "Der Kniefall." In *Deutsche Erinnerungsorte*, ed. Etienne Francois and Hagen Schulze. Munich: Beck Verlag, 2001.

———. "Die schwierige deutsch-polnische Vergangenheitspolitik." *Aus Politik und Zeitgeschichte* B40–41 (2003): 3–5.

Langenbacher, Eric. "Changing Memory Regimes in Contemporary Germany." *German Politics and Society* 21, no. 2 (2003): 46–68.

———. "*Moralpolitik* versus *Moralpolitik*: Recent Struggles over the Construction of Cultural Memory in Germany." *German Politics and Society* 23, no. 3 (2005): 106–34.

Linek, Bernard. "Recent Debates on the Fate of the German Population in Upper Silesia, 1945–1950." *German History* 22, no. 3 (2004): 372–405.

Lutomski, Pawel. "The Debate about a Center against Expulsions: An Unexpected Crisis in German-Polish Relations?" *German Studies Review* 27, no. 3 (2004): 449–68.

Madajczyk, Piotr. "The Centre against Expulsions vs. Polish-German Relations." *Polish Foreign Affairs Digest* 4, no. 2 (2004): 43–78.

Mildenberger, Markus. "Funktioniert die 'Interessengemeinschaft'? Bilanz eines Jahrzehts deutsch-polnischer Beziehungen." In *Die deutsch-polnischen Beziehungen 1949– 2000: Eine Werte- und Interessengemeinschaft?* ed. Wolf-Dieter Eberwein and Basil Kerski. Opladen: Leske und Budrich, 2001.

Moeller, Robert G. *War Stories: The Search for a Usable Past in the Federal Republic of Germany.* Berkeley: University of California Press, 2001.

Nagengast, Emil. "The Beneš Decrees and EU Enlargement." *European Integration* 25, no. 4 (2003): 335–50.

_____. "The German Expellees and European Values." In *Ethnic Cleansing in Twentieth-Century Europe,* ed. Steven Várdy and T. Hunt Tooley. Boulder, Colo.: Social Science Monographs, 2003.

Naumann, Klaus. *Der Krieg als Text: Das Jahr 1945 im kulturellen Gedächtnis der Presse.* Hamburg: Hamburger Edition, 1998.

Petersen, Thomas. *Zeit Fragen: Flucht und Vertreibung aus Sicht der deutschen, polnischen und tschechischen Bevölkerung.* Bonn: Stiftung Haus der Geschichte, 2005.

"Poland's new premier proposes World War II museum in Gdansk." *International Herald Tribune,* December 10, 2007.

Raack, R. C. "Stalin Fixes the Oder-Neisse Line." *Journal of Contemporary History* 25, no. 4 (1990): 467–88.

Rak, Krzysztof, and Mariusz Muszyński. "Recent Claims Against Poland." *Samartian Review* (April 2007): 1300–1304.

Ruchniewicz, Krzysztof. *Zögernde Annäherung: Studien zur Geschichte der deutsch-polnischen Beziehungen im 20. Jahrhundert.* Dresden: Thelem Verlag, 2005.

Rummel, Rudolph J. *Statistics of Democide: Genocide and Mass Murder since 1900.* Münster: Lit Verlag, 1998.

Ryback, Thomas. "Dateline Sudetenland: Hostages to History." *Foreign Policy* 105 (1996– 97): 162–78.

Sayer, Derek. "The Language of Nationality and the Nationality of Language: Prague 1780–1920." *Past and Present* (1996): 164–210.

Schieder, Theodor, ed. *The Expulsion of the German Population from the Territories East of the Oder-Neisse-Line.* Bonn: Federal Ministry for Expellees, Refugees and War Victims, 1956.

Schulze, Rainer. "The Politics of Memory: Flight and Expulsion of German Populations after the Second World War and German Collective Memory." *National Identities* 8, no. 4 (2006): 367–82.

Snyder, Timothy. "Memory of Sovereignty and Sovereignty over Memory: Poland, Lithuania and Ukraine, 1939–1999." In *Memory and Power in Post-War Europe: Studies in the Presence of the Past,* ed. Jan-Werner Müller. Cambridge: Cambridge University Press, 2002.

Spieler, Silke, ed. *Vertreibung und Vertreibungsverbrechen 1945–1948: Bericht des Bundesarchivs vom 28. Mai 1974: Archivalien und ausgewählte Erlebnisberichte.* Bonn: Kulutrstiftung der deutschen Vertriebenen, 1989.

Strzeszewski, Michał. "Opinions about the Polish Situation in the International Arena and Relations with Germany" (Opinie o Sytuacji Polski Na Arenie Międzynarodowej I Stosunkach 2 Niemcami). Warsaw: Centrum Badania Opinii Społecznej, 2007, 1–15.

Süssner, Henning. "Still Yearning for the Lost Heimat? Ethnic German Expellees and the Politics of Belonging." *German Politics and Society* 22, no. 2 (2004): 1–26.

Thum, Gregor. "Cleansed Memory; The New Polish Wrocław/Breslau and the Expulsion of the Germans." In *Ethnic Cleansing in Twentieth-Century Europe,* ed. Steven Várdy and T. Hunt Tooley. Boulder, Colo.: Social Science Monographs, 2003.

Urban, Thomas. *Der Verlust: Die Vertreibung der Deutschen und Polen im 20. Jahrhundert.* Munich: Beck, 2004.

———. "Historische Belastungen der Integration Polens in die EU." *Aus Politik und Zeitgeschichte* 5/6 (2005): 32–39.

Whitlock, Craig. "A Scholar's Legal Peril in Poland: Princeton Historian Could Face Criminal Charges Over Book." *Washington Post,* January 18, 2008.

Wolff, Stefan. "Can Forced Population Transfers Resolve Self-Determination Conflicts? A European Perspective." *Journal of Contemporary European Studies* 12, no. 1 (2004): 11–29.

Wood, Steve. "German Expellee Organisations in the Enlarged EU." *German Politics* 14, no. 4 (2005): 487–97.

Wróbel, Piotr. "Double Memory: Poles and Jews after the Holocaust." *East European Politics and Society* 11, no. 3 (1997): 560–74.

Zernack, Klaus, and Karin Friedrich. "Developments in Polish Scholarship on German History, 1945–2000." *German History* 22, no. 3 (2004): 309–22.

4

Oppression and Vengeance in the Cambodian Genocide

ALEXANDER LABAN HINTON

> *To outsiders, and often to ourselves, Cambodia looked peaceful enough. The farmers bound to their planting cycles. Fisherman living on their boats. . . . The wide boulevards and the flowering trees of our national capital, Phnom Penh. All that beauty and serenity was visible to the eye. But inside, hidden from sight the entire time, was* kum. *Kum is a Cambodian word for a particularly Cambodian mentality of revenge—to be precise, a long-standing grudge leading to revenge much more damaging than the original injury. If I hit you with my fist and you wait five years and then shoot me in the back one dark night, that is* kum. *. . . Cambodians know all about* kum. *It is the infection that grows on our national soul.*
>
> —Haing Ngor, *A Cambodian Odyssey*

> *We cannot cut off their heads in revenge following our anger. I myself used to taste that taste. . . . [Let the matter] be processed in a court case.*
>
> —Chairman of the Cambodian Military Court on prosecuting Ta Mok and Duch, *Phnom Penh Post*, May 1999

In April 2000, the *Phnom Penh Post*, an English-language newspaper, published an interview with a former Khmer Rouge cadre who had studied in Paris with Pol Pot and helped to found the Communist Party of Kampuchea (CPK). When asked why Pol Pot killed millions of people, the former cadre, who chose to remain anonymous, replied, "As far as the killing is concerned, I don't think it was only Pol Pot. It was more about revenge—the revenge with Lon Nol [soldiers] for killing their husbands and wives before 1975."[1] In subsequent parts of the interview, the cadre expanded on this assertion, which seemed to be related to his view that Pol Pot was a "gentle man" with a "good heart" who ultimately shouldn't be blamed for the killing:

So, when Lon Nol soldiers knew that someone was a former Viet Minh [agent], they would shoot and kill them without trial. Then, you can understand that in the Pol Pot regime, they would kill people even though Pol Pot didn't tell them to kill. They just took revenge for their husbands or fathers and put the blame on Pol Pot. . . . Before 1975, there was also a war crime: what happened with the B-52s? . . . I am from Svay Rieng and Prey Veng, where a lot of my relatives were sad. I saw my relatives taking revenge with people from Phnom Penh. They just waited for people from Phnom Penh: if they had a chance to kill, they would kill. . . . I saw that there was more revenge [by people] than official order [from the top].

As the former cadre contends, revenge was an important motivation behind some of the violence that took place during Democratic Kampuchea (DK), the genocidal period of Khmer Rouge rule in Cambodia (1975–79), when roughly 1.7 of Cambodia's 8 million inhabitants died from starvation, overwork, disease, or execution.[2] In fact, revenge was a theme invoked repeatedly by many of the perpetrators and victims I interviewed to explain why the Khmer Rouge killed so many people. However, the cadre's assertion that Pol Pot and other top officials were unaware of and lacked responsibility for the violence (an assertion that these leaders have tried to make) is dubious.

This chapter argues that Khmer Rouge leaders directly and indirectly called for their followers to take subaltern vengeance upon the "class enemies" who had formerly oppressed them. I begin by examining the historical development of the Khmer Rouge Party line (*meakea*), suggesting that Pol Pot and his colleagues came to believe that the "science" of Marxist-Leninism enabled them to discern the origins of, and devise a solution for, the impoverishment and oppression of the Cambodian people. While the Marxist-Leninist and Maoist notions of exploitation made a certain sense to many of Cambodia's poor, the Khmer Rouge leadership attempted to couch such philosophical abstractions in a manner that would inspire them to embrace the Khmer Rouge movement and to take arms against its enemies. To do so, the Khmer Rouge combined the new and the old into ideological palimpsests, sketched upon the lines of cultural understandings, at once transforming and transformed.

Class Hatred and the Khmer Rouge Party Line

The American imperialists and their lackeys
Their lackeys owe us blood as hot as fire.
The hot and angry war ensured that Kampuchea will never forget the enmity
Will not forget the severe oppression.
Seize hold of guns to kill the enemy quickly.

—Khmer Rouge song, "The Motherland of Kampuchea"

One of the Khmer Rouge's key ideological palimpsests centered around the notion of class rage, which played upon ontologically resonant local understandings of disproportionate revenge. In contrast to the often-cited biblical conception of revenge of "an eye for an eye,"[3] the Cambodian model of revenge involves disproportionate retaliation against one's enemy—what we might call "a head for an eye," since disproportionate revenge is usually linked to issues of face and sometimes even decapitation. In an extreme situation like DK, disproportionate revenge could involve an attempt to kill a foe, or even his or her entire family.

To understand the origins of this palimpsest, it is necessary to examine some of the historical processes through which the DK Party line was forged. On September 27, 1977, for example, Pol Pot gave a speech, broadcast throughout the nation, to celebrate the seventeenth anniversary of the founding of the CPK. The speech constituted the first clear public acknowledgment of the CPK's existence, Pol Pot's leadership, and the history of the struggle that had brought the regime to power. Like all party histories, which reconstruct the past to confirm a desired image of the present (for example, Pol Pot's speech excises an alternative history of revolutionary struggle and association with Vietnam dating back to the fight for independence), Pol Pot's is suggestive about the emergence of the party line and the high-modernist orientation of the DK regime.

By "high-modernist orientation," I follow James Scott in referring to an overweening confidence in the possibilities of progress, mastery of nature, and human emancipation through the use of science, reason, and social engineering—a faith that has sometimes inspired authoritarian regimes to attempt to use their highly abstract and oversimplified schemes as a blueprint for radical sociopolitical transformation.[4] Because they tend to oversimplify complex, on-the-ground realities, these projects of social engineering have often ended in catastrophic failure. As was the case with the Khmer Rouge, such high-modernist faith and vision may also provide the building blocks for a revitalization movement, which, in a context of stress and upheaval, is able to attract followers drawn to their promises of a new and better life. I should also note that, in Cambodia, transformative knowledge is viewed as a form of power, one that may give the bearer the aura of potency. If, in the past, revitalization movements in Cambodia and its Southeast Asian neighbors had often been led by charismatic leaders claiming a special endowment of merit and power, Pol Pot and the CPK—particularly as exemplified by their quasi-religious and multivalent pseudonym, Angkar (Ângkar), or "the Organization"—similarly claimed a sort of high-modernist potency that legitimized their claims to power and their subsequent attempt to radically transform and revitalize Cambodian society.

Their sense of having discovered the key to ending oppression and revitalizing Cambodian society seems to have given Pol Pot and his associates a sense of omnipotence and grandeur, one that can be read in the lines of speeches and documents that assert the unique and unprecedented nature of their revolutionary movement. For, like Buddhists who had achieved enlightenment, they had attained secret knowledge that would transform Cambodia and enable its inhabitants to reach a higher state of being. In fact, Khmer Rouge ideology often played upon the theme of enlightenment when depicting Angkar through metaphors of clairvoyance and omniscience. Yet another strand in this sense of grandeur was the French reconstruction of Cambodian history, which provided a narrative of decline from the magnificence of the Angkarean era, when Khmer kings built impressive stone monuments and were a dominant military presence in the region, to the contemporary period, when Cambodia had become a weak country dominated by others.[5] Driven by feelings both of inferiority and of inflation about what was possible, the Khmer Rouge proclaimed that their revolutionary society would surpass even Angkar in greatness, moving more rapidly and successfully toward communist utopia than any other communist regime.

These views and experiences were to give shape to the development and application of the party line. Pol Pot's 1977 speech asserted that Cambodia was plagued by two major contradictions. On the one hand, there existed a contradiction with imperialism, especially U.S. imperialism. Cambodia remained a "semi-colony, in a situation of dependency" on exploitative imperial powers that impoverished the poor and corrupted Cambodian society. On the other hand, Cambodia was plagued by internal class contradictions. While contradictions existed between various classes (workers vs. capitalists, petty bourgeoisie vs. capitalists, capitalists vs. peasants), the dominant one, Pol Pot asserted, was between the landowners and the peasantry, who composed 85 percent of the population.

The solution to these contradictions was to drive out the imperialists and their lackeys, the "feudal-capitalist" government that supported the exploitation of the poor. The DK Party line held that, upon attaining power, the Khmer Rouge would impose new relations of production that ended exploitation. Through this structural reorganization and indoctrination, or what the Khmer Rouge called "seepage" (*karchreap*), the masses would gradually absorb party ideology and be transformed into passionate revolutionaries guided by a proper political consciousness. In addition, the country would avoid foreign dependency and influence by adhering to a strict line of "independence-mastery" (*aekâreach mâchaskar*), one that seemed crucial given centuries of foreign involvement in Cambodian affairs, culminating in the Vietnam War.

To achieve these goals, Pol Pot's 1977 speech contends, requires recognition of "the key problem, the fundamental problem which was decisive for victory," namely, to "arouse the peasants so that they saw [contradictions], burned with class hatred and took up the struggle."[6] If, in the past, such hatred potentially existed, Pol Pot asserted, it was "buried" because of the false consciousness of the masses, who were "deceived" by ruling-class ideology into thinking that their status was due to karma. The party line provided the means of helping the masses see the "contradictions" and the ways in which they were oppressed. For Pol Pot and his colleagues, then, one basic strategy for successfully waging revolution was to make the masses "hot and angry," feelings that would ultimately be transformed into "class hatred" and "class fury."

Class Revenge in Democratic Kampuchea

*To develop ideology, so that there is always the revolutionary attitude
and the class (proletarian) attitude in the party . . . is to conduct
internal ideological indoctrination so that the initial attitude taken is
conserved firmly, and the Marxist-Leninist class leaning and*

> *devotion to class struggle is retained always to win power by*
> *annihilating the enemy regime . . . and to create class ardor and*
> *fury. This ardor and fury must be aroused according to the*
> *contradiction of the day whether it be large or small. Thus,*
> *ideological force will be converted into a burning material*
> *force which will dare to engage in struggle, attack the enemy*
> *and win final victory over the enemy even if he is very strong.*

—Pre-1975 summary of annotated party history,
quoted in Jackson, Cambodia, 1975–1978

> *To dig up grass, one must also dig up the roots.*

—Khmer Rouge saying

To "create class ardor and fury," the Khmer Rouge used notions like exploitation as an ideological "hook," which tapped into preexisting feelings of dissatisfaction, unrest, anger, and spite and provided a foundation upon which revolutionary consciousness could be built. Simple sayings, songs, refrains, and leaflets provided a rudimentary class explanation for this sense of oppression; thus one pre-DK propaganda leaflet explained that capitalists "live in affluence at the expense of the working class and the masses" who "live in misery, bled by them."[7] The revolution, the leaflet asserted, would "liberate" the people from this oppression and revitalize Cambodian society.

More thorough political education texts elaborated upon these points. For example, a August 1973 tract published in the youth periodical *Revolutionary Young Men and Women* asserted that "human society is divided into . . . the oppressor class and the oppressed."[8] The tract went on to discuss who oppressors were (imperialists, feudalists, capitalists, and reactionaries) and how they exploited the oppressed. Through such instruction, the tract proclaimed, the revolutionary youth would "awaken and become aware of the national problem [and] the class problem." Ultimately, such an understanding was supposed to result in rage: "Khmer youth, upon receiving this education in the political principles, the revolutionary consciousness of the party, all found rage strongly mounting. [Their rage] manifested itself as a struggle movement to contest American imperialists and the oppressor classes in whatever guise."[9]

Ith Sarin, who spent nine months with the Khmer Rouge in 1973, provides a detailed example of how such indoctrination proceeded, as the regime attempted to instill "bloody" or "mortal hate" in its followers.[10] At political education seminars, for example, recruits would study a number of documents, including ones on "Class Struggle" and "Revolutionary Hate." Such instruction was supplemented by criticism and self-criticism sessions at which recruits were assessed in terms of their "state of morale [and] feelings." Besides explicit discussion, revolutionary meetings also included artistic performances (or even funerals of those who had been killed in battle) that were designed to foment "revolutionary violence" so that the attendees "burned" with hatred toward the enemy.[11] The ninth of fifteen

Khmer Rouge revolutionary precepts even read, "One must maintain a burning rage (*kamhoeng chap cheh*) toward the enemy."[12]

To recruit cadre and soldiers and to increase their support among the population, then, the Khmer Rouge relied heavily on notions of class struggle and oppression. As Pol Pot noted in his 1977 speech, the goal was to transform popular discontents into class rage that would propel the revolution to victory. By giving preexisting subaltern resentments a focus and target, and by attempting to transform these feelings into a "burning force," the Khmer Rouge effectively encouraged people to hold a class grudge (*kumnum vonnah*) against their "oppressors."

The logic of the Khmer Rouge model of disproportionate revenge was as follows. The oppressors had done "something bad" to the poor by making them suffer and lose face. One or more of these "happenings" led the poor to be "seized with painful anger" (*chheu chap*), which they stored inside themselves. The Khmer Rouge inflamed this hidden resentment into a "burning" class grudge that would motivate many of the poor to want to "eat the flesh and sip the blood" of this enemy. The poor, however, needed a powerful patron to help them exact disproportionate revenge against this hated enemy. Angkar, the "Party Organization," fulfilled this role. This Khmer Rouge ideological model can be schematized as follows:

DK Class Revenge: "A Head for an Eye" ("Disproportionate")

Event:	Oppressors do bad deeds to the poor
Judgment:	The poor lose face and suffer
	Oppressors are "higher than" and "look down upon" the poor
	The poor must return (*sâng*) the bad deed to the oppressors (class grudge, *kumnum vonnah*)
	The poor should try to "completely defeat" the oppressors
Complication:	Oppressors prevent the poor from returning the bad deed
Expectation:	The poor should return the bad deed to oppressors (disproportionately)
Moral Inference:	The poor have a moral obligation to return disproportionately the bad deed to the oppressors
	Oppressors should receive the disproportionate bad deed from the poor (Angkar as the powerful patron)
Status Inference:	The poor will be "higher than" their former oppressors
	The honor of the poor will be cleansed (*star ketteyos*)
	The oppressors will (one hopes) not attempt further retaliation against the poor

It is important to note that the distribution, understanding, internalization, and motivational force of this model could vary. A person living in a Khmer Rouge zone, where various Khmer Rouge indoctrination methods had been instituted, would have much greater exposure to this model than a rich person living in Phnom Penh, which is part of the reason why there was so much interest in Ith Sarin's book when it was published in 1973—many people in Phnom Penh were getting their first look at Khmer Rouge practice and ideology.

Similarly, depending on their personal histories and the social fields through which they moved (for example, their educational, class, or political background), a person might have a relatively deeper understanding of such Khmer Rouge ideological models. Pol Pot, who had been studying Marxist-Leninism since his years in Paris and who was a formulator of Khmer Rouge doctrine, no doubt had a more complex understanding of the regime's ideology than did Ith Sarin. As an educator, Ith Sarin, in turn, likely understood the nuances of Khmer Rouge ideology more deeply than a poor peasant who had little formal schooling and who had received less political training. Reflecting on the way in which he was indoctrinated, one peasant cadre recalled that the Khmer Rouge "told us that the poor were poor because of the rich and the rich were rich because of the poor. They wanted us to become seized with painful anger about this exploitation, to hate and to fight bravely against the capitalist, feudal, and landlord classes, the rich big people who harmed the poor." His basic understanding of class oppression, struggle, and rage was probably similar to that of many poor peasants in Khmer Rouge zones.

The motivational force and contextual salience of Khmer Rouge ideology also varied. Thus, the Khmer Rouge model of disproportionate revenge was likely more compelling to landless peasants who worked the fields of a landlord who paid them little and treated them with disrespect than to the landlord or a relatively wealthy peasant. Similarly, Khmer Rouge ideology was less appealing to most wealthy, educated urbanites, who were classified as "oppressors" and whose relatively privileged life experiences often made it difficult for them to sympathize with the plight of the poor. Moreover, because of the structural position into which "new people" (the urban population that was rusticated immediately after DK) typically were placed (having low status, being subject to dehumanizing discourses and practices, losing their wealth and homes, lacking former rights and access to power), this group had much less reason than poor peasant "old people" (whose structural position typically improved) to "take" and be motivated by Khmer Rouge ideology. This is part of the reason why so many "new people" viewed Khmer Rouge slogans, songs, and meetings with indifference or hostility—in contrast to the recruits that Ith Sarin observed.[13] Even within given socioeconomic groups, the motivational force of the Khmer Rouge model varied depending on life history, personality, and context. Still, the Khmer Rouge model of disproportionate revenge was a strong motive for many cadre, partly because it had an abstractness enabling it to encompass a variety of sources of resentment and discontent (the "bad deeds")—debt, impoverishment, hunger, shame, the destruction of one's home and property, being bombed, the killing of loved ones, and so forth.

During the civil war, the Khmer Rouge attempted to focus these feelings primarily on the Lon Nol regime and the urban areas that it controlled. For the Khmer Rouge, the Lon Nol regime was the corrupt enemy "lackey" that defended the interests of the oppressive social classes and imperialists and protected the capitalist system these groups used to exploit the poor. As a 1973 *Revolutionary Young Men and Women* tract stated, this "traitorous . . . clique is a militarist, fascist representative for the feudal, capitalist, and unparalleled reactionary class that serves as traitorous, country-selling valets of American imperialists."[14] A current government official explained, "The Khmer Rouge brainwashed people to believe that the Lon Nol regime was a capitalist regime, and that the very poor, who had been oppressed and swindled by the rich, had to fight bravely to defeat Lon Nol." Lon Nol had overthrown Sihanouk. He could be blamed for the death and devastation caused by bombing. His soldiers engaged in close combat with Khmer Rouge forces, killing their friends and comrades. Such brutality was memorialized in songs, such as the following one taught to children after the war:

> Baribo village sheds it tears;
> The enemy dropped bombs and staged a coup.
> The screams of a combatant; friend, where are you?
> The hated enemy killed my friend.
> When you died away, friend, you were still naked,
> Chest and stomach asunder, liver and spleen gone,
> You floated them away like a river's current.
> Removal of liver and spleen is cause for sadness.
> The ricelands of my mother are far in the distance.
> The sun slants over the green hills.
> When you died away, friend, you reminded me
> That the hated enemy had swallowed Cambodia.[15]

Through such ideological discourses and practices, the Khmer Rouge helped further inflame emotions, leading many cadre to remain "seized by painful anger" and to maintain a "bloody" and "mortal hate" for the Lon Nol regime.

The cities were similarly vilified as corrupt and immoral centers of undue foreign influence. Even before the war, many peasants already felt somewhat disconnected from and wary of cities. Structurally, there were few institutional links between the urban and rural populations. In her study of Sobay, Ebihara also found that most villagers lived in a fairly insular world that revolved around family, relatives, neighbors, and the wat.[16] While Sobay villagers did travel and have contacts beyond the village (the frequency decreasing dramatically with distance), most remained highly distrustful of strangers.[17] Strangers were often suspected of being "people of bad character," including "robbers, rapists, [and] murderers."[18] If some Sobay villagers, particularly the young, viewed Phnom Penh as exciting, many others found it "a welter of noise, confusion, crowding, unsavory characters, immorality, danger, and expense, to be endured only when absolutely necessary. Some people . . . [brought] back stories of immodest women, attempted or accomplished thievery, physical violence, and other lurid accounts or varied complaints."[19]

This peasant distrust of cities and this structural condition of urban-rural disconnect allowed the Khmer Rouge to crystallize and mark the differences between the urban and rural populations. The Khmer Rouge depicted urbanites as corrupt beings who lived in luxury and sin—residing in huge homes, eating well, drinking cognac, and visiting prostitutes—while the masses were exploited and suffered. Thus, in a May 12, 1975, broadcast, Phnom Penh Domestic Radio proclaimed that in the areas that Lon Nol controlled, "injustice, corruption, hooliganism, burglary, banditry, and prostitution were overwhelming and became a natural and even legal way of life." The "rotten culture" of U.S. imperialism, the broadcast proclaimed, had "poisoned" the urbanites, whose immoral practices were opposed to those of the "clean" peasantry. Such discourses constructed urbanites and peasants as different sorts of beings. A broadcast three days later commented on how, upon entering Phnom Penh, the revolutionary army was "taken aback" by the sight of "long-haired men and youngsters wearing bizarre clothes" such as "skin-tight pants with over-sized bell-bottoms" that stood in stark contrast to the traditional garb of Cambodians.

Such images of strangeness and difference were reinforced by assertions that the cities contained "American lackeys" and foreign imperialists. In fact, the cities were the locales in which more foreigners resided and they contained a disproportionately large number of ethnic minorities. One monograph, published in 1962, reported that Phnom Penh was 42 percent Khmer, 30 percent Chinese, and 27 percent Vietnamese.[20] Such structural divisions resonated with the preconceptions of many peasants who viewed strangers with suspicion and often regarded cities as locales in which sinful deeds took place.

Ideologically, the Khmer Rouge also stigmatized the urbanites as capitalist oppressors who exploited the poor. Slogans and sayings like "Trees in the country, fruit in the town" were used to inflame the anger of the peasantry toward the urbanites. According to Soth Polin, this common Khmer Rouge saying was "cast in the form of an old saying and profit[ed] from the good sense attributed to traditional maxims." He explained that this slogan "engenders jealousy among the peasants against the city-dwellers. Repeated a thousand times, it convinced the former that eliminating the latter was within their rights—better still, an imperative of their culture. Repeated a thousand times, this adage has 'devised' an inextinguishable hatred."[21]

For many peasants, usurers, "those who have" (*neak mean*), or, less frequently, landlords were the familiar oppressors who could serve as a sort of experiential template for abstract Khmer Rouge pronouncements about "class oppressors"— even if their understandings did not always completely parallel the formal DK Party line, which underemphasized usury. Like usurers, who charged high rates of interest, the urbanites consumed the "fruits" of the peasants' land and labor to support their comfortable and "immoral" lives. In all these ways, Khmer Rouge ideology helped manufacture urbanites into an "other" marked as corrupt and targeted for revenge.

Given the intensity of some peasant resentments and the centrality of class rage to Khmer Rouge ideology, it is not surprising that so much violence occurred after liberation. As the "anonymous cadre" suggests, by the end of a brutal civil war the "ignited class anger" was burning at full force and many Khmer Rouge soldiers and cadre were firmly tied in malice toward their enemy. In Battambang Province, for example, Khmer Rouge appeared "contemptuous and aloof" just after liberation and later reportedly admitted that they had been "fired by 'uncontrollable hatred' for members of the 'old society.' 'We were so angry when we came out of the forest,' one speaker allegedly said, 'that we didn't want to spare even a baby in its cradle.'"[22] Some of these cadre even ripped apart a Lon Nol military jet in the Battambang airport by hand.

As this incident suggests, Lon Nol soldiers, police, and government personnel were targets of revenge during the first wave of DK killings. Throughout Cambodia, the Khmer Rouge set out to identify and detain these members of the Lon Nol regime, particularly those who had held high rank. In his confession, Sreng, a high-ranking Northern Zone cadre, asserts that at this time the Party Center "put forward a policy of successively smashing officers, starting from the generals and working down through the lieutenants, as well as government investigative agents, policemen, military police personnel and reactionary civil servants," an order that was later extended to include lower-ranking Lon Nol soldiers.[23]

After taking Phnom Penh, Khmer Rouge radio ordered "all ministers and generals to come to the ministry of information at once to organize the country."[24] Dari, a villager who had fled to Phnom Penh where she lived across from the Ministry, noted that many of these people looked scared, despite Khmer Rouge assurances that they were to help in the reconstruction of the country. Many people thought that the top "supertraitors" of the Khmer Republic would be executed, but few suspected that the Khmer Rouge would execute the entire leadership of the former regime. This is exactly what happened. According to You Kim Lanh, a technician who reported to the Ministry, the Lon Nol officers and officials were asked to write their life histories and then taken to the Monorom Hotel, which was used as a detention center.[25] For several days, You Kim Lanh said, hundreds of people continued to arrive at the hotel, most of whom were loaded into trucks at night and driven away. When You Kim Lanh asked a Khmer Rouge officer he knew what happened to these people, the cadre replied: "We kill them all because they're traitors and deserve to be shot."

As the cities were evacuated, the Khmer Rouge also appealed to high- and low-level soldiers and officials to identify themselves, suggesting that their skills would be of help in the reconstruction of the country or that they would receive an equivalent rank under the new regime. Urbanites being evacuated out of the cities were asked to give background information about their former occupations. Many people who told the truth were taken away to be killed. Others who remained silent were recognized or discovered through investigations.

Up to two hundred thousand people—ranging from Lon Nol soldiers to civilians who made "mistakes"—may have perished during this first wave of DK killing immediately after the regime took power.[26] For many Khmer Rouge cadre, the Party Center's call to "execute all leaders of the Lon Nol regime beginning with the top leaders"[27] provided them with a warrant to take revenge upon the "oppressor enemy" against whom they were tied in malice for so many reasons.

Instead of ending the vengeance after this initial period of violence, the Khmer Rouge attempted to keep this class grudge inflamed. "Burning rage" remained a central part of revolutionary consciousness. Sometimes this connection was explicit, as in a July 1977 issue of *Revolutionary Flags* stating that, as one's "standpoint" (*kol chumhor*) was "clarified and sharpened," one would be "pushed" to have a political consciousness (*sâtiarâmma*) that included:

1. A constantly burning rage (*kamhoeng chap cheh*) for the enemy.
2. An extremely deep revolutionary sentiment toward the oppressed classes.
3. A strong spirit of love for the nation, revolution, collective, and party.[28]

These three forms of consciousness constituted the "basis" of the "daily fighting spirit," which would ideally make one "hot" (*kdav*) so that one would "stand on the base of anger toward the enemy." And, ultimately, this revolutionary consciousness, including "anger for outside enemies, class enemies, and enemies burrowing from within," would inspire one to "work hard to research, investigate, seek out, and clean up these enemies."

More concretely, the DK regime attempted to generate this "constantly burning rage" through frequent reminders of the "bad deeds" that the oppressor classes had done to the oppressed. On the local level, cadre were instructed to continue emphasizing oppression in their political propaganda. A regional deputy secretary stated that this meant encouraging the peasantry to remember that the city people "had an easy life" in contrast to their own suffering, "were exploiters," "shirked productive work," and were "not pure and clean."[29] Khmer Rouge speeches, publications, and radio broadcasts reinforced this message. Thus, a January 20, 1976, radio broadcast reminded its listeners of how the city people had caused them to suffer and feel humiliated:

> Our brothers and sisters lived a most miserable life, enduring all manner of hardships, including shortages of food and clothing while under the most barbaric, ferocious and fascist oppression of the imperialists, colonialists and their lackeys of all stripes, including their ringleader, Lon Nol. They never had enough food, never were happy and never had an opportunity to receive [an education]. Our brothers and sisters were looked down upon, regarded as animals or as the most ignorant class in national society. Remembering all this, our brothers and sisters have a great hatred for the traitorous clique.[30]

Similarly, in a speech marking the first anniversary of the revolution in April 1976, Minister of Information Hu Nim harped on the devastation inflicted upon the rural areas during the war by guns, napalm and other chemical agents, and bombs. Hu Nim's speech is striking for its detailed and exaggerated statistics, including 400,000 peasants killed, more than 20,000 maimed or disabled, and 200,000 injured; 80 percent of Cambodia's factories destroyed; and 80 percent of the fields and almost all the homes close to battlefields ravaged.[31] On the same occasion, Khieu Samphan proclaimed: "Nothing can erase or make us forget . . . [this] dark past."[32]

Such discourse was incorporated into Khmer Rouge song and dance. To help keep the class grudge inflamed, for example, Khmer Rouge dances, performed at meetings, frequently involved harsh, militaristic demeanor and violent imagery. Sometimes the theme of subaltern revenge was quite explicit. Haing Ngor recalled how, at the end of a propaganda dance, costumed cadre—some of whom wore red headbands and red krama sashes around their waists—formed a line and then began shouting

"BLOOD AVENGES BLOOD!" at the top of their lungs. Both times when they said the word "blood" they pounded their chests with clenched fists, and when they shouted "avenges" they brought their arms straight out like a Nazi salute, except with a closed fist instead of an open hand.

"BLOOD AVENGES BLOOD! BLOOD AVENGES BLOOD! BLOOD AVENGES BLOOD!" the cadre repeated with fierce determined faces, thumping their fists on their hearts and raising their fists. They shouted other revolutionary slogans and gave the salutes and finally ended with "Long Live the Cambodian revolution!"

It was a dramatic performance and it left us scared. In our language, "blood" has its ordinary meaning, the red liquid in the body, and another meaning of kinship or family. Blood avenges blood. You kill us, we kill you. We "new" people had been on the other side of the Khmer Rouge in the civil war. Soldiers of the Lon Nol regime with the help of American weapons and planes had killed many tens of thousands of Khmer Rouge in battle. Symbolically, the Khmer Rouge had just announced that they were going to take revenge.[33]

Besides the overt call for vengeance, this dance embodies various movements signifying "burning rage"—loud shouts associated with anger; fierce faces showing that one was *dach chett* (resolute); clenched fists indexing the "knot" of malice; chests pounds (with the clenched fists) evoking the image of a person who is "seized with painful anger."

Blood imagery was also central to this dance. In fact, the color of blood was a prominent theme in Khmer Rouge propaganda, providing a metaphoric call for revenge. The DK national anthem contained numerous references to spilled blood, which provided a reason for people to maintain their "unrelenting hatred." In a September 27, 1977, speech, Pol Pot explained that a "blood call has been incorporated into our national anthem. Each sentence, each word shows the nature of our people's struggle. This blood has been turned into class and national indignation."[34] Similarly, the Khmer Rouge flag was red and glorified by "The Red Flag" song, often sung in unison before meetings:

THE RED FLAG

Glittering red blood blankets the earth—
Blood given up to liberate the people:
Blood of workers, peasants, and intellectuals;
Blood of young men, Buddhist monks, and girls.
The blood swirls away, and flows upward, gently, into the sky,
Turning into a red, revolutionary flag.

Red flag! Red flag! Flying now! Flying now!
O beloved friends, pursue, strike and hit the enemy.
Red flag! red flag! Flying now! Flying now!
Don't leave a single reactionary imperialist (alive)
Seething with anger, let us wipe out all enemies of Kampuchea.
Let us strike and take victory! Victory! Victory![35]

Like the national anthem, "The Red Flag" song, with its analogy between blood sacrifice and the color red and its encouragement to "seethe with anger" and "strike and hit the enemy," urged cadre to maintain their class grudge until not "a single reactionary imperialist" was left alive.

The invocation of blood imbues such songs with powerful ontological resonance. On the one hand, blood is central to health. In Khmer ethnophysiology, the proper flow of blood leads to a balanced state of well-being. The disruption of this flow signifies social and somatic disequilibrium, often diagnosed as maladies of excess heat or cold. Anger, in turn, is conceptualized as having heating properties and may make the blood "burn."[36] More concretely, the loss of blood signifies injury and a threat to one's well-being, possibly even the loss of one's life. Blood is also a powerful, embodied symbol of violence, which often results in bloody injury or death.

Through such frequent invocations of spilled blood, then, Khmer Rouge songs and other ideological discourses and symbols condense a number of powerful themes: existential threat, bodily and social disequilibrium, anger and rage, sorrow and loss, and violence against the enemy. Moreover, as Haing Ngor notes, blood is also a kinship idiom signifying similarity and difference. By focusing on the spilled blood of beloved comrades, Khmer Rouge ideology implied there was a kinship-like bond between the revolutionaries (Angkar being the "parent") that was opposed to their enemy "others"—the oppressor classes. Blood imagery thereby also helps to manufacture difference, providing a symbolic manifestation of more explicit us/them discourses. In the context of the dances and songs, the blood imagery implies that "something bad" has been done to one, a sentiment that leads to imbalance and makes one become hot and "seized with painful anger." The ensuing knot of malice, in turn, generates hatred and a desire for vengeance or, as the Khmer Rouge dancers cried out, for blood to avenge blood. The threat of revenge was clear to Haing Ngor, leaving him, and many other members of the "oppressor enemy" who listened to the performance, terrified.

While such ideological messages clearly had a different "take" among different segments of the population, they were effective in motivating many cadre, particularly poor and uneducated cadre like Boan, the village chief at Trâpeang Trah, to seek revenge against their class enemies. As Vong, who resided at Trâpeang Trah during DK, noted, "At first Boan was like us. After they had brainwashed him, however, his heart and thoughts changed. He became angry at the people, particularly the rich and soldiers. Boan was an ignorant person and couldn't write much . . . but he loved *Ângkar* and would report on people who were then killed." Similarly, the relatives of the "anonymous cadre" were likely influenced by such discourses as they took "revenge with people from Phnom Penh" because of their anger over the loss of loved ones and the B-52 bombings: "They just waited for people from Phnom Penh: if they had a chance to kill, they would kill." (His assertion that such revenge killings were not driven by an "official order [from the top]," however, is problematic given the DK leadership's explicit policy of annihilating "hidden enemies" and ideological call for vengeance.) Haing Ngor once made a pun to some other "new people" in his work group that such Khmer Rouge cadre were not "communist" (*kommuyonis*) but "revenge people," or *kum monuss:* "'That's what they are at the lower level,' I said, 'revenge people.' 'All they know is that city people like us used to lord it over them and this is their chance to get back. That's what they are, communist at top and *kum-monuss* at the bottom.'"[37]

Long work hours, starvation rations, a lack of freedom, miserable living conditions, and constant terror soon erased the humanity of "new people." As Someth May recalled, "We were hungry, too tired to wash or clean our clothes, and we lost all sense of hygiene. We didn't care what we ate as long as we could put something in our stomachs. We didn't mind where we had a shit, or who saw us. Disease spread through the village—cholera, malaria, dysentery, diarrhoea and skin infections."[38] Such conditions often reduced a person into an animal-like state of being. Like water buffalo, "new people" were sometimes even required to pull a plow or cart and might be whipped if they failed to work hard enough.[39] A soldier told one "new person" that it would be better for her sick mother to die "than [it would be for] a cow. The cows are good. They help us a lot and do not eat rice. They are much better than you pigs."[40] Since "new people" were less than fully human, there were fewer moral inhibitions in harming them. A "new person" who did something wrong could therefore be "discarded" (*veay chal*)—a euphemism for execution—without much of a qualm, an attitude captured by the chilling Khmer Rouge threat, "To keep you is no gain; to destroy you is no loss" (*tuk min chomnenh yok chenh min khat*).

This dehumanization, combined with Khmer Rouge ideology that fomented malice against the oppressor classes and glorified revolutionary violence, were key factors that contributed to the revenge killings that continued to take place long after the first wave of DK executions had ended. Having annihilated most of the Lon Nol government's leadership, the Khmer Rouge began to seek out and kill off other "class enemies," such as rich "capitalists," intellectuals, professionals, and lower-ranking Lon Nol soldiers, police, and government employees. By the end of March 1976, the Party Center had made the decision to authorize the use of violence to "smash" people "inside and outside" the revolutionary ranks,[41] initiating a second wave of violence that peaked in 1977 in most areas but continued to ebb and flow until the end of DK. Throughout Cambodia, orders were passed down the Khmer Rouge civilian and military chain of command instructing local cadre to research the backgrounds of the people under their control and find the "hidden enemies burrowing from within."[42]

Entire Cambodian family lines were destroyed during DK. In some cases, the Khmer Rouge would simply load families of "new people" into trucks and take them to execution centers. The Khmer Rouge adopted a Maoist saying that encouraged such slaughter: "To dig up grass, one must also dig up the roots" (*chik smav trauv chik teang reus*).[43] Echoing the explanation of many others, a former DK village chief told me that this phrase meant that cadre were supposed to "dig up the entire family line. Not just the [nuclear family] of husband, wife, and children, but the entire line of descent, the entire clan, from the grandparents on, to take the entire string at once." He confirmed that he was ordered to research the background of the people living in his village and that, at meetings, Rom, a Khmer Rouge official, spoke of a plan to seek out "soldiers, the rich, and government workers and to kill all of them and their families." The village chief explained that this was done so that "none would be left to take revenge on a later day."

Much of the killing that occurred during DK was motivated by a Khmer Rouge ideological model that drew heavily upon preexisting notions of disproportionate revenge. Many of the poor were angry at the rich and powerful "oppressors" who looked down upon them, exploited them, and made them suffer. The Khmer Rouge used this ideology to inflame the feeling of resentment even further, trying to make its followers "burn with rage" and be "seized with painful anger" (*chheu chap*), feelings that would motivate them to seek revenge and destroy their class enemies. As Khieu Samphan's brother explained in an interview with me: "The destruction of the Cambodian people can be understood in terms of the resentment (*chheu chap*) of the destitute (*neak ât*) who suffered and were looked down upon. . . . Their resentment became a grudge that was repaid (*sâng*) when they had power. . . . They repaid [this debt] by killing people in return."

As illustrated by the revenge killings that took place at the end of DK, the Khmer Rouge were not completely successful in preventing retaliation. Thus, while some cadre fled before the Vietnamese invasion, others like Phat—a woman known for her brutality—were not able to escape. After hiding in the jungle for a few days, Phat tried to sneak into a village to steal food one night and was shot and wounded. A crowd soon gathered and beat Phat to death. One villager whose husband had been killed by Phat told me, "More and more people kept coming, including grandfathers and grandchildren. They really hated her because she had killed so many people. I hit her two times, too. I hated her because she had killed my husband. We wanted revenge." Many Cambodians witnessed the post-DK revenge killing of former Khmer Rouge cadre. In this way the cycle of revenge was perpetuated.

As the chairman of the Cambodian Military Court suggested in one of the epigraphs with which this essay began, local understandings of revenge have continued to be invoked in relationship to the Khmer Rouge, but they have also shifted with the currents of history. Just after DK, the People's Republic of Kampuchea pursued a two-pronged strategy with regard to the Khmer Rouge, stating that former Khmer Rouge might be imprisoned briefly, but ultimately should be accepted back into society. Anyone who sought vengeance against these individuals would be arrested. On the other hand, the PRK regime based its legitimacy on having "liberated" the country from the Khmer Rouge and attempted to keep popular anger toward the "Pol Pot—Ieng Sary clique," which had fled to the Thai border and was now fighting the PRK regime, inflamed through education, commemorations, a trial, memorials, holidays, literature, film, and other media that dramatically foregrounded this deviant "clique's" campaign of mass murder.[44] Implicitly, the PRK regime encouraged the populace to remain "tied in anger" toward the "Pol Pot—Ieng Sary clique" and take vengeance by fighting these evil enemies.

After the 1993 UN election, the genocidal past was again rewritten as the new Cambodian government attempted to entice the Khmer Rouge to defect and, in the name of reconciliation, deemphasized the Khmer Rouge atrocities. In the domain of education, for example, virtually all mention of DK was removed from textbooks that had previously foregrounded them intensively.[45] When, in late 1998, former Khmer Rouge leaders Nuon Chea and Khieu Samphan defected to the government, Prime Minister Hun Sen announced, "We should dig a hole and bury the past."[46] Khieu Samphan himself urged people "to forget the past so our nation can concentrate on the future. Let bygones be bygones."[47] While some Cambodians still spoke of the desire for revenge, others might invoke the need for reconciliation or Buddhist forgetting during this period.

Even as the Cambodian government advocated reconciliation, the United States and other Western powers—that had barely acknowledged the Cambodian genocide while the PRK regime, which was aligned with the Soviet bloc and thus a Cold War enemy of the West, was in power—suddenly began advocating for an international tribunal. The chairman of the Cambodian Military Court's remarks about possibly prosecuting former high-ranking Khmer Rouge officials were made in the context of this shift toward consideration of a Khmer Rouge tribunal. It was not until 2006 that the Khmer Rouge tribunal finally got off the ground. Even now, while most Cambodians generally appear to favor the trial of a handful of former Khmer Rouge leaders, some continue to talk of revenge, or even to view the tribunal itself as a form of vengeance against these former enemies. It remains to be seen whether these perceptions will shift as the trials proceed, the past is reworked yet again, and ordinary people seek to make sense of it all.

Notes

1. Sainsbury and Sotheacheath, "Good Intentions Paved Road to Mass Murder."

2. See Chandler, *The Tragedy of Cambodian History*; Hinton, *Why Did They Kill?*; and Kiernan, *The Pol Pot Regime*.

3. Of course, alternative models of more disproportionate revenge also exist in the Judeo-Christian tradition, as a reading of the Old Testament or Greek tragedy illustrates.

4. Scott, *Seeing Like a State*.

5. See Chandler, *The Tragedy of Cambodian History*; Chandler, *Facing the Cambodian Past*.

6. Pol Pot, "Long Live the 17th Anniversary of the Communist Party of Kampuchea," 28.

7. Reproduced in Kiernan, *How Pol Pot Came to Power*, 231–32.

8. Carney, "The Communist Party of Kampuchea and the Problem of Khmer Young Men and Women," 30.

9. Ibid., 32.

10. Ith Sarin, quoted in ibid., 39.

11. Ith Sarin, *Srânah Proleung Khmaer*, 68; Carney, *Communist Party Power*, 52.

12. Ith Sarin, *Srânah Proleung Khmaer*, 63; see also Carney, *Communist Party Power*, 51.

13. Ith Sarin, *Srânah Proleung Khmaer*.

14. Carney, *Communist Party Power*, 31.

15. Cited in Kiernan, *The Pol Pot Regime*, 422.

16. May Mayko Ebihara, "Kin Terminology and the Idiom of Kinship in Cambodia/ Kampuchea," 186, 348, 579.

17. Ebihara, "Kin Terminology," 584.

18. Ibid., 562.

19. Ibid., 569.

20. Tooze, *Cambodia: The Land of Contrasts*, 90. See also Kiernan, *The Pol Pot Regime*, 5.

21. Soth Polin, "Pol Pot's Diabolical Sweetness," 43–45.

22. Chandler, Kiernan, and Lim, *The Early Phases of Liberation in Northwestern Cambodia*, 2, 9.

23. CMR 12.25, quoted in Heder and Tittemore, *Seven Candidates for Prosecution*, 31.

24. Ponchaud, *Cambodia: Year Zero*, 29. On the round-up and execution of the Khmer Rouge leadership in Phnom Penh, see also Becker, *When the War Was Over*, 192–93; Pin Yathay, *Stay Alive, My Son*, 16.

25. Ponchaud, *Cambodia: Year Zero*, p. 28.

26. Thion, *Watching Cambodia*, 166.

27. One of eight key components of the Party Center's plan that was allegedly discussed by Pol Pot at a conference on May 20, 1975 (Kiernan, *The Pol Pot Regime*, 55).

28. *Revolutionary Flags* (*Khmer Rouge* magazine), 1977, 21–22. See also *Foreign Broadcast Information Service* (microfilm of government broadcast, hereafter *FBIS*), April 14, 1978, H5.

29. Kiernan, interview with Ouch Bun Chhoeun, in *The Pol Pot Regime*, 62.

30. *FBIS*, January 20, 1976, H1; see the same source on how oppression "fired the anger of our poor brothers and sisters." On the Khmer Rouge construction of the urban/ rural divide, see McIntyre, "Geography as Destiny," 30–58.

31. *FBIS*, March 31, 1976, H2–3; *FBIS*, April 16, 1976, H8.

32. *FBIS*, January 16, 1976, H3.

33. Ngor, *A Cambodian Odyssey*, 140. On Khmer Rouge song and dance, see Locard, "Khmer Rouge Revolutionary Songs and the Cambodian Culture Tradition," 308–48.

34. *FBIS*, October 4, 1977, H25.

35. This translation by Chandler is from Chandler, Kiernan, and Lim, *The Early Phases of Liberation*, 14, and Locard, "Khmer Rouge Revolutionary Songs," 324–26.

36. Gosananda, *Step by Step*.

37. Ngor, *A Cambodian Odyssey*, 159.

38. May, *Cambodian Witness: The Autobiography of Someth May*, 165.

39. See Ngor, *A Cambodian Odyssey*, 165f.; Stuart-Fox, *The Murderous Revolution*, 60; Szymusiak, *The Stones Cry Out*, 147.

40. Moyer, *Escape from the Killing Fields*, 123.

41. "Decisions of the Central Committee on a Variety of Questions," in Chandler, Kiernan, and Boua, *Pol Pot Plans the Future*, 3.

42. See Heder and Tittemore, *Seven Candidates for Prosecution*, 42f.

43. See Locard, *Le "Petit livre rouge" de Pol Pot ou les paroles de l'Angkar*, 55.

44. See Hinton, "Truth, Representation and the Politics of Memory after Genocide," 62 81.

45. Ibid.

46. "Khmer Rouge Leaders Arrive in Phnom Penh, Won't Be Tried."

47. "Apology from Two 'Killing Fields' Leaders."

Works Cited

"Apology from Two 'Killing Fields' Leaders." CNN.com. December 29, 1998. http://www.cnn.com/WORLD/asiapcf/9812/29/cambodia.02/index.html.

Becker, Elizabeth. *When the War Was Over: Cambodia and the Khmer Rouge Revolution.* New York: Public Affairs, 1998.

Carney, Timothy. "The Communist Party of Kampuchea and the Problem of Khmer Young Men and Women." In Timothy Carney, *Communist Party Power in Kampuchea (Cambodia): Documents and Discussion.* Ithaca: Cornell University Southeast Asia Program, 1977.

Chandler, David P. *Facing the Cambodian Past: Selected Essays, 1971–1994.* Chiang Mai, Thailand: Silkworm Books, 1996.

_____. *The Tragedy of Cambodian History: Politics, War and Revolution since 1945.* New Haven: Yale University Press, 1991.

Chandler, David P., Ben Kiernan, and Chanthou Boua, eds. *Pol Pot Plans the Future: Confidential Leadership Documents from Democratic Kampuchea, 1976–1977.* Monograph Series 33. New Haven: Yale University Southeast Asia Studies, 1988.

Chandler, David P., Ben Kiernan, and Muy Hong Lim. *The Early Phases of Liberation in Northwestern Cambodia: Conversations with Peang Sophi.* Melbourne: Monash University Centre of Southeast Asian Studies Working Papers, 1976.

"Duch and Ta Mok Face Charges Under 'Anti-KR' Law." *Phnom Penh Post.* May 1999.

Ebihara, May Mayko. "Kin Terminology and the Idiom of Kinship in Cambodia/Kampuchea." Paper presented at the SSRC/Indochina studies Program Workshop on Kinship and Gender in Indochina, University of Northern Illinois, July 26–27, 1986.

Gosananda, Maha. *Step by Step: Meditations on Wisdom and Compassion.* Berkeley, Calif.: Parallax Press, 1992.

Heder, Steve, and Brian D. Tittemore. *Seven Candidates for Prosecution: Accountability for the Crimes of the Khmer Rouge.* Washington, D.C.: War Crimes Research Office, American University, 2001.

Hinton, Alexander. "Truth, Representation and the Politics of Memory after Genocide." In *People of Virtue: Reconfiguring Religion, Power and Morality in Cambodia Today,* ed. Alexandra Kent and David Chandler. Copenhagen: NIAS Press, 2008, 62–81.

Ith Sarin. *Srânah Proleung Khmaer [Regrets for the Khmer Soul].* Phnom Penh, 1973.

Jackson, Karl D., ed. *Cambodia, 1975–1978: Rendezvous with Death.* Princeton: Princeton University Press, 1989.

"Khmer Rouge Leaders Arrive in Phnom Penh, Won't Be Tried." CNN.com, December 29, 1998. http://www.cnn.com/WORLD/asiapcf/9812/29/cambodia.01/index.html.

Kiernan, Ben. *How Pol Pot Came to Power: A History of Communism in Kampuchea, 1930–1975.* London: Verso, 1985.

_____. *The Pol Pot Regime: Race, Power, and Genocide in Cambodia under the Khmer Rouge, 1975–79.* New Haven: Yale University Press, 1996.

Locard, Henri. "Khmer Rouge Revolutionary Songs and the Cambodian Culture Tradition, or, The Revolution Triumphant." In *Khmer Studies,* vol. 1, ed. Sorn Samnang. Phnom Penh: Ministry of Education, Youth, and Sports, 1998, pp. 308–48.

_____. *Le "Petit livre rouge" de Pol Pot ou les paroles de l'Angkar.* Paris: Harmattan, 1996.

McIntyre, Kevin. "Geography as Destiny: Cities, Villages and Khmer Rouge Orientalism." *Comparative Studies of Society and History* 38, no. 4 (1996): 30–58.

Moyer, Nancy. *Escape from the Killing Fields: One Girl Who Survived the Cambodian Holocaust.* Grand Rapids, Mich.: Zondervan, 1991.

Ngor, Haing. *A Cambodian Odyssey.* New York: Warner Books, 1987.

Pin Yathay. *Stay Alive, My Son.* New York: Touchstone, 1987.

Pol Pot. "Long Live the 17th Anniversary of the Communist Party of Kampuchea." Phnom Penh: Ministry of Foreign Affairs, 1977.

Ponchaud, François. *Cambodia: Year Zero.* New York: Holt, Rinehart and Winston, 1978.

Sainsbury, Peter, and Chea Sotheacheath. "Good Intentions Paved Road to Mass Murder." *Phnom Penh Post,* April 2000.

Scott, James C. *Seeing Like a State: How Certain Schemes to Improve the Human Condition Have Failed.* New Haven: Yale University Press, 1998.

Someth May. Cambodian *Witness: The Autobiography of Someth May.* New York: Random House, 1986.

Soth Polin. "Pol Pot's Diabolical Sweetness." *Index on Censorship* 5 (1980): 43–45.

Stuart-Fox, Martin. *The Murderous Revolution: Life and Death in Pol Pot's Kampuchea Based on the Personal Experiences of Bunbeang Ung.* Chippendale, Australia: Alternative Publishing Cooperative, 1985.

Szymusiak, Molyda. *The Stones Cry Out: A Cambodian Childhood, 1975–1980.* Trans. Linda Coverdale. New York: Hill and Wang, 1986.

Thion, Serge. *Watching Cambodia: Ten Paths to Enter the Cambodian Tangle.* Bangkok: White Lotus, 1993.

Tooze, Ruth. *Cambodia: The Land of Contrasts.* New York: Viking, 1962.

5

From Jasenovac to Srebrenica
Subaltern Genocide and the Serbs

David B. MacDonald

In cases of subaltern genocide, oppressed and victimized groups employ genocidal strategies against their oppressors. What, though, of instances where a group's victimization and its adoption of genocidal strategies are separated by decades or even centuries? What happens when the targets of those genocidal strategies share no meaningful connection to the perpetrators of past acts of victimization? And what happens in situations where subaltern identifications become national myths, fueling a sense of vulnerability, humiliation, and fear that in turn helps to foment genocidal wars of aggression "in self-defense"? To what extent are such cases reasonably considered within a framing of "subaltern genocide," and how do they serve to amplify and deepen the concept?

The case of Yugoslavia/Serbia in the twentieth and twenty-first centuries offers one of the most striking instances of a genocidal campaign fueled by past victimization experiences and the subaltern identifications they spawned. It shows as well how such identifications may be marshaled and nurtured by unscrupulous political leaders, to strengthen their legitimacy and justify aggressive war and genocide. From 1941 to 1945, part of the Croatian/Bosnian Serb population was targeted with extermination by the Croatian Ustasha fascist regime, which the Nazis had installed as puppets following their invasion of Yugoslavia in June 1941. The Ustasha established a network of concentration camps designed expressly to exterminate its ethnic enemies. In 1995, during the wars in Bosnia-Herzegovina, Bosnian Muslim men and boys in the city of Srebrenica were subjected to what the International Criminal Tribunal for the former Yugoslavia (ICTY) has called genocide at the hands of Bosnian Serb forces under the control of General Ratko Mladic. In August 2001, Bosnian Serb General Radislav Krstic was found guilty of genocide by the ICTY for the killing of some 8,000 men and boys at Srebrenica in 1995.[1] This has been rightly described as "the largest single war crime in Europe since the Second World War."[2]

If we accept that groups may commit or support violent acts against other groups when motivated by fear or threat, then the more real the threat appears, the more likely a group is to be motivated to commit abhorrent acts in "self-defense," launching "preemptive" strikes allegedly to avoid impending attack. However, fear and trauma are often misplaced and redirected. As such, while Croats were the aggressors in the 1940s and Serbs the victims, Muslims, not Croats, were Serbs' primary targets of the 1990s. The problem of using past victimization to understand present crimes is that we may develop a tendency to "understand" them, which can lead to excusing such actions as somehow inevitable. But there was nothing inevitable about the Bosnian genocide, or the wider war in Croatia, Bosnia-Herzegovina, and Kosovo. At best, we can say that many Serbs, due to past victimization and trauma, had a psychological predisposition to a subaltern identification, and to fear for their personal safety during periods of social or political uncertainty; they were thus more easily swayed by nationalist rhetoric than perhaps the average Czech or Belgian would be. This, however, can in no way justify or excuse the horrendous crimes that some Serbs committed, and that many Serbs at least tacitly supported, in the 1990s.

This chapter is divided into three parts. I begin by examining the longevity of the effects of group trauma and victimization, and their potential impact on the nation, both as a psychological problem for the group and a rhetorical arsenal for nationalists. I then discuss the World War II genocide, before turning to the second, more contemporary outbreak of genocide in Bosnia-Herzegovina at the city of Srebrenica. Of equal interest is how Serbian history has been manipulated and instrumentalized in the political sphere, the subject of the final part of the chapter. I end on a cautionary note. While the Srebrenica events were gruesome, the verdict of genocide passed by the ICTY has had a negative effect on Serbs in terms of their historical memory, and their likelihood of owning up to the crime. This is because the verdict has redefined the nature of a victim group (now localized to a city) and has thus significantly reduced the "in part" criteria of the 1948 UN Genocide Convention. As a more general observation, Serbian nationalists have serious "memory problems" with regard to the 1990s. Coupled with a high degree of willful ignorance, this precludes a serious reckoning with the horrors of the recent past.

Thinking Like a Victim: The Serbian Case

Jones and Robins signal that "genocidal assaults that contain a morally plausible element of revenge, retribution, or revolutionary usurpation are less likely to be condemned, and are often welcomed."[3] In the Serbian case, subaltern identifications and past victimization experiences were invoked time and again to justify the renewal of Serbian nationalism in the 1980s and the expansion of Serbia's borders beyond the republic, to include parts of Croatia and Bosnia-Herzegovina. A "Jewish trope" also developed during this time. As Zivkovic paraphrased the emergent Serbian view: "Both Serbs and Jews are the 'chosen peoples'—slaughtered, sacrificed, denied expression, yet always righteous, always defending themselves, never attacking."[4]

From the Battle of Kosovo in 1389, which subjected Serbs to five centuries of Ottoman rule, to severe losses in the world wars, Serbs have felt themselves (to some extent correctly) to be victims of their neighbors—even if the identities of their aggressors have changed over time. Several Serbian writers have characterized their nation as one that is continually alert to the threat of war and destruction, while similarly pervaded by a sense of victimhood. Popov, for example, describes war as a "way of life": "not just a myth, [but] a legend and an epic." Historically, the nation prided itself on being constantly prepared for war, with the warrior's vocation held in especially high regard. In this narrative, Popov reveals, "peace merely appears as a deceptive break between clashes and fierce battles."[5]

Instrumentally, Bosnian Serb psychiatrist Dusan Kecmanovic has argued that myths of victimhood were vital in cementing political power in a context of civil strife and breakdown. "Being a victim means having the moral and material right to reprisal," as "everyone seems to expect the victim to settle accounts sooner or later, to return tit for tat, and to punish those who have made them a victim." Victimhood thus gives one a special status—"a moral and psychological advantage."[6] It becomes a means of legitimating any strategy deemed necessary to "protect" the self against injury and injustice, at present or in the future. Since the victim is deemed "not responsible for his or her unfortunate fate," no soul-searching is required as to "whether and how much he or she might have contributed to this quite unenviable position."[7]

Serbian Trauma?

For groups which have suffered from genocide or other collective tragedy, a heightened sense of fear and trauma may be transmitted intergenerationally. In its most basic sense, trauma can be defined as "an event in the subject's life defined by its intensity, by the subject's incapacity to respond adequately to it, and by the upheaval and long-lasting effects that it brings about in the psychical organization."[8] Some effects of trauma include "disassociation," where salient chunks of information about the traumatic event may be confused or even forgotten. "Emotional numbing" is also common, as is "interpersonal vigilance," which can lead to violence, injury, and even death. "Suicide thinking and risk-taking behavior" can result from the trauma as a sufferer enters into a self-destructive spiral.[9]

If individuals can suffer from trauma, so too can groups. Parents effectively externalize their trauma by passing it on to their children. The child becomes "a reservoir for the unwanted, troublesome parts of an older generation." It is then the child's designated responsibility to absorb their parents' expectations and frustrations; eventually the child is obliged to "mourn, to reverse the humiliation and feelings of helplessness pertaining to the trauma of his forebears."[10]

For many Serbs, chief among the past's traumatic events was their attempted genocide at the hands of the Croatian Ustasha. Bogosavljevic has called these crimes "the unresolved genocide," tying past and lingering traumas to the anger and frustration of the 1980s and the violence of the 1990s. It is no surprise, then, that "retaliation for what had been done earlier, and the fear of a renewal of genocide (irrespective of whether this fear was justified or not), were, at the same time, if not the moving force behind the war, then certainly an important element in motivating the masses."[11] Others, too, have seen the genocide beginning in 1941 as an "important contributory factor" in the uprising of Serbs in Croatia. Mirkovic depicts a mixture of three elements as laying the foundation for the convulsions of the 1990s:

> (1) Collective trauma rooted in [the] genocidal experience of a victimized group and expressed as fear and threat resulting from disorientation following the disintegration of the state. (2) The politics of memory through [the] so-called "media war" in the 1980s aimed at fanning fear and hatred. (3) Revival of ultra-nationalist ideologies of [the] *Ustashism* and *Chetnikism,* respectively [in Croatia and Serbia], as genocidal ideologies.[12]

It should be noted that Mirkovic was dealing with Croatian Serb fears in the 1990s, and had little to say about the Bosnian conflict. In the Croatian case, moreover, he was critical of what he saw as the "manipulation of consciousness through mass media in order to revive the memories of genocide of 50 years ago, with the specific purpose of enhancing conflict and justifying the use of force."[13] One should add that, psychologically speaking, there is no axiomatic link between suffering from past traumas and violence committed against others. Fear and resentment may to some extent predispose individuals from a designated victim group to engage in future atrocities, but this is by no means inevitable.

Genocide in World War II

On April 5, 1941, Yugoslavia was invaded by Italian and German forces and split into different spheres of influence. In Serbia, General Milan Nedic formed a quisling "Government of National Salvation." The regime was unpopular, and Serbs divided their loyalty between the fledgling communist Partisans (whose ranks Croats also joined) and the Serbian Chetniks under General Draza Mihailovic. These were paramilitary bands loyal to the Yugoslav government-in-exile, which was allied with the Western powers. Much of Croatia and Bosnia-Herzegovina was given over to the Croatian fascist Ustasha-controlled "Independent State of Croatia" (or NDH) under the leadership of Ante Pavelic.

Some Croat writers have downplayed Ustasha crimes, but the scale of these atrocities was immense. Large numbers of Serbs, Jews, Gypsies, communists, and Croatians hostile to the regime were interned in concentration camps, while countless others were massacred in towns and villages. The Ustasha were directly involved in the administration and in the orchestration of the killings. In addition, some 200,000 Serbs were forcibly converted to Catholicism.[14] According to the Ustasha blueprint, one-third of Serbs were to be killed, another third expelled, and a final third converted to Catholicism.[15]

The Ustasha founded a series of concentration/death camps, from smaller ones at Dakovo, Lepoglava, Lobor, and Sisak, to Jasenovac, the largest and best known. Jasenovac was a complex of five camps, which operated from August 1941 to April 1945. Staffed by Croatian political police and Ustasha militiamen, conditions for prisoners were atrocious, causing the deaths of tens of thousands of Serbs and some 20,000 Jews.[16] At Jasenovac, Dedijer reveals a variety of killing methods including revolvers, carbines, machine guns, bombs, knives, axes, hatchets, wooden hammers, iron bars, iron hammers, hoes, trampling, belts and leather whips, hanging, burning, cremation, scorching of sensitive body parts, freezing, poison gas, suffocating, starvation, and disease.[17]

Serbs themselves by no means had clean hands during the war. The Chetnik royalist forces perpetrated massacres of Croatian and Bosnian Moslem populations in Bosnia-Herzegovina, making them as hated there as the Ustasha. Chetnik reluctance to engage the Germans for fear of reprisals, and their violent conflicts with communist forces, eventually lost them Allied favor.[18] While the wartime records of some Serbs and Croats were dubious, there were nevertheless qualitative differences between the Allied-backed Chetnik monarchists and their small-scale massacres, and the Nazi-backed Ustasha with their concentration camps-cum-death camps. While there is indisputable evidence of Chetnik massacres of Croats and Moslems, there is no concrete proof that the Chetniks aimed to exterminate the entire Croatian nation. The only letter to this effect, describing a plan to create an "ethnically pure Greater Serbia," was a forgery.[19] However, it seems clear that the Ustasha aimed to exterminate at least a *part* of the Serbian nation, and the legal definition of genocide emphasizes destruction "in whole or in part" of a target group. How large a part must be targeted for the label of genocide to apply? In his recent book, Jones argues in favor of a "substantial part" of the group, perhaps numbering in the tens or hundreds of thousands.[20] Certainly the Serbian case fits this requirement, though the cited range of total deaths is rather wide, from 100,000 to 750,000.[21]

The tide turned against Germany and its Ustasha supporters in 1943 with the surrender of Italy. By the end of 1943, the Partisans under Josip Broz (Tito) had gained Allied support and were able to inflict significant damage on German and Ustasha targets. By 1944, they had liberated the country, and by May 1945 Tito and the Communist Party of Yugoslavia had laid the basis for a new federal state designed to foster "brotherhood and unity."[22]

Prelude to the Bosnian War

The rise of nationalism in the former Yugoslavia is by now extremely well documented. For most of the lifetime of the Socialist Federal Republic of Yugoslavia (SFRY), Serbian nationalism was subordinate to communism and did not become an important factor until Tito's death in 1980. The power vacuum at the federal center would be filled by aspiring nationalists at the republic level, beginning in Kosovo with movements for Albanian secession in 1981.[23]

In reaction to Albanian nationalist demands, the Serbian Academy of Sciences and Arts (SANU) drew up its famous Memorandum in 1986—a list of

Serbian grievances against their treatment within the Federation. SANU decried the "genocide" of Serbs in Kosovo—the first time the term had been deployed in reference to contemporary events or perceived threats within the federation, and an explosive usage indeed. More generally, it articulated a need for Serbs throughout Yugoslavia to assert themselves as a collectivity. The Memorandum's architects played a prominent role in spurring Serbian nationalism. Slobodan Milosevic rose to power in 1987 by appealing to an emerging sense of Serbian unity, and claimed to speak for Serbs throughout Yugoslavia.[24]

In Croatia, the former general and historian Franjo Tudjman emerged as head of the Croatian Democratic Movement (HDZ). By 1990, this had become the primary nationalist force in the republic, winning the elections in April of that year.[25] Tudjman's party, while appearing western and progressive, soon began discriminating against the republic's Serbian population.[26] Largely funded by Croatians in the diaspora, the HDZ was anti-communist and unsympathetic to Serbian demands. The 1990 constitution conspicuously omitted Serbs as a constituent nation; on a practical level, jobs, property rights, and even residence status depended on having Croatian citizenship, which was not automatically granted to non-Croats.[27] In this context, renewed fears arose of a Croatian-led genocide against Serbs.

War in Croatia and Bosnia-Herzegovina

In 1990, Tudjman tried to pull Croatia out of the SFRY, precipitating a Serbian invasion of Croatian territory. In 1990, with Serbia's backing, Serbs in the Krajina region declared a "state of war" against the Croatian state. Open fighting broke out in April, and a referendum on Serbian independence resulted in a call for Serbian secession. Between February and June 1991, rebellion escalated. Serbian paramilitary units such as Arkan's "Tigers" and Vojislav Seselj's "White Eagles" arrived in Croatia, trained and funded by the Serbian Ministry of the Interior. The situation grew more dramatic when Yugoslav People's Army forces intervened under the pretext of protecting Serbian minority rights.[28] By September 1991, Serbian forces had leveled Vukovar and other eastern towns, and controlled almost one-third of Croatian territory. By October, they had pushed south to Dubrovnik, which they shelled with abandon.[29]

By January 1992, a ceasefire was agreed. UN troops created a series of buffer regions, and the fighting moved to Bosnia-Herzegovina. The seven-month campaign had cost some 10,000 lives and resulted in 700,000 displaced persons.[30] While "ethnic cleansing" entered the journalistic lexicon at this time, genocide and allusions to World War II were not prominent in media discourse.

The Bosnian conflict proved to be far more protracted and bloody than its predecessor. While fighting bitterly over Croatia, both Tudjman and Milosevic had dreamed of creating expanded national homelands. Serbs composed 31.1 percent of the Bosnian population and the Croats 17.3 percent. Muslims (43.7 percent) were loyal to neither side.[31] A further quandary in dividing Bosnia was the paucity of ethnically homogenous enclaves. According to the 1991 census,

Serbs could be found in 94.5 percent of the republic's territory, Muslims in 94 percent, and Croats in 70 percent.[32] Into this ethnic mosaic must be factored some 90,000–100,000 Serbian fighters, including Yugoslav People's Army units and irregulars who were transferred from Croatia. They surrounded the major population centers—Sarajevo, Mostar, Tuzla, and Bihac.[33]

While Alija Izetbegovic's Party of Democratic Action (SDA) favored a unitary Bosnia, Serbian and Croatian leaders were more hostile to the idea. The Serbian Democratic Party (SDS) was founded two months after the SDA, led by Radovan Karadzic. A Bosnian branch of the Croatian HDZ was formed under Stjepan Kljuic.[34] After the referendum in August 1991 signaled Moslem and Croatian support for independence, Bosnian Serbs created four autonomous units in the republic. Bosnian Serbs held their own referendum in November, resulting in near-unanimous support for separation from Bosnia-Herzegovina and union with the SFRY.[35]

By early 1992, both Serbian and Croatian leaders had created autonomous ethnic regions and laid the groundwork for the bloody dismemberment of the republic. A variety of paramilitary organizations began operating in the region, such as the Tigers and White Eagles (Serbian) and Autumn Rain and the Croatian Defence Forces-HOS (Croatian). Bosnian Serbs also formed a separate army (the BSA), led by General Mladic and closely tied to the SDS. Fighting began in 1992 and quickly escalated into bloody ethnic war. Villages and towns were "cleansed" of ethnic "enemies."[36] Serbian forces appeared to follow a five-stage process which began with "concentrating" target populations, "decapitating" their leadership through executions, "separation" or division of civilians into men of fighting age and others, "evacuation" of women, children, and the elderly, and finally "liquidation" of men of fighting age and disposal of their bodies.[37] This process would also be used at Srebrenica.

Cultural destruction played an important role in the campaign: some 1,400 churches and mosques were destroyed during the first years of the war. Organized rape was also common on the Serbian side, with "rape camps" established in many conflict zones. These were designed not only for perverse sexual gratification, but to humiliate "enemy" women—rendering them, in the context of their patriarchal society, unfit for marriage.[38] Both Serbs and Croats also ran "detention centers" and "collection camps" where prisoners were housed, frequently beaten and terrorized, sometimes sexually violated, and often killed. Of the larger camps, Serbs controlled thirteen and Croats four, although the Red Cross documented a total of fifty-one camps in all, many of them small and impromptu—located in camp grounds, schools, and even movie theaters.[39]

Srebrenica

In 1995, Serbs committed what the ITCY has confirmed as genocide at Srebrenica—paradoxically, in one of six UN safe areas created under a Security Council mandate in 1993. While I use the term genocide, I raise questions below about its specific applicability in this case, of interest to genocide scholars. This was not the first time Serbs had deliberately attacked UN safe areas. In April 1994 Gorazde was shelled, and Moslem homes were burned while the British commanding officer stood by. Srebrenica, a former silver mining town, was in the heart of a region of Bosnia that abutted Serbia proper, and was thus a prime target for Serbian predation from the beginning of the war. The town proved difficult to defend. It was a small enclave with a large civilian population. The Bosnian Muslim forces present were poorly armed, and UN forces were also below optimum strength and located in easily targeted positions.[40] Although the army of the Republic of Bosnia-Herzegovina had twice the number of soldiers, they had no heavy weapons. The Bosnian Serb Army, by contrast, had between 1,000 to 2,000 troops from the Fifth "Drina" Corps, as well as additional units and special forces. These were well equipped with artillery and mortars, tanks, and tracked armored vehicles. Their military intelligence, communications, and command-and-control capacities were far superior to the Muslims', and they thus enjoyed "an overwhelming military advantage over the Bosnian Government forces in the enclave."[41]

From February, the BSA began to restrict humanitarian aid into the safe area, and in April Dutchbat peacekeeping forces were restricted from entering or leaving the enclave. Fuel, food, and other supplies were also strictly managed. By early July, the UN High Commission for Refugees (UNHCR) reported that it had managed to achieve only 30 percent of its food target for June. The BSA had effectively boxed in the peacekeepers.[42]

The BSA attack began on July 6 primarily from the southern part of the enclave. Dutchbat observation posts were targeted and shells lobbed into the enclave. The following day, things were quiet due to bad weather, but by July 8, BSA forces had surrounded two other observation posts and were beginning to tighten their hold on the enclave. As the BSA advanced, some 3,000 residents of the Swedish Shelter Project, located in the southern part of the enclave, fled to Srebrenica town to escape. By July 10, some 2,000 civilians were clustered around the hospital, hoping its special status would protect them from Serbian attacks. By the following day, Dutchbat forces had retreated further into the town, while thousands of civilians sought refuge in the peacekeeping compound at Potocari. Dutchbat forces let approximately 5,000 enter, but refused admission to the rest, who remained camped outside the compound. Altogether, the Dutchbat commander concluded by July 11 that there were some 15,000 people in or around the compound.[43] At this stage, 70 percent of the Srebrenica population were civilians from elsewhere who had been "ethnically cleansed" and internally displaced by Serbian forces.[44]

UN forces allowed BSA forces access to the compound and put up little resistance as Mladic's forces moved out civilians in buses, separating the men and the boys from the rest of the population. By July 11, thirty-one Dutch peacekeepers were being held hostage by the BSA.[45] The Dutch were intimidated by the Serbs, and many later reported fearing for their lives. Most were told they would not be harmed if they cooperated, and seemed to accept the false assurances given them by Serbian officials concerning the fate of the Muslim civilians.[46]

Mladic did allow some fifty to sixty buses to evacuate women, children, and the infirm, but a different fate was planned for the men. Mladic demanded that all males ages sixteen to sixty-five be questioned as potential "criminals" before being allowed to leave. Of the 239 men listed by the Dutchbat as inside the compound, few would survive the next several days. Many outside the compound were put in the so-called "White House" directly adjacent; 50 were killed on the first night. The small number of men who were initially allowed to board evacuation buses were later removed and housed in a school in the town of Luka, where a number were later shot.[47]

The sorting process continued into July 12–13, with most of the men sent to the town of Bratunac, where they were housed in an old school and a warehouse, in buses and trucks, and on a football field. Over the next four days they were systematically executed. After detainees were assembled at the school complex of Karakaj, thousands were shipped out to killing locations near the town. Later reports identified five locations where mass executions took place: Orahovac, the "dam" near Petkovici, Branjevo farm, the Pilica Cultural Center, and Kozluk. In the case of the Branjevo farm, men were brought in by buses, blindfolded with their hands tied; they were then shot and dumped in mass graves. Others were taken to the agricultural warehouse in Kravica, where they were killed by small arms and grenades. Another seventy people were killed in a meadow near Kravica, and several hundred more in the football stadium in Nova Kasaba.[48]

The ICTY has estimated that most victims were buried in mass graves within forty-eight hours of their execution. In the months to follow, BSA forces attempted to cover their tracks by reburying the bodies in some thirty-three "secondary sites" containing smaller numbers of bodies.[49] Stray clothing, bags, and other things were burned or otherwise disposed of. Dutchbat forces witnessed bodies being removed and evidence of the killings destroyed. No trace was to remain of the killing operation.[50]

Sensing the danger, many of Srebrenica's men had chosen by July 12 to escape toward the Bosnian stronghold at Tuzla, some fifty kilometers away. This carried them directly through Serbian lines. Some 15,000 men began the trek. A third were armed and positioned at the front of the exodus, followed by a long column of unarmed men. In time, several thousand were attacked by Serbian heavy weapons. BSA forces exhorted the Muslim men to surrender; when they did, they were routinely beaten, then killed almost down to the last captive. Those who made it to safety—disproportionately from the armed part of the column—estimated that approximately 3,000 of their number had been killed, either directly by BSA forces or by stepping on landmines.[51] Throughout, a high level of organization and systematic implementation prevailed in the selection, "cleansing," and killing operations.

What were the motives? On one level, Srebrenica was strategically valuable. It was part of the territory Bosnian Serbs sought to incorporate into their own republic. Mladic's goal was to ethnically cleanse the entire eastern portion of Bosnia, making it a Serbian preserve. Zepa, another putative safe area, was subjected to ethnic cleansing a week later. Ironically, genocide helped Serbia accomplish its geostrategic goals. While the region was supposed to become Muslim-controlled under the Dayton Peace Accord, both Srebrenica and Zepa became part of the Bosnian Serb Republic.[52]

Srebrenica was also a symbol. As a major refugee center for Muslims from across Bosnia, it was strategically important for Mladic to "cleanse" it. The targeted men and boys were killed to ensure that Muslims could never return and reestablish a viable community.[53] Destroying Srebrenica served as a warning and a humiliation to the Bosnian Muslim leadership.

David Rohde also touches on a more visceral dimension: namely, residual fear stirred up by Serbian propagandists. The circulation of the previously banned novel *Bloody Hands of Islam* described Muslim and Croat atrocities against Serbs around Srebrenica during World War II—stoking fears of renewed bloodshed. Such fears seemed justified by Srebrenica strongman Naser Oric's supposed execution of 120 Serbs in 1992. Whether the nature and scale of Oric's crimes were accurately conveyed, the accounts captured the imagination of many Serbian combatants, convincing them that Bosnian Muslims posed a genuine military threat.[54] Interestingly, Oric would be indicted at the ICTY for violations of the laws or customs of war, namely for seven murders of Serbs, the beating of several others, and the destruction by "Muslim armed units in the Municipalities of Bratunac, Srebrenica and Skelani . . . [of] a minimum of fifty predominantly Serb villages and hamlets" in attacks launched mostly from the Srebrenica "safe area."[55]

Ultimately, Oric faced a much reduced sentence: he was not convicted of the murders, nor of the destruction of villages and hamlets.[56] Whether he was actively resisting Serbian genocidal plans stemming from 1992 (as his lawyer suggested) or instigating his own brand of terror remains in dispute.[55] Serbs circulated many other stories of Muslim atrocities—46 dead in May 1992 and another 120 dead in July 1992 in Zalaje, with another 100 Serbs burned alive in January 1993 in the town of Kravica. Whatever the veracity of individual accounts, they spawned anger and fear. For some Serbian commanders like General Milenko Zivanovic, the resulting "bitterness was deeply personal."[58]

Indictment for Genocide

Both Mladic and Karadzic would later be charged with genocide, crimes against humanity, and violations of the laws or customs of war. Pertinent to this chapter are the genocide charges, which relate specifically to Srebrenica. As ICTY prosecutor Richard Goldstone outlined the case:

> Between about 12 July 1995 and 13 July 1995 . . . Bosnian Serb military personnel, under the command and control of RATKO MLADIC and RADOVAN KARADZIC, summarily executed many Bosnian Muslim refugees who remained in Potocari. . . . Between about 13 July 1995 and 22 July 1995, Bosnian Serb military personnel, under the command and control of RATKO MLADIC and RADOVAN KARADZIC, summarily executed many Bosnian Muslim men who fled to the woods and were later captured or surrendered. . . . On or about 14 July 1995, Bosnian Serb military personnel, under the command and control

of RATKO MLADIC and RADOVAN KARADZIC, transported thousands of Muslim men from this school complex [near Karakaj] to two locations a short distance away. At these locations, Bosnian Serb soldiers, with the knowledge of RATKO MLADIC, summarily executed these Bosnian Muslim detainees and buried them in mass graves.[59]

In indicting suspects for a gender-based, city-based genocide, it was crucial for the ICTY to clearly articulate what the Genocide Convention's provision for destruction "in part" of a targeted group meant in this context. The tribunal had to begin by identifying Bosnian Muslims as a separate people. During the *Krstic* trial, the court argued that Krstic indeed "intend[ed] to destroy a part of the Bosnian Muslim people as a national, ethnical, or religious group." It argued further that "the Bosnian Muslims were a specific, distinct national group, and therefore covered by Article 4." The court further recognized that "it is well established that where a conviction for genocide relies on the intent to destroy a protected group 'in part,' the part must be a substantial part of that group."[60]

So far so good; but how can one leap from defining genocide as targeting a minority group *as such* (the Convention requirement) to targeting a small proportion of that population living in a specific city and its environs? It was clear that Krstic had not attempted to exterminate the entire Bosnian Muslim nation. Thus, the Srebrenica ruling of genocide seems at first glance to violate many of the precedents of the ICTY and ICTR (International Criminal Tribunal for Rwanda). For example, the issue of "substantial" was addressed carefully by the ICTY in 2004. In previous decisions like *Jelisić* and *Sikirica*, a "substantial part" or a "substantial number relative to the total population of the group," respectively, needed to be targeted for an allegation of genocide to be sustained. Similarly, before the ICTR, in *Kayishema,* the Trial Chamber determined that a "considerable number of individuals who are part of the group" needed to be targeted for destruction before the Genocide Convention could be invoked. This was further upheld in *Bagilishema* and *Semanza.* The court on the basis of these decisions upheld the applicability of the Convention.[61]

The Srebrenica case, however, seems to have moved the goalposts to some extent. While the "protected group" was defined as "the national group of Bosnian Muslims," Krstic was accused of targeting "the Bosnian Muslims of Srebrenica, or the Bosnian Muslims of Eastern Bosnia." As such, 8,000 individuals represented a *substantial* part of the 40,000-strong Bosnian Muslim population of *Srebrenica.* The ICTY, however, saw this as genocide, in part due to the strategic importance of the city and its surrounding territory to the Bosnian Serb leadership, as well as its symbolism as a UN safe haven. As the court argued: "The elimination of the Muslim population of Srebrenica ... would serve as a potent example to all Bosnian Muslims of their vulnerability and defenselessness in the face of Serb military forces."[62]

Genocide scholars should, I argue, carefully examine the court's rationale here. Obviously, Srebrenica men and boys were deliberately targeted with massacre and were systematically killed. The court's reasoning is interesting but not entirely convincing. Does a finding of genocide depend on the strategic or symbolic importance of the place where the killing occurs? If so, why? This is not really explained, and it places some victims in a different category under international law than others—not so much because of *who* they are, but *where* they are. Further, the decision throws into question the significance of the "in part" criterion. Can the massacre of 8,000 civilians really be genocide? Where does the remaining Bosnian Muslim population fit in the mix?

Second, classifying Srebrenica as genocide opens a Pandora's box for almost any other crime of similar numerical or proportional magnitude to be similarly classified, from the "rape of Nanking" to the firebombing of German cities during World War II. Third, the decision reinforces the widely held Serbian view that there is one law for Serbs and another for non-Serbs. The view that the Convention has been stretched to target the Serbs does not sit well in Serbia, and has tarnished the image of the tribunal process.

Lastly, we have the Oric debacle. On trial for his own brand of ethnic cleansing, Oric and his forces arguably did not have the means to inflict the same level of destruction as BSA forces. Their atrocities were primarily reactive and less well organized. Nevertheless, the traditional view that the victim group in genocide is "innocent" or "defenseless" is challenged when we consider the attacks that Oric led against Serbian communities. Katherine Southwick, in a recent edition of the *Yale Human Rights and Development Law Journal,* raises a question as to whether the ICTY successfully proved specific intent or *dolens specialis* in the Krstic decision. She argues that the tribunal never took seriously the defense's claim of having been challenging a military threat. It would, she posits, have been more accurate to indict Krstic for crimes against humanity.[63] This in no way excuses Serbian conduct, which was brutal, bloodthirsty, and completely unacceptable. Rather, it raises questions about the legal finding of genocide, though further exploration of these issues lies beyond the scope of the chapter.

Denouement: The Politics of Serbian Genocide Scholarship

In the aftermath of the 1995 Dayton Peace Accord, Bosnia-Herzegovina was divided into a Serbian Republic and a Croat-Muslim Federation. The accord gave Serbs much of the land they had "cleansed" by force, reinforcing the view that while democracy was a goal of the accord, ethnic separation was a reality.[64] Sixty percent of Bosnia's inhabitants were forced from their homes, and more than 1.3 million people (some 30 percent of the population) were dispersed in sixty-three countries.[65] This was in addition to a death toll of perhaps 280,000 by the war's end.[66]

Croatia achieved a measure of stability following Dayton. In 1995, Milosevic effectively abandoned the Bosnian Serbs, looking on as Croatian forces retook Croatian Serb strongholds.[67] In late April 1995, the Croatian Army launched an attack on western Slavonia, and within thirty-six hours managed to take back the region.[68] By August, the Croatian Army seized the Krajina region in a campaign lasting just eighty-four hours.[69]

Of interest to historians is how the events of Jasenovac in an earlier war, and Srebrenica in a later one, will shape Serbian identity in the future. My conclusions are unfortunately pessimistic: Jasenovac and other historical events will continue to be viewed through a lens of Serbian victimology. In contemporary Serbian accounts of the era, Jasenovac was but one aspect of a much older hatred of the Serbs, which has been dubbed "Serbophobia." The term denoted a historic fear, hatred, and jealousy of Serbs, often likened to antisemitism in terms of its ideological motivation and fury."[70]

Predictably, many Serbian nationalists and scholars pushed the World War II death tolls as high as they could reach. The numbers of Serbs killed at Jasenovac was intensively debated, with estimates ranging (on the Serbian side) from 700,000 to 2 million, far out of proportion to more impartial appraisals.[71] Milan Bulajic, who served as the director of the Museum of the Victims of Genocide in Belgrade, became famous for his theorizing about an eliminationist racism directed toward Serbs. For Bulajic, the motivations of Croats and the Vatican never changed. As they had in the nineteenth century, these two groups still sought to destroy the Orthodox Church in order to expand Roman Catholicism throughout the Balkans.[72]

Older studies were reedited in line with new government priorities. Vladimir Dedijer's thought-provoking account of Jasenovac received a Holocaust gloss designed primarily to heighten its propaganda value. The original Serbo-Croatian title, *Vatikan i Jasenovac,* had morphed by 1992 into *Jasenovac: The Yugoslav Auschwitz and the Vatican.*[73] In the process, Jasenovac was explicitly compared to the paragon of the Nazis' death-camp system, and the number of alleged Serbian dead grew threefold. While Dedijer provides a figure of 200,000 killed at Jasenovac, primarily Serbs (a figure echoed in Gottfried Niemietz's foreword to the German edition, and roughly in keeping with other scholarly estimates), Belgrade University's Mihailo Markovic, in his preliminary note, gives a figure of 750,000 Serbian victims, followed by Jews and Gypsies. This was, he avers, to be a "'final solution' for Serbs."[74] In order to give the book a timely wartime context, Markovic declared of Tudjman's Croatia: "The world must not forget that during World War II the fate of Serbs in Croatia was very similar to that of the Jews. With [a] little imagination one can guess how a Jewish minority in Germany would feel if another pro-Nazi, racist government would come to power and begin to make militant anti-Semitic moves."[75]

The problems of interpreting and representing the 1940s invariably spilled over into the 1990s and after. The idealized image of Serbs as history's leading victims (alongside European Jews) makes sober reflection and self-criticism exceedingly difficult. Even in the post-Milosevic era, a staggering lack of remorse for Serbian crimes is evident in Srebrenica and elsewhere.[76] One might have assumed that Milosevic's handover to the ITCY would help Serbs engage with their nation's guilt. The reverse proved to be true. The trial bolstered widely held perceptions that the West was punishing Milosevic as a way of punishing Serbia. President Vojislav Kostunica, who opposed the extradition of Milosevic, expressed the view of most Serbs—that domestic trials needed to take place first. When Milosevic was charged exclusively with crimes against non-Serbs committed outside Serbia, many felt that justice had been denied.[77]

Public opinion polls conducted in 2001 revealed that over 52 percent of respondents "could not name a single war crime committed by Serb forces in Bosnia, Croatia, or Kosovo. Nearly half, however, could name at least three crimes committed against Serb civilians by other forces." Further, Karadzic and Mladic continued to be heralded as the two "greatest defenders of the Serb nation."[78] The 2003 elections demonstrated clearly the memory problems still present in Serbia. The Serbian Radical Party of warlord Vojislav Seselj drew broad support, and T-shirts of Mladic and Karadzic were sold throughout the campaign.[79]

Then, in June 2005, a video from the Srebrenica massacres stunned the Serbian public. The film captured the murder of six civilians by a Serbian paramilitary group known as "The Scorpions." President Boris Tadic averred that "Serbia is deeply shocked." Yet as far as he was concerned, the crimes, though committed "in the name of our nation," were the responsibility of *individuals* who did not represent Serbian interests. A survey held in late May 2005 showed that only half of Serbs believed the Srebrenica massacre had even taken place.[80] The Ministry of Information continued its oblique reaction to the video, referring to it in mid-2005 as "a film of the crime in Srebrenica," following this later by describing Srebrenica as "that shameful crime." But no details were forthcoming about the crime, or the guilty parties.[81]

At present, then, the Serbian past through to Jasenovac is viewed as an evolving campaign of Serbophobia culminating in the Ustasha genocide. The post-Jasenovac era, for its part, is depicted as a time of continued repression and victimization, with frequent analogies drawn between World War II and the 1990s. It is doubtful that Serbian nationalists will thus learn anything from history, save for the lessons they selectively choose to interpret through a narrow nationalist lens. With a subaltern identification so deeply embedded in nationalist narratives, and so regularly deployed for political purposes, the chances of a moral reckoning seem slim. This is doubly so in the context of Kosovo's bid for independence, which threatens to further energize Serbia's political right. In the February 2008 elections, for example, the Radicals under Tomislav Nikolic almost came to power with 47.9 percent of the vote.[82]

One may perceive similar dynamics at work in other genocides and post-genocidal contexts. The Rwandan government under President Kagame since 1994 has regularly deployed the mass slaughter of Tutsis as grounds for evading acknowledgment of crimes committed by Tutsi-led forces against Hutu civilians in the later stages of the genocide, and in Zaire/Congo thereafter. As chapters in this volume by Evelin G. Lindner, Eric Langenbacher, and Adam Jones explore, the Nazis drew heavily on German suffering and humiliation after the First World War to wage their genocidal campaigns of the Second World War; victimized populations then drew upon their suffering at Nazi hands to justify the brutal treatment and mass expulsion of ethnic Germans from the formerly occupied territories. Many such instances could be cited, and they serve as reminders of the destructive dynamics that subaltern identifications may generate, particularly when harnessed by political leaders and directed to bellicose and genocidal ends.

Notes

1. Transitions Online, "Guilty of Genocide."
2. Honig and Both, *Srebrenica: Record of a Crime*, xix.
3. See introduction to this volume.
4. Zivkovic, "The Wish to Be a Jew," 73.
5. Popov, "Traumatology of the Party State," 81–83.
6. Kecmanovic, *Ethnic Times*, 54–56.
7. Ibid., 56.
8. Hendershot, "From Trauma to Paranoia."
9. McFarlane, Golier, and Yahuda, "Treatment Planning for Trauma Survivors with PTSD," 10–13.
10. Volkan, *Bloodlines: From Ethnic Pride to Ethnic Terrorism*, 43.
11. Bogosavljevic, "The Unresolved Genocide," 146.
12. Mirkovic, "The Historical Link between the Ustasha Genocide and the Croato-Serb Civil War: 1991–1995," 365–67.
13. Ibid., 370.
14. Ridley, *Tito*, 164.
15. Dedijer, *The Yugoslav Auschwitz and the Vatican*, 129; Jelinek, "Nationalities and Minorities in the Independent State of Croatia," 196–97.
16. United States Holocaust Memorial Museum, *Genocide in Yugoslavia During the Holocaust*; Dedijer, *The Yugoslav Auschwitz and the Vatican*, 225–65.
17. Dedijer, *The Yugoslav Auschwitz and the Vatican*, 225–65.
18. Tanner, *Croatia: A Nation Forged in War*, 160.
19. Judah, *The Serbs: History, Myth and the Destruction of Yugoslavia*, 120.
20. Jones, *Genocide: A Comprehensive Introduction*, 22–23.
21. MacDonald, *Balkan Holocausts?*, chapter 5.
22. Djilas, *The Contested Country*, 150–59.
23. Banac, *Eastern Europe in Revolution*, 173–75.
24. Magas, *The Destruction of Yugoslavia*, 110.
25. Cohen, *Broken Bonds*, 95.
26. Cigar, *Genocide in Bosnia*, 88, 98–99.
27. Cohen, *Broken Bonds*, 18.
28. Laura Silber and Alan Little, *The Death of Yugoslavia*, 100–11, 146–47.
29. Ibid., 195–201.
30. Power, *"A Problem from Hell,"* 247.
31. Bringa, *Being Muslim the Bosnian Way*, 26.
32. Mahmutcehajic, "The Road to War," 141.
33. Divjak, "The First Phase: 1992–1993," 155.
34. Silber and Little, *The Death of Yugoslavia*, 230–31.
35. Campbell, *National Deconstruction*, 58–59.
36. Gutman, *Witness to Genocide*, 23; Malic, "Herceg Camp."
37. This is according to journalist Mark Danner, cited in Jones, *Genocide*, 216.
38. Ronayne, *Never Again*, 109.
39. Gutman, *Witness to Genocide*, 23.
40. Honig and Both, *Srebrenica: Record of a Crime*, 4–5.
41. United Nations Secretary General, "Report of the Secretary-General Pursuant to General Assembly Resolution 53/35: The Fall of Srebrenica," 55.
42. Ibid., 56–7.

43. Ibid., 59–61, 64, 67, 70–72.
44. Rohde, *Endgame: The Betrayal and Fall of Srebrenica*, 107.
45. United Nations Secretary General, "Report of the Secretary-General," 74–75.
46. Honig and Both, *Srebrenica: Record of a Crime*, 30, 35.
47. United Nations Secretary General, "Report of the Secretary-General," 74–76.
48. Ibid., 79–80, 82; International Tribunal for the Former Yugoslavia (ICTY), "The Prosecutor of The Tribunal Against Radovan Karadzic and Ratko Mladic."
49. United Nations Secretary General, "Report of the Secretary-General," 83.
50. Honig and Both, *Srebrenica: Record of a Crime*, 60.
51. United Nations Secretary General, "Report of the Secretary-General," 71–72, 86, 90.
52. Ronayne, *Never Again*, 111; Holbrooke, *To End a War*, 68–69.
53. Honig and Both, *Srebrenica: Record of a Crime*, 176–77.
54. Rohde, *Endgame: The Betrayal and Fall of Srebrenica*, 14.
55. ICTY, "The Prosecutor of The Tribunal Against Naser Oric."
56. "Bosnian Muslim Guilty but Freed."
57. "Srebrenica Muslim Chief on Trial."
58. Rohde, *Endgame: The Betrayal and Fall of Srebrenica*, 215.
59. ICTY, "Naser Oric."
60. ICTY Appeals Chamber, "Prosecutor v. Radislav Krstic," 2.
61. Ibid., 3.
62. Ibid., 5–6.
63. Southwick, "Srebrenica as Genocide?"
64. Udovicki and Stitkovac, "Bosnia and Hercegovina: The Second War," 198–99.
65. Campbell, *National Deconstruction*, 221.
66. Glover, *Humanity: A Moral History of the Twentieth Century*, 127–29.
67. Holbrooke, *To End a War*, 160–62.
68. Tanner, *Croatia: A Nation Forged in War*, 294.
69. Judah, *The Serbs*, 195–98.
70. Cosic, *L'éffondrement de la Yougoslavie*, 44.
71. MacDonald, *Balkan Holocausts?*, chap. 5.
72. Bulajić, "Never Again: Genocide in the NDH."
73. Dedijer, *The Yugoslav Auschwitz and the Vatican*.
74. Ibid.
75. Markovic, in ibid., 14.
76. Lyon, "Words of War," 224.
77. Karadjis, "Yugoslavia: The Milosevic Regime without Milosevic."
78. Devic, "War Guilt and Responsibility."
79. Nikolic-Solomon and Tanner, "Shadow of Hague Falls Over Serbian Election."
80. "Serbian Leader 'Shocked' by Video."
81. Serbian Ministry of Information, "Del Ponte Commends Government's Action."
82. Bilefsky, "Tadic Wins Serbian Re-election as President."

Works Cited

Banac, Ivo. *Eastern Europe in Revolution*. Ithaca: Cornell University Press, 1992.
BBC News. "Bosnian Muslim Guilty but Freed." June 30, 2006.
BBC News. "Serbian Leader 'Shocked' by Video." June 3, 2005.
BBC News. "Srebrenica Muslim Chief on Trial." October 6, 2004.

Bilefsky, Dan. "Tadic Wins Serbian Re-election as President." *International Herald Tribune.* February 3, 2008.

Bogosavljevic, Srdan. "The Unresolved Genocide." In *The Road to War in Serbia: Trauma and Catharsis,* ed. Nebojsa Popov, 146–60. Budapest: Central European University Press, 2000.

Bringa, Tone. *Being Muslim the Bosnian Way: Identity and Community in a Central Bosnian Village.* Princeton: Princeton University Press, 1995.

Bulajić, Milan. "Never Again: Genocide in the NDH: Ustashi Genocide the Independent State of Croatia NDH From 1941–1945." Belgrade: Serbian Ministry of Information. http://www.yugoslavia.com/Society_and_Law/Jasenovac/ndh.htm. Accessed June 18, 1998.

Campbell, David. *National Deconstruction: Violence. Identity, and Justice in Bosnia.* Minneapolis: University of Minneapolis Press, 1998.

Cigar, Norman. *Genocide in Bosnia: The Policy of "Ethnic Cleansing."* College Station: Texas A & M University Press, 1995.

Cohen, Lenard. *Broken Bonds: Yugoslavia's Disintegration and Balkan Politics in Transition.* Boulder. Colo.: Westview Press, 1995.

Cosic, Dobrica. *L'éffondrement de la Yougoslavie: positions d'un resistant.* Paris: Age 'Homme, 1994.

Dedijer, Vladimir. *The Yugoslav Auschwitz and the Vatican: The Croatian Massacre of the Serbs during World War II.* London: Prometheus Books. 1992.

Devic, Ana. "War Guilt and Responsibility: The Case of Serbia: Diverging Attempts at Facing the Recent Past." *GSC Quarterly* (Spring 2003). http://www.ssrc.org/programs/gsc/gsc_quarterly/newsletter8/content/devic.page. Accessed September 20, 2004.

Divjak, Jovan. "The First Phase: 1992–1993." In *The War in Croatia and Bosnia-Herzegovina, 1991–1995,* ed. Branka Magas and Ivo Zanic, 152–78. London: Frank Cass, 2001.

Djilas, Aleksa. *The Contested Country: Yugoslav Unity and Communist Revolution. 1919–1953.* Cambridge, Mass.: Harvard University Press, 1996.

Glover, Jonathan. *Humanity: A Moral History of the Twentieth Century.* New Haven: Yale University Press, 2001.

Gutman, Roy. *Witness to Genocide.* New York: Lisa Drew Books, 1993.

Hendershot, Catherine. "From Trauma to Paranoia: Nuclear Weapons, Science Fiction, and History." *Mosaic* 32, no. 4 (1999): 73–90.

Holbrooke, Richard. *To End a War.* New York: Random House, 1999.

Honig, Jan, and Norbert Both. *Srebrenica: Record of a Crime.* London: Penguin, 1996.

International Criminal Tribunal for the Former Yugoslavia. "The Prosecutor of the Tribunal Against Naser Oric." Case no. IT-03-68 (PT third amended indictment). The Hague: ICTY, June 2005. http://www.un.org/icty/indictment/english/ori-3ai050630e.htm. Accessed February 2, 2007.

International Criminal Tribunal for the Former Yugoslavia. "The Prosecutor of the Tribunal Against Radovan Karadzic and Ratko Mladic." Case no. IT-95-5-I. The Hague: ICTY, 1995. http://www.un.org/icty/indictment/english/kar-ii951116e.htm. Accessed February 2, 2007.

International Criminal Tribunal for the Former Yugoslavia Appeals Chamber. "Prosecutor v. Radislav Krstic." Case no. IT-98-33-A. The Hague: ICTY, April 19, 2004. http://www.un.org/icty/krstic/Appeal/judgement/krs-aj040419e.pdf. Accessed March 2, 2008.

Jelinek, Yeshayahu. "Nationalities and Minorities in the Independent State of Croatia." *Nationalities Papers* 8, no. 2 (1980): 195–210.

Jones, Adam. *Genocide: A Comprehensive Introduction.* London: Routledge, 2006.

Judah, Tim. *The Serbs: History, Myth and the Destruction of Yugoslavia*. New Haven: Yale University Press, 1996.

Karadjis, Marko. "Yugoslavia: The Milosevic Regime without Milosevic." *Green Left Weekly* (July 18, 2001). http://www.greenleft.org.au/back/2001/456/456p19.htm. Accessed September 20, 2004.

Kecmanovic, Dusan. *Ethnic Times: Exploring Ethnonationalism in the Former Yugoslavia*. Westport, Conn.: Praeger, 2002.

Lyon, Philip. "Words of War: Journalism in the Former Yugoslavia." *SAIS Review* 23, no. 2 (Summer–Fall 2003).

MacDonald, David. *Balkan Holocausts? Serbian and Croatian Victim Centered Propaganda and the War in Yugoslavia*. Manchester: Manchester University Press, 2002.

Magas, Branka. *The Destruction of Yugoslavia: Tracing the Breakup 1980–1992*. London: Verso, 1993.

Mahmutcehajic, Rusmir. "The Road to War." In *The War in Croatia and Bosnia-Herzegovina 1991–1995*, ed. Branka Magas and Ivo Zanic, 133–52. London: Frank Cass, 2001.

Malic, Gordan. "Herceg Camp." *Feral Tribune*. April 29, 1996. http://www.cdsp.neu.edu/info/students/marko/feral/fera131.html. Accessed June 18, 1995.

McFarlane, Susan, Julia Golier, and Rachel Yahuda. "Treatment Planning for Trauma Survivors with PTSD: What Does a Clinician Need to Know Before Implementing PTSD Treatment?" In *Treating Trauma: Survivors with PTSD*, ed. Rachel Yahuda. Washington, D.C.: American Psychiatric Publishing, 2002.

Mirkovic, Damir. "The Historical Link between the Ustasha Genocide and the Croato-Serb Civil War: 1991–1995." *Journal of Genocide Research* 2, no. 3 (2000): 163–73.

Nebojsa, Popov. "Traumatology of the Party State." In *The Road to War in Serbia: Trauma and Catharsis*, ed. Nebojsa Popov, 81–109. Budapest: Central European University Press, 2000.

Nikolic-Solomon, Dragana, and Marcus Tanner. "Shadow of Hague Falls Over Serbian Election." *BCR* 502 (June 10, 2004). http://www.iwpr.net/index.pl?archive/bcr3/bcr3_200406_502_1_eng.txt. Accessed September 20, 2004.

Power, Samantha. "*A Problem from Hell*": America and the Age of Genocide. New York: Harper Perennial, 2003.

Ridley, Jasper. *Tito*. London: Constable, 1994.

Rohde, David. *Endgame: The Betrayal and Fall of Srebrenica. Europe's Worst Massacre Since World War II*. Boulder, Colo.: Westview, 1997.

Ronayne, Peter. *Never Again: United States and the Prevention and Punishment of Genocide since the Holocaust*. Lanham, Md.: Rowman and Littlefield, 2001.

Serbian Ministry of Information. "Del Ponte Commends Government's Action in Apprehension of Srebrenica Suspects." June 2, 2005. http://www.srbija.sr.gov.yu/vesti/vest.php?id=12880&q=srebrenica. Accessed September 20, 2006.

Silber, Laura, and Alan Little. *The Death of Yugoslavia*. London: BBC, 1996.

Southwick, Katherine. "Srebrenica as Genocide? The Krstic Decision and the Language of the Unspeakable." *Yale Human Rights and Development Law Journal* 1 (January 2005): 88–227.

Tanner, Marcus. *Croatia: A Nation Forged in War*. New Haven: Yale University Press, 1997.

Transitions Online. "Guilty of Genocide." August 7, 2001. http://balkanreport.tol.cz/look/BRR/article. Accessed June 2003.

Udovicki, Jasminka, and Ejub Stitkovac. "Bosnia and Hercegovina: The Second War." In Burn *This House: The Making and Unmaking of Yugoslavia*, ed. Jasminka Udovicki and James Ridgeway, 174–215. Durham, N.C.: Duke University Press, 2000.

United Nations Secretary General. "Report of the Secretary-General Pursuant to General Assembly Resolution 53/35: The Fall of Srebrenica." New York: United Nations, November 15, 1999.

United States Holocaust Memorial Museum. *Genocide in Yugoslavia during the Holocaust.* Washington, D.C.: USHMM, 1995.

Volkan, Vamik. Bloodlines: *From Ethnic Pride to Ethnic Terrorism.* London: Farrar, Strauss and Giroux, 1997.

Zivkovic, Marko. "The Wish to Be a Jew: The Power of the Jewish Trope in the Yugoslav Conflict." *Cahiers de L'URMIS* no. 6 (2000): 69–84.

6

Visions of the "Oppressor" in Rwanda's Pre-Genocidal Media

CHRISTOPHER C. TAYLOR

On April 6, 1994, the flames of the twentieth century's last genocide were ignited when Rwanda's president, Juvénal Habyarimana, was killed when his plane was downed by a shoulder-held missile. I was present in Rwanda and working as a behavioral research specialist for Family Health International (a contractor to USAID). Less than three days later, along with other members of the American expatriate community, my Rwandan Tutsi fiancée and I were evacuated from Rwanda by a land convoy headed for Bujumbura, Burundi. We stayed there for several days. Each day we learned, from the few Rwandan refugees who managed to make it there, who among our friends and acquaintances had been killed and who was still alive. From Bujumbura we flew to Nairobi, where we spent the next four months. There as well, refugees of Rwanda's crisis were arriving in small numbers. Each passing day brought news of survivors, but more frequently, news of those who had been killed.

Although killings on a massive scale began just hours after Habyarimana's assassination, rumors of widespread massacres had been in the air for months. One of my closest Rwandan friends, killed on the first night of the genocide, often argued, "It's not possible for anyone to wipe out an entire people." "Oh yes it is," I would reply, "so you had better do your best to get out of here or keep a low profile." Although my friend was Tutsi, he, like many others of his ethnicity, had not been in favor of the invasion that the Rwandan Patriotic Front (RPF) had mounted from Uganda in 1990. Moreover, in an indirect way he was tied to the regime, as his Hutu wife was the sister-in-law of someone highly placed in the Habyarimana government. Months later, that same government, in an effort to blame the RPF invasion on Tutsi in general, imprisoned many of them, though most had not supported the RPF in any way. My friend was among them. Subjected to daily abuse, he was finally released after his wife's brother-in-law intervened. After his release, he made no attempt to conceal his pro-RPF sympathies. Today, it is the brother-in-law who is a prisoner. Accused of crimes against humanity, he is in the custody of the International War Crimes Tribunal on Rwanda in Arusha, Tanzania. Months before the genocide, he had warned my friend on several occasions. There were going to be massacres, he said, and they would make those that occurred in 1959 seem small by comparison.[1] He advised my friend to leave while he could. That large-scale massacres were being planned was hardly in doubt among Rwandans whom I spoke with during the early months of 1994. Only American diplomats and employees of USAID seemed to think that the peace agreement between the warring sides still had a chance of success.

Although the war between Rwandan Government Forces (RGF) and the RPF had temporarily abated with the signing of the Arusha accords in August 1993, later that year the political situation began to deteriorate. The propaganda campaign on the part of all the interested parties was heating up, and this was especially apparent on Rwanda's infamous "hate radio," Radio-Télévision Libre des Mille Collines (RTLM). For years before, however, Rwanda's print media had been fanning the fires of ethno-nationalist passion. A "free press" was something new in Rwanda. Before the democratization initiative pushed by France and other Western powers in the late 1980s and early 1990s,[2] Rwanda had had only a handful of printed news sources, and these were very cautious in tone. By the early 1990s—with widespread discontent at home, war with the RPF on its northern border, and pressure from Western donor states abroad—the Rwandan government was forced to accept opposition political parties and an open press.

Although a free press came to life, it had no history, few precedents to follow, and little constraints on its actions. Consequently fantasy, rumor, and slander all took their places at the table with fact, and all appeared to be drinking from the same chalice. Distinguishing between truth and falsehood was difficult. In every rumor and every allegation there was an element of plausibility, and many found their way into print. The print media consisted of dozens of cheap news magazines. Almost every one of Rwanda's numerous political parties had a magazine, and many of the factions within these parties had magazines as well. Some had only the most ephemeral existence; others had been around for years. Selling for modest sums, they did a brisk business, and because many of their readers were not fully literate, they relied heavily on photos, illustrations, and cartoons. In both the illustrations and the printed stories, we see evidence of the rekindling of colonial stereotypes concerning Tutsi. Perhaps this was to be expected, but what was more surprising was that these often betrayed envy, as well as fear and resentment.

In this chapter I discuss aspects of Rwanda's social imaginary where issues of sex, gender, and leadership are concerned. First, I discuss what I mean by the terms "social imaginary," and then show how this was deployed in media sources. In order for the genocide to occur, it was necessary to arouse the passions of Hutu extremists. In other violent conflicts, information sources of one form or another have served to fan the sentiments of hate and disgust against targeted groups.[3] Quite often, the targeted groups are convenient as scapegoats because of their remoteness or defenselessness. In this instance, however, the targeted group was a minority that had once been masters of Rwanda. Their dominance in some parts of Rwanda can be traced back about three hundred years.[4] In other parts of Rwanda, most notably northern Rwanda, Tutsi dominance was recent and imposed only with the aid of European colonial powers.[5] In both cases, the memory of Tutsi control had yet to fade. The speed and ferocity of Rwanda's genocide can be traced to the fact that even though Hutu had controlled Rwanda since the early 1960s, many of them did not feel confident that their dominance was secure.

As for Tutsi, despite decades of being treated as second-class citizens, discriminated against in employment, and denied access to higher education, many had managed to do quite well. Moreover, many highly placed Hutu notables had Tutsi wives or mistresses.[6] This was a thorn in the side of Hutu extremism, and indicative of its contradictory sentiments of desire, fear, and envy—something one expects more from an oppressed group than from a dominant group. It is in these contradictory passions and imaginings that we see Rwanda's exterminatory violence as a "genocide by the oppressed," and not simply as a genocide perpetrated by a dominant majority against a vulnerable minority.

Violence and the Social Imaginary

When the state implements a campaign of violence, it spares no expense to legitimize its actions according to local moral perceptions that are more or less in harmony with subjacent cultural codes. The state's organized violence is supported and institutionalized by ideologies which make destructive acts appear justified for the maintenance of collective well-being. Frequently, public media serve as the means by which these ideologies are communicated to the mass of the state's citizens, and in which the purported validity of the associated ideologies is expressed and enacted. However, these media also convey deeper, less immediately apprehensible desires and fears, especially when they rely on nonverbal means of communication. These latter are less accessible to conscious apperception, more archetypal in nature, and less likely to be construed by social actors as having obvious and clear-cut ideological content. One could think of them as infra-ideological.

Following Aijmer's discussion of violence,[7] the analytical scheme of which bears a close resemblance to that used by Godelier in an apparently unrelated context[8]—the ambiguities left unresolved in Mauss's discussion of the gift—one could posit the existence of three dimensions to state violence and to the persuasive means that serve to justify it: the imaginary, the symbolic, and the real. At the least apprehensible level is what Aijmer and Godelier term the "imaginary." This consists of iconic images organized into diffuse cultural codes and shared for the most part among members of a single group. These constitute the base of the social imaginary in its envisioning of possible worlds. This material is only intuitively cognized by social actors, and consists of what Roy Wagner would call "symbols that stand for themselves"[9]—in other words, symbols that are not readily translatable into a verbal or discursive idiom. These symbols and diffuse codes constitute a collective body of implicit knowledge reflecting the group's profoundest fears and desires. This is also the level least accessible to the social actors themselves and their exegesis. Despite the relative inaccessibility of this iconic imaginary base to the persons who embody it, it precedes and conditions everything that is more conscious in nature. In this respect Godelier explicitly marks his difference from both Lacan and Lévi-Strauss, who see the symbolic as logically prior to both the imaginary and the real.

At the next level, what Aijmer terms the "discursive" and Godelier terms the "symbolic," verbal elements come to the fore. It is here that agentive phenomena are manifest as social actors verbalize what their intentions are, and act these out in consonance with avowed pragmatic ends. This is the domain of language, discourse, and narrative. People will usually be able to identify and verbalize what the ideologies of their supporters and opponents are, and explain the pragmatic ends that are served with any particular statement or action. It is here that strategizing is most apparent, as social actors weigh the consequences of one course of action over another and then behave accordingly. This is also the level where disagreement, conflict, and struggle are most manifest.

The most visible level of state violence is what Aijmer calls the "ethological" and Godelier calls the "real." Violence has very real biological and psychological effects upon its victims—suffering, pain, injury, and death. Yet even this level must interact with the other two levels if violent acts are to attain their full amplitude of social meaning. It may not be sufficient, for example, to kill one's opponent; it may be necessary to mutilate, to destroy, or to dispose of the body in such a way that the victim's spirit not return to wreak vengeance on the perpetrator of the violence. As Aijmer puts it, while physical death may be irrevocable and non-negotiable, social death may not be.

Both Godelier and Aijmer posit the primacy of the imaginary, but the three levels are interconnected. It is possible for people to become aware of the iconic symbols that constitute their imaginary. It is possible for certain members within a collectivity, as with individuals in psychoanalysis, to have a "prise de conscience" in which the deeper levels of their socially shared fears and desires become manifest. When this happens, the iconic enters the realm of the symbolic and becomes susceptible to verbalization. The pre-discursive rises to the discursive. In like fashion, the process can be reversed. Discursive material that had once been verbalized in the form of ideological statements and narratives can become so habitual as to become virtually unconscious. What was once stated and debated becomes tacit and implicit, joining the ranks of other phenomena constituting the *habitus* or the "things that go without saying."[10] It is my contention that many of the darkest "things that go without saying" receive expression during times of violence, as all curbs on transgression evaporate.

Violence Divined

At around 3 AM on the morning of April 7, 1994, several hours after the downing of President Habyarimana's plane,[11] we heard the sound of gunfire as the RGF attacked the RPF garrison in Kigali.[12] The shaky truce that had endured for less than nine months was over—but this time, along with war came genocide. Some time later, Rwandan radio announced the president's death and advised everyone to stay at home. Kigali's neighborhoods turned into killing fields. For the next sixty hours, we remained ensconced in our house, and at times when the explosions seemed frighteningly near, we sheltered in the innermost corridor with mattresses on either side. Occasionally when there was a lull in the fighting, I ventured out onto our front porch to have a look. From there, I could see just above the courtyard wall and into the street. Every now and then, a loaded car or pickup truck raced by. At other times, I could make out the bobbing heads of looters carrying away booty on their heads, as people in the neighborhood were killed and their houses pillaged.

Following my evacuation and then my arrival in Nairobi, I began to visit Rwandan refugees housed at the Shauri-Moyo YMCA. From them, I learned about a diviner named Magayane, who two years earlier had predicted the genocide, the president's death, and a number of other occurrences. These predictions had been printed in one of Rwanda's numerous cheap political magazines. One of Magayane's predictions was that Habyarimana would be killed and that he would be the last of Rwanda's Hutu kings. This was intriguing, because during the time of the monarchy (pre-1962), the king had always been Tutsi. Magayane's prediction was thus suggestive of a Tutsi restoration.

The presentiment that Habyarimana would not live beyond March 1994 was stated more than once in the popular political literature of the time, and not just by the diviner Magayane. Here in *Kangura*, one of the more infamous and widely

FIGURE 6.1   In this political cartoon from Hutu extremist publication Kangura, Habyarimana is depicted as doing the bidding of RPF leader, Paul Kagame. The caption reads, "Tutsi ingratitude. Habyarimana will die in March 1004."

read Hutu extremists' organs, Habyarimana's death was predicted four months in advance. He was also depicted as doing the bidding of the RPF leader Paul Kagame. I was first shown this cartoon (Figure 6.1) by a Hutu friend in January 1994. His comment was that there was more than a bit of truth to the idea that Habyarimana had become Kagame's beast of burden. For many extremist foes of the Arusha accords, Habyarimana by early 1994 was no longer to be trusted as the champion of Hutu ethno-nationalism.

Kingship

About eighty popular journals, each with a distinct point of view, arose in the period between 1990 and 1994—quite extraordinary for a country with a population of about seven million. Some of these journals employed symbols of kingship in their depictions of Habyarimana, but it was more often the case that Hutu extremist journalists explicitly accused the Rwandan Patriotic Front of wanting to restore the monarchy, its trappings, and its rituals. Hutu extremist journalists routinely referred to RPF members as "feudo-monarchists." Several of their cartoons recall the former custom of emasculating slain enemies and then using these body parts to adorn the royal drum (see Figure 6.2).

In the cartoon from an extremist Hutu magazine, *La Medaille-Nyiramacibiri*, RPF soldiers are depicted crucifying, impaling, and castrating Melchior Ndadaye, neighboring Burundi's first democratically elected Hutu president. Elected in October 1993, he was subsequently killed by Burundian army officers (all of whom were Tutsi) in an abortive coup attempt.[13]

This image condenses a great deal of violence at both the discursive and imaginary levels. At the discursive level, we see a clear iteration of the oft-repeated charge by Hutu extremists that the RPF were "feudo-monarchists" intent upon restoring kingship, the royal rituals, and the monarchy's principal emblem—the drum named Karinga. Another ideological claim is advanced by depicting Hutu victims of the RPF as Christ-like martyrs, for Ndadaye is being crucified. Beneath these claims, however, a subtler message is conveyed: one rooted in the social imaginary. By impaling Ndadaye, the RPF torturers are turning his body into an obstructed conduit and as such transforming his person into an inadequate, unworthy embodiment of *imaana* (the principle of life and fertility).[14] In former times, Rwandans killed cattle thieves in this manner.[15] During the genocide, some victims were impaled from anus to mouth or from vagina to mouth. In fact, at one of Rwanda's genocide memorials, one can view the remains of a Tutsi woman who was killed in that way. In the second cartoon, use of this cruel technique is foreshadowed. Moreover, specifically Rwandan symbols with deep historical roots have merged with those that are the more recent product of Christian evangelization.

The democratic Hutu opposition press also used sexual imagery in its attacks on Habyarimana and his allies. Another use of the castration image, for example, appears in *Umurangi*, a magazine that represented the point of view of

FIGURE 6.2   A civilian RPF supporter: "Kill this stupid Hutu and after you cut off his genitals, hang them on our drum."

the Mouvement Démocrate Republicain (MDR), a southern Hutu party. Here (Figure 6.3) a woman named Habimana, a close associate of Habyarimana's and head of the Rwandan Office Nationale de la Population, instructs a doctor with scissors to castrate each man standing in line. Mme. Habimana commands: "Castrate them in the name of the *umwami w'akazu* [i.e., Habyarimana, king of the *akazu* or "little house"—the small clique of people who were Habyarimana's closest supporters and most favored clients]. He has his aim in mind. Don't ask questions." The doctor in the cartoon replies: "You don't have to tell me about the [dangers of] *inyenzi* (RPF). Don't we take money from the same project?"

The Imagining of Sexual Violence

In the months leading up to the genocide, violent sexual imagery depicting both males and females abounded in the iconography of Hutu extremist literature, while actual sexual violence against Tutsi women occurred with increasing frequency. Of course, as with many scapegoated groups, sexual violence against the

128

FIGURE 6.3 Published in the magazine Umurangi a woman named Habimana, a close associate of Habyarimana's and head of the Rwandan Office Nationale de la Population, instructs a doctor with scissors to castrate each man standing in line.

group's women increases during conflict. This does not explain, however, why so much ambivalence and so much of the extremists' energy was concentrated on Tutsi women. This was apparent in the popular press, as we shall see below in the infamous "Hutu Ten Commandments."

Here we encounter one of the regime's thorniest contradictions. Despite all measures to discourage the practice, it found that it could not keep Hutu men from being attracted to and occasionally establishing long-term sexual relationships with Tutsi women. Widely reputed by Europeans to be more beautiful than Hutu, Tutsi women were even held to be more attractive by many Hutu as well. I frequently heard statements to this effect in the 1980s, during my first period of fieldwork in Rwanda. It is also discussed by Liisa Malkki in her book about Burundian Hutu refugees.[16] Two of the "mythico-histories" that she analyzes are entitled "Beautiful Tutsi Women as Bait into Servitude" and "The Death Trap of Tutsi Women's Beauty."[17] The gist of these stories is that Tutsi use the beauty of their women to trick Hutu into marriage. Once ensnared, the unfortunate Hutu man is said to become the virtual slave of his wife's Tutsi parents. It may be argued that beyond readily apparent and standard determinants of beauty, the question of beauty is a political one. The dominant standards of human beauty in any given social system, such an argument would assert, are the standards of the dominant class. Where the poor are emaciated, "Rubenesque" fleshiness is likely to be perceived as beautiful. Where the poor are obese, slimness is likely to be perceived as desirable.

Such an explanation seems dubious in the Rwandan context, where it was the women of the dominated group who were said to be more beautiful than those of the dominating group. The belief in the beauty of Tutsi women has a long precedent. Nineteenth-century European explorers, following the received wisdom of the Hamitic hypothesis, believed that the Tutsi were the descendants of Ham, one of Noah's sons. Of supposed Middle Eastern origin, they were almost Caucasian rather than Negroid. Therefore, the Tutsi were thought to have higher intelligence and greater physical beauty. G. Prunier cites Father van den Burgt's comments on the Tutsi from Burgt's French-Kirundi dictionary: "We can see Caucasian skulls and beautiful Greek profiles side by side with Semitic and even Jewish features, elegant golden-red beauties in the heart of Ruanda and Urundi."[18]

Just as the "Black is beautiful" slogans of the 1960s in the United States may have failed to erase the profound and fearful self-doubt lurking in the minds of many black people, after centuries of intellectual and aesthetic disparagement, so it was with many of Rwanda's Hutu. The Hutu Revolution of 1959–62 never directly addressed the psychic corollaries of Hamitism. The question of power, of who was to rule, may have been settled by that revolution, but little else. The premises of physical beauty, associated with European colonialism and pitting one group against the other, persisted in Rwanda and Burundi well after decolonization. In part this was reinforced by the fact that Europeans who entered into romantic involvements with Rwandan or Burundian women, or who married them, more frequently did so with Tutsi women. There was certainly an impetus on the part of Tutsi women to establish such relationships. Marrying a European man usually meant a dramatic rise in the woman's social and economic status, and carried with it a substantial measure of protection. Such a woman could more readily leave the country, and she could usually help other members of her family to do so as well. She was also in a better position to help them financially. These advantages were so compelling that it was not at all uncommon in pre-genocide Rwanda to see some of the most beautiful young Tutsi women married to European men more than twenty or thirty years their senior.

Unfortunately, because of their high visibility, such marriages contributed to the impression that the sexual and matrimonial destinies of beautiful Tutsi women were determined more by the laws of the marketplace than by Rwandan social norms. The marriages also incited resentment and jealousy among Hutu extremists. Some of the latter might have wished that Hutu women would also be chosen by Europeans; others might have resented the fact that the most beautiful Rwandan women often spurned marriage with Rwandan men and sought husbands from Europe or North America. In 1982–83, sentiments such as these had led to the imprisonment of scores of Tutsi women on charges ranging from "vagabondage" to prostitution. In the years shortly before the genocide, the image of the alluring Tutsi woman appeared once again. In extremist literature, Hutu cartoonists depicted Tutsi women as prostitutes capable of enlisting Western support for the RPF cause through the use of their sexual charms. One cartoon (Figure 6.4) shows Canadian general Roméo Dallaire, the head of the United Nations peacekeeping force in Rwanda before and during the genocide,

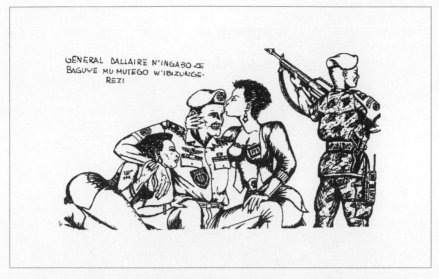

FIGURE 6.4   In extremist literature, Hutu cartoonists depicted Tutsi women as prostitutes capable of enlisting Western support for the RPF cause through the use of their sexual charms. One cartoon shows Canadian General Roméo Dallaire, the head of the United Nations peacekeeping force in Rwanda before and during the genocide, in an amorous embrace with two Tutsi women. The caption on the cartoon reads: "General Dallaire and his army have fallen into the trap of fatal women."

in an amorous embrace with two Tutsi women. The caption on the cartoon reads: "General Dallaire and his army have fallen into the trap of fatal women."[19]

Another cartoon depicts three Belgian paratroopers in various sexual acts with two Tutsi women (Figure 6.5).[20] This cartoon merits further comment. In 1983 and 1984, I had occasion to discuss the 1982–83 repression against young urban women consorting with European men. Many of my interlocutors expressed dismay that the Western press seldom printed anything at all about Rwanda, and when it did, as in 1983, it chose to cast the country in a bad light. One of them asked me how I expected Rwandan parents to raise morally upstanding daughters, if the children had the example before them of prostitutes grown rich from their escapades with European men. Another man expressed disgust at the type of sexual practices that he claimed were being transmitted to Rwandan women through contact with Europeans: notably, anal intercourse, cunnilingus, and fellatio. In this cartoon, not only are these acts pictured, but they are also being done in a group, compounding the violation of Rwandan sexual norms. Similar to food taboos, perceived differences in the sexual practices between one group and another are important in delineating the boundaries between the groups. Sexual practices are also, of course, highly invested with emotion. In this cartoon, Hutu extremists are by implication distinguishing their own sexual practices, procreative and moral, from European and Tutsi practices, non-procreative and immoral.

FIGURE 6.5   Belgian paratroopers depicted with two Tutsi women.

Yet at the same time, Hutu extremists appear to be attempting to purge their ambivalence toward Tutsi women via symbolic violence, even as they project their own erotic fantasies upon them. On one level, they were certainly aware that to preserve the racial purity of Hutu, they had to categorically renounce Tutsi women as objects of desire. At the same time, they knew that they themselves were not free of the forbidden desire. They were not impervious to the allure of Tutsi women, and indeed knew that many of the most prominent Hutu men had succumbed to the temptation. If the choice between Hutu and Tutsi women was non-problematic for Hutu extremists, narratives to the effect that Tutsi use the beauty of their women to ensnare Hutu men would be unnecessary. One can only speculate about the possible cognitive dissonances in the minds of many Hutu extremists where Tutsi women were concerned. What is most important for our purposes is that these sentiments received social expression.

For example, in December 1990, the Hutu extremist magazine *Kangura* printed what is perhaps the most succinct statement of Hutu extremist ideology: the infamous "Hutu Ten Commandments." Although this document has been cited often and widely discussed by scholars who have written about the genocide, notably Prunier and Chrétien, no one has pointed out that gender preoccupations were very much on the minds of the extremists. Hutu extremists clearly accorded high priority to the question of relations between Hutu men and Tutsi women, for the first three of the ten commandments concern this subject and this alone. They read as follows:

1. Every Muhutu [Hutu male] should know that wherever he finds Umututsikazi [a female Tutsi], she is working for her Tutsi ethnic group. As a result, every Muhutu who marries a Mututsikazi, or who takes a Mututsikazi for a mistress or employs her as a secretary or a protégée, is a traitor.
2. Every Muhutu should know that our Bahutukazi [female Hutu] are more worthy of, and conscious of their roles as woman, spouse, and mother. Are they not pretty, good secretaries, and more honest!
3. Bahutukazi [Hutu women], be vigilant and bring your husbands, brothers, and sons back to the path of reason.[21]

Would it have been necessary to recall Hutu men to order in this way, if the women of the opponents' group had not exerted such a compelling attraction? Why was it necessary for the extremists to assert that Hutu women are pretty, unless there were doubts to the contrary? The third commandment is also very telling: Hutu men cannot be expected to resist the attractions of Tutsi women alone; they need their Hutu wives, sisters, and mothers to call them back to reason!

Another commandment, the seventh, declares that the Rwandan Army must remain Hutu, but adds an additional warning against Tutsi women. Apparently, Hutu extremists were so preoccupied by this issue that no amount of redundancy or overemphasis could ever be deemed excessive.

7. The Rwandan Armed Forces must be exclusively Hutu. The experience of the October 1990 war teaches us this. No soldier should marry a Mututsikazi.[22]

Lurking beneath this ambivalence, one cannot help but sense imagery reflecting the "Hamitic hypothesis"—a tragic yet unacknowledgeable conviction on the part of the extremists that when all was said and done, early Europeans had indeed been correct in depicting Tutsi as "golden-red beauties" and Hutu as inferior (and less attractive) Negroids. The "Hutu Ten Commandments" are not the only evidence of this type of sentiment. In June 1994, after months of inaction on the part of the United Nations and the international community, the French decided to intervene in Rwanda through "Operation Turquoise." Too little, too late, the operation saved few threatened Tutsi and may have actually facilitated escape into Zaire for the beleaguered remnants of Rwandan Government Forces and their allied extremist militias. Perceived as "friends" by the latter, the Hutu extremist radio, Radio-Télévision Libre des Mille Collines (RTLM), called upon the population to welcome the French. Their appeal to young Hutu women was especially revealing: "You Hutu girls wash yourselves and put on a good dress to welcome our French allies. The Tutsi girls are all dead, so now you have your chance."[23] The beauty of Hutu women, it would seem, could only be expected to shine in the absence of competition from Tutsi women.

As Prunier points out in a footnote in his book,[24] such evidence of a lingering inferiority complex may partly account for the degree of sadism unleashed by Hutu death squads against Tutsi. Indeed, special measures of terrorism were reserved for Tutsi women by the extremists. Many Tutsi women suffered breast oblation, or were raped before being killed. Others, as noted, were impaled with spears from vagina to mouth. Many were forced to commit incest with a male family member before being killed. Pregnant women were often eviscerated. Still other Tutsi women were spared and taken as "wives" by their persecutors and brought into the refugee camps of eastern Zaire. There they became sexual slaves to their captors. In the events that transpired in eastern Zaire during the last days of the Mobutu regime, some of these women managed to escape and to return to Rwanda, pregnant and seeking abortion in a country that prohibits it.

The Rwandan genocide cannot be understood solely in political or even ethnic terms. Although recent contributions to the study of ethno-nationalism in Rwanda are obviously of great importance in comprehending this tragedy, they tend to accord little weight to what I have called the "social imaginary." My contention here has been that one of the best ways for gaining access to this is to examine both verbal and nonverbal means of communication—text, certainly, but also cartoons and images—that appeared in Rwanda's pre-genocidal media. When we look beneath the surface of ideology and the avowed intentions of social actors in the genocide, we uncover some of the deeper fears and desires of the *génocidaires*.

Contradictory in nature, these deeper fears and desires indicate a preoccupation with sex and gender. Fears of inadequacy in one form or another haunt the texts and the images. Would it have been necessary to remind Hutu extremists of the beauty of their own women if the fear had not lurked somewhere in their minds that Tutsi were what nineteenth-century Europeans had said they were—more beautiful? Would it have been necessary to depict one's enemies as castraters if one did not simultaneously fear them as sexual rivals and desire their castration? Gender concerns and sexual fears interacted in complex ways, extending to the demarcation of social boundaries and local notions of racial purity. Although these notions were ultimately of nineteenth-century European origin and were associated with the Hamitic hypothesis, they became internalized by many Rwandans and were later used ideologically by ethnic extremists in both Rwanda and Burundi. Many of the stereotypes of Tutsi women that one observes in pre-genocide Hutu extremist literature also owe their existence to preexisting Hamitic models.

The Rwandan genocide of 1994 differs from earlier incidents of massive violence in the country's history in that women were targets of violence much more than they had been in earlier incidents of ethnic strife there. This was especially true where Tutsi women were concerned, but it was not confined to them. The ethnic war in Rwanda's media aimed at reasserting an imagined past condition of patriarchy as well as the perpetuation of Hutu dominance, but it could not do this without betraying its unmentionable fear—that perhaps Tutsi really were superior in both beauty and intelligence.

Envy, resentment, and humiliation are perhaps the most social of emotions, and when these emotions concern traits like intelligence and physical beauty, they are not easily expunged. One can seize wealth and power from those that one envies; but one cannot appropriate another's intelligence and beauty. When Hutu took control of Rwanda in 1959, their revolution did nothing to reverse the ethnic stereotypes inherited from colonialism. Conceiving themselves as the oppressed made it easier for Hutu participants in the genocide to commit unspeakable crimes against their once real, now imagined oppressors.

Notes

1. Until 1960, Rwanda was ruled by a Tutsi king under the tutelage of the Belgian colonial administration. The pastoralist Tutsi were a minority in Rwanda, composing about 15–20 percent of the population. Agricultural Hutu constituted about 80–85 percent. In addition, there was a third group called Twa who were potters or foragers, and who counted for about 1 percent or less of the total population. Tutsi held the overwhelming majority of posts in the indirect-rule state apparatus under the Belgians. In the 1950s, educated Hutu sought a greater role in the Rwandan government and became politically active and vocal. Their movement, aided by the Rwandan Catholic Church and later supported by the Belgian colonial administration, culminated in the replacement of Tutsi administrators with Hutu under Governor General Jean-Paul Harroy. Shortly thereafter, the Tutsi king was overthrown along with the system of Tutsi dominance. The violence of this transition, between 1959 and 1964, claimed the lives of tens of thousands of Tutsi; many thousands more fled to neighboring African countries, creating a large diaspora. During the 1980s the sons and daughters of the original refugees sought to return to Rwanda. When their overtures to the Habyarimana government met with little substantive action in their favor, they decided to return to Rwanda by force. A group calling itself the Rwandan Patriotic Front, about 70 to 80 percent Tutsi in membership, invaded Rwanda from Uganda in October 1990. Peace accords ending this war were signed in Arusha, Tanzania, in August 1993 and gave the RPF most of what it had fought for. Implementing the accords, however, proved to be another matter. Hostilities between the two sides resumed on April 7, 1994, and resulted in an RPF victory by July 1994. In the intervening period, approximately one million Rwandans lost their lives—mostly Tutsi, although many Hutu opponents of the regime were also killed.

2. The democratization wave pushed by Western powers during the late 1980s and 1990s also touched Rwanda. Feeling that it would have to open its political system in order to continue receiving aid from Western donors, Rwanda allowed other political parties besides the ruling MRND (Mouvement Revolutionnaire pour le Développement et la

Démocratie) to come into being, although most power continued to rest with the president. Many different political parties quickly saw the light of day, but the principal ones besides the MRND were the Mouvement Democrate Republicain (MDR), the Parti Liberal (PL), and the Parti Social Democrate (PSD). In an effort to scramble the situation, the MRND also created other parties that were in effect clones of itself, such as the Parti Ecologiste. The CDR party, Coalition pour la Défense de la République, was an MRND splinter party that was more openly anti-Tutsi and anti-RPF than the MRND. Later in the 1990s, President Habyarimana and other Hutu extremists managed to split off anti-RPF factions from the MDR and the PL parties that became known as "Hutu Powa" (Hutu power) factions. Many later supporters of the genocide were recruited from the "Hutu Powa" groups.

3. See Dower, *War without Mercy*.

4. See Vansina, *Le Rwanda ancien*.

5. See Nahimana, *Le Rwanda, emergence d'un état*. During the pre- and early colonial era, Rwanda was ruled by a Tutsi king. But because many Rwandan kings assumed this function at a tender age, in reality the king ruled in conjunction with a queen mother. Rwandan queen mothers were often politically prominent, prompting some early European explorers to speak of Rwanda as a territory ruled by a queen. One of the most famous queen mothers in Rwanda's history was Rwabugiri's favorite wife, Kanjogera. After Rwabugiri's death, Kanjogera managed to engineer a coup d'état at Rucunshu (ca. 1896) and put her own son, Musinga, on the throne in place of Rwabugiri's personally designated successor. Biographical sketches of women whose lives straddled the pre- and early colonial period are also indicative that women's lives did not improve under colonialism. See Codere, *The Biography of an African Society*.

6. Locally, the institution of keeping a mistress was referred to as "deuxieme bureau" or "second office."

7. Aijmer and Abbink, *Meanings of Violence*.

8. Godelier, *L'énigme du don*.

9. Wagner, *Symbols That Stand for Themselves*.

10. Bourdieu, *Outline of a Theory of Practice*.

11. According to most students of Rwandan politics and history, Habyarimana's plane was probably shot down by elements within his own coterie who were even more extreme in their anti-Tutsi racism. This seems likely. With the bulk of their forces concentrated in northern Rwanda, several days away from Kigali, it is unlikely that the RPF would have acted so brashly. As for the extremists, they could hope for an angry, generalized response by Hutu against Tutsi following Habyarimana's death. Although many Hutu did not have such a response, due to the genocide's careful planning and organization, probably somewhere between sixty and eighty percent of Rwanda's resident Tutsi population died in about one hundred days.

12. As part of the Arusha accords, the RPF was allowed to station one battalion of its troops in Kigali in order to protect its political representatives. Although the first violent incidents that followed the president's assassination were against prominent Hutu opponents of the genocide and some individual Tutsi, the RPF garrison was attacked early on April 7, 1994. It then asked and received permission from the United Nations Mission to Rwanda to leave the confines of its garrison in order to defend itself.

13. Under the Habyarimana government, Tutsi were not allowed to serve in the military. Some Tutsi who had managed to fake Hutu ethnic identity, however, managed to enter the military. Most were later found out and purged during the 1980s.

Melchior Ndadaye was Burundi's first democratically elected president and its first Hutu president. Elected in June 1993, Ndadaye was taken prisoner in late October and then executed (not by impalement) by Burundian Tutsi army officers in a coup attempt. Almost universally condemned by other nations, the coup eventually failed, but not before it had provoked reprisal killings in which thousands of Tutsi civilians died, as well as counter-reprisal violence in which thousands of Hutu were also killed. The coup and Ndadaye's death served the cause of Hutu extremism in Rwanda quite well, and extremists lost no time in exploiting it. Unfortunately, the extremists' point that the Tutsi could never be trusted as partners in a democracy gained enormous credibility in Rwanda in the wake of Ndadaye's tragic death.

14. See Taylor, *Milk, Honey, and Money.*
15. Taylor, *Sacrifice as Terror,* 136–40.
16. Malkki, *Purity and Exile.*
17. Ibid., 82–87.
18. Prunier, *The Rwanda Crisis,* 9.
19. Chrétien, *Rwanda: Les médias du génocide,* 274.
20. Ibid., 366.
21. Ibid., 141. My translation.
22. Ibid., 142. My translation.
23. Quoted in Prunier, *The Rwanda Crisis,* 292.
24. Ibid.

Works Cited

Aijmer, Göran, and Jon Abbink, eds. *Meanings of Violence.* Oxford: Berg Press, 2000.

Bourdieu, Pierre. *Outline of a Theory of Practice.* Cambridge: Cambridge University Press, 1977.

Chrétien, Jean-Pierre. *Rwanda: Les médias du genocide.* Paris: Karthala, 1995.

Codere, Helen. *The Biography of an African Society: Rwanda 1900–1960: Based on Forty-Eight Rwandan Autobiographies.* Tervuren: Musée royal de l'Afrique centrale, 1973.

Dower, John W. *War without Mercy: Race and Power in the Pacific War.* New York: Pantheon Books, 1986.

Godelier, Maurice. *L'énigme du don.* Paris: Fayard, 1996.

Malkki, Liisa. *Purity and Exile.* Chicago: University of Chicago Press, 1995.

Nahimana, Ferdinand. *Le Rwanda, emergence d'un etat.* Paris: L'Harmattan, 1993.

Taylor, Christopher C. *Milk, Honey, and Money: Changing Concepts in Rwandan Healing.* Washington, D.C.: Smithsonian Institution Press, 1992.

_____. *Sacrifice as Terror: The Rwandan Genocide of 1994.* Oxford: Berg Press, 1999.

Vansina, Jan. *Le Rwanda ancien: le royaume nyiginya.* Paris: Karthala, 2001.

Wagner, Roy. *Symbols That Stand for Themselves.* Chicago: University of Chicago Press, 1986.

7

Genocide, Humiliation, and Inferiority
An Interdisciplinary Perspective

EVELIN G. LINDNER

This chapter argues that the root of genocides does not lie in ethnic fault lines, dwindling resources, "rational" conflicts of interest, or any general "evil" of human nature or modernity, but rather in complex psychological mindsets and behavioral clusters that exhibit their own homicidal—and also often suicidal—"rationality." History offers many examples of ethnic diversity having stimulating and enriching effects; dwindling resources may inspire cooperation and innovation; and "rational" conflicts can be solved by mutually beneficial negotiation. However, all these contexts may turn sour, acquire a greater emotional intensity, and become essentialized because of another, underlying dynamic: that of humiliation.

Humiliation is related in complex ways to shame, scapegoating, and the depiction of other humans as "beyond the pale." Genocide may involve acts of humiliation carried out in response to fear of humiliation—more precisely, to fear of *future* humiliation, based on an experience of past humiliations and habitual submission. In part for this reason, genocidal perpetrators are not always drawn from long-established elites. Rather, they are often recently risen subaltern actors, caught in a complex web of elements sometimes labeled as an "inferiority complex." They may be consumed by feelings of shame, along with a lingering admiration for the targets of the genocide. These dynamics are relevant not only for the study of genocide (especially subaltern genocide), but also for terrorism worldwide. They represent an important field of inquiry for all students of human security.

At the outset, we need to raise a number of puzzling questions and observations. For example: What is genocide? We often conceive of the phenomenon as an atrocity in which a powerful group selectively targets a less powerful group (characterized by ethnic or other markers), and we view this as reflecting either "rational" self-interest or "irrational" evil. Strikingly, however, almost every aspect of this framework is open to question. Consider the fact that genocide often seems to be less about "mere" killing and more about humiliating the targeted victims. Victims often are killed only after elaborate humiliation rituals; they are not slaughtered as honorable "enemies," but are dehumanized, degraded to the level of "pollution," "rats," or (as in Rwanda) *inyenzi,* "cockroaches." Is it conceivable, then, that genocide is more about humiliation than about actual killing? Perhaps killing is part of the humiliation process, rather than vice-versa?

The assumption that genocide's victims belong to a less powerful group also needs to be destabilized. Is it not curious that minorities such as the Isaaq in Somalia, Tutsi in Rwanda, or Jews in Nazi Germany, even when they were objectively rather subdued and politically marginalized, still seemed so threatening to genocidal perpetrators that exterminating them seemed the only "solution"? Why was it not sufficient simply to marginalize them? Why did the perpetrators feel a need to go to elaborate lengths to "send messages" to the victims—messages, that is, of humiliation? Does a simple scapegoat explanation suffice?

We should look more closely, as well, at the element of conflicts of interest over dwindling resources, with genocide posited as the outcome of rational, self-interested calculations. In both African cases that this author has studied in depth, namely Somalia (a quasi- or proto-genocide in 1988) and Rwanda (full-scale genocide in 1994), the countries in question were regarded as beacons of development until shortly before the genocides occurred. International experts flocked to them and sang their praises. Both countries had every reason to continue along their existing path and to work to resolve resource conflicts in constructive ways. Most observers probably would have placed Somalia and Rwanda far down the list of African countries most likely to suffer genocides.

Furthermore, the rational self-interest of the perpetrators was typically undermined—not bolstered—by the genocides that ensued. Many perpetrators of genocides have ended up much worse off than they were prior to the genocide. In several instances, genocide can even be considered a *suicidal* strategy for its instigators. To the outside observer, apart from being immoral, genocide often seems self-defeating.

As for ethnic markers, in pre-Nazi Germany, Jews were much more integrated than they were in Eastern Europe. Somalia, likewise, constitutes the most ethnically homogenous country in Africa (a single ethnic background; a unifying language and religion). In Rwanda, too, historical-anthropological analysis turns up more in the way of ethnic similarity than the ethnic differences that were accentuated by colonial rulers to buttress their dominance. Other countries in Africa are much more fragmented than Somalia and Rwanda.

Does this mean, then, that *homo sapiens* is hopelessly evil by nature, imbued with destructive instincts that regularly burst through the thin veneer of civilization? Or is it, in fact, the other way round? Are humans peaceable by nature, and corrupted by a modernity that spurs them to mayhem?

This chapter argues that the dichotomy of human "nature" versus "culture" is misleading. Human nature is neither savage nor noble, because human nature *is* culture. And culture is not an automaton. It mediates the environment that humans inhabit in a variety of ways, both driving emotions and being driven by them. Humiliation is perhaps the strongest force in this dynamic. Feelings of humiliation, and fear of humiliation, are "the nuclear bomb of the emotions." As with other emotions, humiliation is a historical-cultural-social-emotional construct: one that changes over time, wields considerable force, and can be directed to destructive ends.

I begin by sketching the background of research on humiliation. I then take a step back and examine the human condition through a historical lens, discussing the transition in human affairs from societies based on "ranked honor" to those proclaiming an "equal dignity," and the relevance of this framing for genocide studies. I then turn to consider genocide, and subaltern genocide specifically. How does humiliation lend its own "rationality" to genocide? How does genocidal "cleansing" represent a ghastly means of purging feelings of inferiority and shame, derived from concepts of elite admiration?

The Background of Humiliation Research

My scholarly research has focused on the phenomenon of humiliation for the past decade. A doctoral project explored "The Feeling of Being Humiliated: A Central Theme in Armed Conflicts," focusing on the African cases of Somalia and Rwanda and the European case of Germany.[1] These investigations included 216 qualitative interviews in the three countries, focusing on their history of genocidal killing. These interviews, some of them filmed, were carried out in Africa and Europe in 1998–99.

As the title of the project indicates, I focused on conflictive parties in Somalia and Rwanda and on those who sought to intervene. The results confirmed my hypothesis that, indeed, humiliation played a key role in war and genocide—not only in the distant past, but at present. In all cases, a fear of imagined future destitution, and of humiliating subjugation at another's hands, figured as a core justification for genocidal killing. In the German case, this fear took the form of a future *Weltherrschaft des Judentums*—a world dominated by Jews. In Rwanda, the fear was of democratic power-sharing with Tutsi, interpreted as meaning a return to Tutsi domination. Somalia's future was also regarded as threatened by the "arrogant" Isaaq tribe.[2]

Since the conclusion of doctoral studies in 2001, my research has expanded to include other cases in Europe, Southeast Asia, and the United States. I seek to construct a theory of humiliation that is transdisciplinary in nature, drawing on anthropology, history, social philosophy, social psychology, sociology, and political science.[3] I see humiliation not as an ahistorical phenomenon rooted in human "nature," but as a historical, cultural, social, and emotional construct that changes over time. I contend that present generations occupy a transitional world-historical juncture, between an "honor world" grounded in conceptions of ranked honor (with a concomitant experience of honor-humiliation) and a future world of equal dignity (with a quite distinct experience of dignity-humiliation).

In traditional hierarchical societies, elites were socialized to translate feelings of humiliation into an urge to react violently. They defended their honor against humiliation—whether with a sword, in duel-like conflicts, or in duel-like wars employing increasingly lethal weaponry. Subaltern actors, namely women and male underlings, were expected to accept their subjugation humbly, subserviently, and obediently, without invoking or expressing feelings of humiliation. This conceptualization first arose around ten thousand years ago, when hierarchical societal systems emerged alongside complex agricultural societies.[4] Until recently, such hierarchical societal systems were regarded as legitimate, even divinely ordained. Even today, in many parts of the world, populations still subscribe to these concepts.

Humiliation in general can be described in a threefold sense, pointing simultaneously to an act, a feeling, and a process. Humiliation means the enforced lowering of a person or group: a process of subjugation that damages or strips away pride, honor, and dignity. To be humiliated is to be placed, against one's will (or occasionally by consent—for example, in cases of religious self-abnegation or sadomasochism), and often in a deeply hurtful way, in a situation that is markedly at odds with one's sense of entitlement. Humiliation may involve acts of force, including violence. At its heart is the idea of pinning or putting down, of holding to the ground. Indeed, one of the defining characteristics of the process of humiliation is forcing the victim into passivity—a state of being acted upon and made helpless.

People react in different ways when they feel unduly humiliated. Some simply become depressed: anger turned inward against oneself. Others become enraged; still others hide their anger and carefully plot revenge. The person motivated by revenge may rise to become leader of a movement that instigates mass violence—by forging narratives of humiliation, and inviting the masses to invest their grievances in those narratives. Feelings of humiliation and fear of humiliation, if instigated and harnessed in malign ways by "humiliation entrepreneurs," may fuel mass atrocities in an enormously powerful and highly efficient manner.

The most potent weapon of mass destruction is thus the humiliated mind (whether the feeling of humiliation preexists or is manipulated). That mind may be ready to transgress all "normal" calculations of self-interest in response. A relatively small number of people so inclined can humble large armies—not least because cycles of humiliation, if kept in motion, may preempt the need for sophisticated weapons. In Rwanda, household tools such as machetes often sufficed; many victims paid to be shot instead of hacked to death. (In part, this was viewed as a more "honorable," less humiliating death.) Note also that the destruction of the World Trade Center on September 11, 2001, was achieved without access to high-tech bombs or missiles. Modern technology may thus serve as a magnifier of the humiliated mind—as in the Nazi Holocaust, where it enabled mass killing on an industrial scale.

Many elements of this equation merit attention I must unfortunately deny them here, for space reasons. To take one example: What is the difference between a humiliation felt "innately" and such a feeling when culturally prescribed or instigated by means of propaganda? If humiliation is felt at the individual level, how is it transmitted to the group, if indeed it is?[5]

Relatively few researchers have studied humiliation directly and explicitly. Among the few exceptions are Donald C. Klein, and Linda M. Hartling and Tracy

Luchetta.[6]Many scholars, for instance, fail to differentiate humiliation from other concepts. Humiliation and shame are often deployed interchangeably.[7]Donald L. Nathanson describes humiliation as a combination of three innate affects out of nine altogether: namely, as a combination of shame, disgust, and dissmell [*sic*].[8]

My own work addresses humiliation in its own right, not simply as a sub-variant of shame. Shame carries a host of prosocial connotations. People who are "shameless," for example, are not seen as fit for constructive coexistence.[9] Shame is an emotional state that is only salient when we accept it—however painfully. Humiliation, on the other hand, is an assault that we typically seek to repulse and which enrages us. Thus, in my conceptualization, Hitler managed to transform feelings of shame into feelings of humiliation among the German population. In interviews with Germans, Stephan Marks and Heidi Mönnich-Marks asked subjects about their motives for supporting Hitler.[10] One interviewee, born in 1917, described the hard, boring life in his village, and how Hitler's vision had lifted him out of his lowly condition. Hitler, he reported, showed him that his lowliness was not a *shame* to be accepted, but a *humiliation* to be rejected and fought.[11]

The view that humiliation may be a particularly powerful force is supported by the research of Thomas J. Scheff and Suzanne Retzinger, who studied shame and humiliation in marital quarrels.[12] They demonstrated that the bitterest divisions and suffering have their roots in feelings of humiliation and shame. Jan Smedslund developed the concept of "psychologic," which included emotions of anger, forgiveness, and humiliation.[13] William Vogel and Aaron Lazare likewise document humiliation as a serious obstacle in the treatment and counseling of couples.[14] In his recent book, *On Apology*, Lazare writes: "I believe that humiliation is one of the most important emotions we must understand and manage, both in ourselves and in others, and on an individual and national level."[15] His claim is supported by Robert Jay Lifton[16] and Jessica Stern.[17] Robert L. Hale explored the subject in his book *The Role of Humiliation and Embarrassment in Serial Murder*.[18] Humiliation has also been studied in fields as diverse as love, sex, and social attractiveness; depression, society and identity formation; sports, history, literature, and film.

Of particular interest here is Scheff and Retzinger's extension of their work on violence and the Holocaust,[19] which examined the role of "humiliated fury"—a term coined by Helen Block Lewis[20]—in escalating conflicts between individuals and nations.[21] Vamik Volkan, Joseph V. Montville, and colleagues carried out important psychopolitical research on intergroup conflict and its traumatic effects.[22] In his book *Blind Trust*, Volkan argues that a trauma experienced as humiliating is not adequately mourned, leading to a desire for revenge and, under the pressure of fear/anxiety, to collective regression.[23]

In the realm of psychology, sociology, and trauma, Ervin Staub's work continues to be highly significant.[24] Staub makes the point that bystanders need to stand up—and not stand by—when humiliation is perpetrated on their neighbors. Avishai Margalit, for his part, argues that we must not only oppose individual acts of humiliation, but build societal institutions that do not humiliate their citizens.[25] Notions of honor and humiliation are addressed by Richard E.

Nisbett and Dov Cohen, who examine the particular form of honor operative in traditional branches of the Mafia and, more generally, in blood feuds.[26] Bertram Wyatt-Brown has studied the history of concepts of honor in the American South,[27] while William Ian Miller's book *Humiliation and Other Essays on Honor, Social Discomfort, and Violence* links humiliation to honor as it is understood in historical and literary classics like *The Iliad* and Icelandic sagas.[28] One should also note the research on mobbing and bullying, which touches on the phenomenon of humiliation, and on trauma and post-traumatic stress disorder (PTSD).

With these framings in mind, let us consider humiliation in historical context, with reference to the transition from ranked honor to equal dignity, or from honor-humiliation societies to dignity-humiliation societies.

The Historic Transition from Ranked Honor to Equal Dignity

According to William Ury, most of human history passed relatively peacefully, with small bands of hunter-gatherers cooperating in noticeably egalitarian societal structures, amidst abundant resources. By roughly ten thousand years ago, *homo sapiens* had populated the entire globe—at least its more easily accessible regions—and uninhabited land became scarce. No longer could people just wander off to the next virgin valley; it was likely to be populated already (the anthropological term is *circumscription*). Increasingly, people had to stay in place, become more sedentary, and make do with the resources immediately available, primarily through a process of agricultural *intensification*.

Agriculture introduced a profoundly new way of life: much more malign than previously, because land belongs either to oneself or to another. This win-lose logic, in turn, fuels war. International relations theory uses concepts like the "security dilemma" to describe how arms races and war were all but inevitable in this atmosphere of fear of attack from outside one's community.[29] In response to these novel circumstances, hierarchical societies evolved, with masters at the top and lesser beings at the bottom. Human worthiness became ranked, with different degrees of honor attached to each stratum.

Very recently, however—just a few hundred years ago—humankind faced a second deep transition, as profound as the one that occurred millennia ago. Technological innovations allowed humans to relate to their home, the planet Earth, in new ways. Increasingly, knowledge and not land is the essential resource for sustainable livelihoods. Ury suggests that humankind is on the verge of creating a global knowledge society—"for the first time since the origin of our species, humanity is in touch with itself"[30]—thus returning to the win-win frame of the hunter-gatherers (since knowledge, unlike land, is an expandable resource). Human beings may thereby regain the potential for relatively peaceful and egalitarian societal structures.

Some of the predicted changes may already be seen in the growing acceptance of human-rights ideals, which have wrought a profound shift in the hierarchical

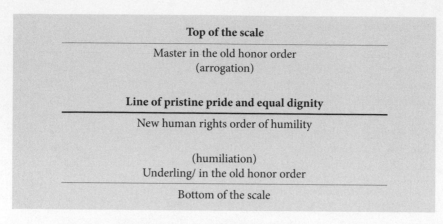

FIGURE 7.1 The Historic Transition to Equal Dignity

order. In the course of this process, the notion of humiliation has changed its point of attachment. The change is marked by the emergence of the modern meaning of the word "humiliation." William Ian Miller informs us that "the earliest recorded use of to humiliate, meaning to mortify or to lower or to depress the dignity or self-respect of someone, does not occur until 1757."[31] Under this new framework, the downtrodden and the subaltern *gains the right to feel humiliated*. Humiliation moves from being the privilege of the elite to becoming the right of the disadvantaged at the bottom of the ladder. Subaltern actors around the world today are socialized to feel humiliated by their lowliness—now defined as an illegitimate affront to their dignity rather than a legitimate humbling. The elites, by contrast, are called on to regain humility and are no longer permitted to resist such demands by labeling them as humiliating.

The human rights revolution could be described as an attempt to collapse the master-slave dynamic of the past ten thousand years to a midpoint of equal dignity and humility (see Figure 7.1).

The following section investigates the relevance of this historic transformation for the study of genocide, including subaltern genocide.

Genocide and the Historic Transition

In periods of transition, trends and tendencies are typically blurred and indistinct. So it is with the transition now underway from the traditional paradigm of ranked honor to a novel paradigm of equal dignity. Therefore, when we speak of "human rights based societies" in this discussion, we do so in the spirit of a Weberian ideal-type approach.[32] Perhaps genuinely human-rights based societies will emerge in a century or two. So far, we see only seedlings—but growths that nonetheless merit attention.

An important trend is that the more that concepts of human rights permeate a society, the more humiliation becomes hurtful; the more important it becomes as a topic for research; and the more relevance it gains for policy planning. This is because the four basic kinds of subjugation known to honor cultures become conflated in a single kind of humiliation when viewed through a human rights lens.

Subjugation in honor societies can be categorized in four variants.[33] A master uses *conquest subjugation* to drive formerly equal neighbors into a position of inferiority. When the hierarchy is established, the master uses *reinforcement subjugation* to keep it in place. This may range from rituals such as seating orders and bowing rules, to brutal measures such as customary beatings and killings. A third form of humiliation, *relegation subjugation,* is used to push an already subaltern individual still further down. *Exclusion subjugation* anathematizes its targets altogether—by exiling or even killing them.

In honor societies, all these variants are regarded as legitimate tools. The hint of violation that the word "humiliation" carries in contemporary parlance is present solely in relationships among equal aristocrats, not in the attempt to subjugate subaltern others. Attempting to debase others is always legitimate in a ranked society, which dictates that "might is right." Equals, however, will often oppose such debasement—we may label it "honor-humiliation"—and respond, for instance, by a challenge to a duel.

Human rights frameworks turn all four types of subjugation into utterly illegitimate *exclusion humiliation.* Attempts at subjugation of whatever kind are now regarded as a human-rights violation that excludes the victims from humanity. This situation produces intense pain and suffering, because losing one's dignity means being excluded from the human family altogether. In the absence of moderating forces—a Nelson Mandela, for example (see the conclusion to this chapter)—this pain may provoke violence, up to and including terrorism and genocide. Table 7.1 seeks to summarize this argument and to explore its relevance to genocide.

As sketched in Table 7.1, the more societies are influenced by ideals of human rights, the more salient feelings of humiliation become—in a threefold fashion. First, subalterns feel more humiliated in a system where elites are no longer accepted as benevolent patrons, but come to be viewed as evil oppressors. Second, feelings of inferiority may provoke feelings of *shame* at such inferiority. Third, subalterns may feel *retrospective* shame—that is, shame that they ever admired elites and bowed before them. All three elements may be translated, in the absence of countervailing influences, into an urge to purge and "cleanse" shame and humiliation, along with the people who are seen as triggering these emotions.

Rwanda and Nazi Germany

Rwanda provides an excellent example of this dynamic in action. My research there made it clear that the country does not agree on its history. Rather, it has two core historical narratives. My friends of Tutsi background tended to emphasize the ethnic homogeneity of all Rwandans, the benevolent patronage of their

TABLE 7.1   THE HISTORIC TRANSITION OF HUMAN HISTORY AND
ITS RELEVANCE FOR GENOCIDE

The Historic Transition and Its Relevance for Genocide		
	Options for dissatisfied members of a group	Relevance for genocide
Prior to 10,000 years ago: Pristine, egalitarian hunter-gathering context	Dissatisfied members of a group had the option to wander off and find unoccupied land with abundant resources, while maintaining egalitarian societal structures.	There is no archaeological evidence that systematic genocidal killing occurred prior to ten thousand years ago.*
During the past 10,000 years: Agricultural context of ranked honor	Since unoccupied land was no longer easily accessible, the option of wandering was foreclosed. The remaining options were acquiescence to a master's domination, or attempting to replace the master. Dissatisfied masters, for their part, could force subaltern actors into alternative societal structures, and conquer neighboring groups.	There is ample archeological evidence of systematic war during the past ten thousand years, much of it taking the form of conquest of neighboring territory. Masters reinforced their domination of subaltern actors, but usually without excluding them entirely—e.g., to retain them as part of a workforce. Subalterns who succeeded in replacing masters tended to adopt their ways. In sum, conquest and oppression, though often very brutal, were less systematic and fanatical than the term "genocide" normally implies.
Vision for the future: Global knowledge society with equal dignity for every global citizen	Human rights frameworks call on societies to transform themselves in order to provide adequate subsistence to all citizens, so that they may enjoy equal rights and dignity. Humankind is depicted as a single family of equals. The traditional system of ranked honor is delegitimized.	1. Human rights transform the lowly position of subalterns into utterly illegitimate *exclusion humiliation*; the resulting "nuclear bomb of the emotions" may be translated into genocide. 2. Subalterns (former or present) may feel inferiority to masters as *shameful*, as something to be "cleansed" through killing and genocide. In sum, the delegitimization of traditional rank transforms old emotional scripts of submission into new shameful scripts of humiliation. Formerly obedient underlings become angry victims of humiliation. Strong feelings of humiliation may be translated into a call for genocide as a "cleansing act."

* See, for example, Haas, Warfare and the Evolution of Culture, 8; Ury, Getting to Peace, 35.

Tutsi forefathers over the centuries, and how happily Hutu clients accepted such patronage. Friends with a Hutu background, in contrast, have a tendency to deemphasize ethnic homogeneity and deny that their forefathers ever acquiesced to Tutsi domination—which, they suggest, was not benevolent at all.

There might be a problem with both these views: one that helps to explain a genocidal outcome. Perhaps both perspectives are correct, at least in part. Might Tutsi rule in the past have been less benevolent than today's defenders wish to portray it? Might Hutu have acquiesced, even admired their patrons/oppressors more than they later chose to admit? Tutsi women, for example, were still highly sought-after trophies for wealthy Hutu men (see Taylor's chapter in this volume). In field research in 1999, I frequently heard it said that a Hutu man who gets rich "buys a house, gets a Mercedes, and marries a Tutsi woman."[34] In other words, a degree of habitual Hutu admiration for Tutsi superiority lived on after the Tutsi had been deposed from formal power, suggesting that voluntary submission to, and admiration for, a Tutsi elite might well have existed earlier as well.

Why was the Hutu revolution of 1959, which overturned the traditional ethnic order, not sufficient to transform the Hutu-Tutsi relationship at an existential level? How could the enthusiastic sense of liberation and dignification among Hutu after the revolution of 1959, which deposed the Tutsi rule in favor of the majority population, be transformed into one of the most extreme genocides on the historical record?

As noted above, many genocidal perpetrators have ended up worse off than they were prior to the genocide. To the outside observer, viewed through a lens of self-interest, genocide—apart from being morally repugnant—hardly seems worth the effort. Hitler brought ruin not only upon the world, but upon his own followers and himself. He led an entire society into the abyss, as if this had been his aim. Many Hutu *génocidaires* live miserable lives today. Somalian dictator Siad Barre died in exile—hated, not venerated, in his own country.

Yet Hitler, in taking his own life, declared himself satisfied. Eberhard Jäckel reports Hitler's last words, on April 2, 1945: "The world will be eternally grateful to National Socialism that I have extinguished the Jews in Germany and Central Europe."[35] In other words, it seems Hitler's "gain" was a glory lying somewhere beyond this Earth and beyond physical death. His and his followers' physical preservation on Earth was not necessarily the desired endpoint of his calculus. The "proud and dignified Germany" he sought to build might not take a physical form, but could receive its validation from *die Vorsehung* (providence), where humiliation and its redress would be recognized as meritorious.

Moreover, Hitler is said to have expressed satisfaction at the destruction of Germany in the war's later stages, because he judged that "his" Germans had failed him and did not deserve to survive. For Hitler, by being destroyed *das Deutsche Vaterland* got what it deserved for failing to heed and implement his vision. After all, as Hitler explained in detail in his book *Mein Kampf,* the German fatherland had neglected, overlooked, and humiliated the German minority in Austria (where Hitler was born and grew up). The elite of the German fatherland had miserably failed in World War I through unintelligent strategies, thus bringing humiliation upon their entire people. In addition, Germany (and also England, in Hitler's view) was insufficiently alert to the supposed "threat" posed by Jewish world domination and world humiliation. In Hitler's mind, he had tried to teach Germans nobility and grandeur—but in vain. Now Germans were reaping what they had sowed: downfall. Hitler's twofold satisfaction could be formulated as him having saved German greatness and protected the world against future humiliation—even if this would be recognized only in the afterlife, and even if everyone else had failed him, including his own people.

We may hypothesize, then, that humiliation—as both act and feeling—is so powerful that it overrides calculations of earthly well-being. It may transform what is regarded as "rational" self-interest (before death) into redress of humiliation and protection against future humiliation, as a quasi-religious achievement (realized only after death). The "nuclear bomb of the emotions" may encourage adoption of extreme strategies that pursue a mystical transcendence, and which hamper pragmatic, "here-and-now" solutions. Dynamics of humiliation may thus be as potent and consuming as any addiction: "getting the fix" of redress for humiliation may override all other rationales.

Genocide as a "Cleansing" of the Inferiority Complex

Are not genocide's victims usually members of subaltern minorities? But if so, why are resources mobilized to humiliate and kill people who are already subordinate or powerless? Would not continued marginalization be more "efficient"? *What turns powerless people into such a threat?* In Rwanda, Somalia, and Germany, the elite would surely have gained more by incorporating the minority that they feared (whether Isaaqs, Tutsi, or Jews). Instead, they ascribed preposterous powers and abilities to the minority—namely, its ability to dominate and subjugate the rest—and surprisingly low abilities to themselves, namely their inability to integrate this minority peacefully. Why so little self-confidence?

What we observe here seems to have its roots in the dynamic known as the *inferiority complex*. In psychology, the term is connected with the Viennese psychiatrist Alfred Adler (1870–1937). Thomas J. Scheff explains that "the concept of an inferiority complex can be seen as a formulation about chronic low self-esteem, i.e., chronic shame."[36]

Consider, in this context, the situation in Somalia under President Mohammed Siad Barre. Siad Barre initially gave people new hope. He condemned tribalism and clannism. He seemed to stand for a government that would attend to all Somalis' needs, not those of one clan alone. At least this was his rhetoric; perhaps, at the outset, it was also his conviction. He developed the economy and gave Somalis some years of relative peace.

Then Siad Barre set out to fulfill Somalia's great dream of unification. In 1978, he invaded Ethiopia to capture the Ogaden territory and bring the ethnically Somali Ogaden "home" to Greater Somalia. Somalia's defeat in this conflict constituted a devastating humiliation. Siad Barre, however, survived the humiliation by locating scapegoats. He targeted his fellow countrymen from the north, accusing them of having caused the defeat. The first objects of his campaign were the Majerteen, whose villages and wells he destroyed; later he turned on the Isaaq people.

In January 1986, the Morgan Report was issued, the work of General Mohammed Sidi Hersi "Morgan," Siad Barre's son-in-law of Majerteen background. Officially it was a top secret report on "implemented and recommended measures" for a "final solution" to Somalia's "Isaaq problem." Morgan writes that the Isaaq and their supporters must be "subjected to a campaign of obliteration" in order to prevent them "rais[ing] their heads again." He continued: "Today, we possess the right remedy for the virus in the [body of the] Somali State." Among the "remedies" he proposed: "Rendering uninhabitable the territory between the army and the enemy, which can be done by destroying the water tanks and the villages lying across the territory used by them for infiltration"; and "removing from the membership of the armed forces and the civil service all those who are open to suspicion of aiding the enemy—especially those holding sensitive posts." (A worn copy of this report, in English, was shown to me in Hargeisa in November 1998.)

Why did Siad Barre choose first the Majerteen and then the Isaaq as scapegoats? Not because they were easy targets. On the contrary, they were among the most challenging targets possible (and he paid the price: the Isaaq-dominated Somali National Movement [SNM] was among the leading forces that eventually toppled Siad Barre in 1991).

During colonial times, prior to independence in 1960, the north of Somalia had been the "British Protectorate of Somaliland," while the rest of present-day Somalia was under Italian rule. Through their traditional occupation as traders, northern Somalis had acquired greater managerial skills than southerners and had learned English under their colonial masters—internationally more useful than Italian after independence was achieved. Siad Barre, an autodidact like Hitler (intelligent, but lacking formal education), hailed from the formerly Italian south—the part of Somalia that was surpassed in education and efficiency by the northerners. One Isaaq woman reported to me during fieldwork in 1998 that she had met the dictator to plead for her imprisoned family members. "You Isaaq, you are so arrogant," Siad Barre allegedly told her. It confirmed her belief that the dictator may have suffered personal humiliation at the hands of Isaaq colleagues more educated than he was.

By choosing not weak scapegoats but strong ones, Siad Barre turned scapegoating into a double victory for himself, at least in the short term. First, he survived politically, by pointing the finger at others for Somalia's disastrous defeat in the Ogaden war. Second, he settled a score—his feelings of humiliation at the hands of the scapegoats.

From the genocide in Cambodia, to Rwanda and Germany, and in innumerable other cases, it is the skilled, the intellectuals, the knowledge carriers who are the first to be exterminated, by those who thereby cleanse themselves of feelings of inferiority and triumph over past humiliations. Thus, the commonly used term "ethnic cleansing" may refer to more than the expulsion or eradication of another ethnic group. It may reflect subalterns' need to purge and eradicate their own unacceptable feelings of humiliation and shame.

Genocide as the "Cleansing" of Shame over Elite Admiration

This chapter took as its starting point genocide's many perplexing characteristics. One question raised was if genocide is about killing, why are so many victims not only killed, but elaborately humiliated before death? Genocide seems to be about humiliating the personal dignity of the victims, depicting a group as "sub-human," then reducing them to that level. The Rwandan genocide of 1994 offers an intricate and gruesome catalogue of practices aimed at destroying victims' dignity. The most literal way to achieve this was to cut short the legs of Tutsi (whose "superiority" was symbolized by their height, on average greater than that of Hutu), or to sever their Achilles tendons so they would be forced to crawl. These actions not only shortened Tutsi bodies, but "cut them down to size" in a metaphorical sense, obliterating the source of their alleged arrogance.

The driving force behind these actions may be what I term *elite admiration*. In *Mein Kampf*, Hitler describes at length the Austrian political personalities whom he most admired—many of them Jews.[37] Reading his text, it becomes obvious to the reader that he once admired Jews, even if only early in life. Later, Hitler attempted to expunge every trace of Jews—along, perhaps, with his admiration for them. Cognizant of their talents and aptitudes, he was convinced that they had the capacity to dominate the world if he did not prevent them from doing so. His fear of this "global elite" and his desire to exterminate them were founded at least in part on admiration of their competence.

Elite admiration and imitation is deeply inscribed in the culture of rank that has dominated the world for the past ten thousand years. It has been taught to, and learned by, subaltern actors through the millennia. Imitating masters was one way that subalterns could ascend in rank (another way was to replace their masters in uprisings). Still today, despite the fact that these mindsets are losing their structural underpinnings, elite admiration and imitation are widespread. Modern celebrity culture attests to this. The most recent "high culture," that of the French court of Versailles, was not only imitated throughout Europe and its colonies, but is today imitated in the French-castle style adopted for millionaires' mansions in Texas, or the dwellings of the newly rich in contemporary China.

At first glance, such imitation seems to be a quite innocent phenomenon. But it is often dysfunctional and highly inappropriate to the environment to which it is transposed. The urge for imitation, moreover, is often so strong that even disability and self-mutilation may be accepted as consequences. Chinese foot-binding, for example, began as a "luxury" among the idle rich, who did not require women to be mobile enough for housework. But it was soon adopted by the subaltern classes, becoming a prerequisite for marriage—even though the female's reduced physical capacity and mobility had a negative impact on poorer households that could not afford servants. Foot-binding lasted for a thousand years, during which time about one billion women suffered its mutilations.[38]

Earlier, we mentioned the Hutu revolution in Rwanda in 1959, which produced an enormous outpouring of enthusiasm among the subaltern masses. How could this enthusiasm later turn into genocide? What is it about a liberation movement that can carry it too far? What transforms saviors (and even Hitler and Siad Barre were initially welcomed as saviors) into other- and self-destroyers, when "mere" oppression would have maintained them in power more efficiently? Perhaps what takes place is that *shame becomes unbearable*—shame rooted in subalterns' admiration of former elites, a dynamic accentuated further by the advent of modern concepts of human rights.

Briefly revisiting the difference between shame and humiliation is relevant at this point. Shame may be defined as a humbling experience that a person agrees she has caused, while humiliation describes experiences imposed by others—those that the victim has *not* caused. Shame, in contrast with humiliation, is often prosocial—shamelessness is not a virtue! But there is an exception: a special and emotionally destructive type of shame, namely *unacknowledged and bypassed shame*. This is so unbearable that it cannot even be acknowledged and is accordingly denied and disavowed. For Scheff, bypassed shame is the motor of all violence,[39] the source of what Lewis calls "humiliated fury."

Human rights ideals amplify this phenomenon, because they call not only for an end to tyrants, but for an end to rank altogether. This turns elite admiration into a doubly shameful voluntary self-lowering and self-humiliation. In former times, subalterns rose and stepped into the shoes of their envied masters, taking over as objects of subaltern admiration and imitation. But when the master-subaltern dyad is dismantled, there is no place left for elite veneration. Therefore, shame for elite admiration in subalterns—particular bypassed shame—may explain why such particularly extreme cruelties and humiliations are inflicted when subaltern actors rise up to take "revenge."

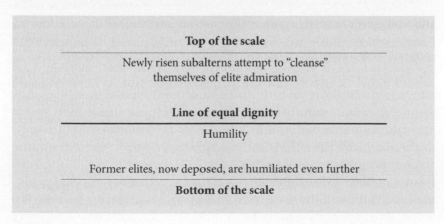

Top of the scale

Newly risen subalterns attempt to "cleanse"
themselves of elite admiration

Line of equal dignity

Humility

Former elites, now deposed, are humiliated even further

Bottom of the scale

FIGURE 7.2   Genocidal "cleansing"

Notions of "cleansing," ethnic and otherwise, thus may also point to sub-alterns' need to cleanse and eradicate their own elite admiration. The obsession with tearing even the babies out of mothers' wombs, to wipe out "root and branch" every trace of the formerly admired elite, may derive from this shame. For entrenched elites, the "mere" oppression of subalterns might suffice. Rational considerations may prevail; excessive humiliation or killing is simply "not worth the bother." But former subalterns—now risen to power—often seem obsessed with "total cleansing" and may perpetrate extreme forms of violence and humiliation on the former (and, one suspects it is feared, *future*) elites.

For the study of genocide, Figure 7.1 may be adapted to arrive at Figure 7.2. The cruelest behavior may not be exhibited by long-established elites, but rather by subaltern actors attempting to "cleanse" themselves of inferiority and elite-admiration.

"Getting the fix," in the case of humiliation, may also be conceptualized as resolving dissonance and self-doubt and gaining "purity."[40] "How can I feel sympathy, let alone admiration, for oppressors I ought to hate!"—this is the dilemma. It may be that genocide's victims are dehumanized and humiliated before being exterminated not so much because perpetrators actually believe they merit this, but *because they have doubts and need to persuade themselves through the infliction of atrocity.* They may feel a need to go as far as total extermination, precisely because they do not trust their own ability to always hate. They may fear that weakness on this score will lead to a return of the oppressors, and to a fresh round of humiliation.

This doubt is analogous to what Paul Rusesabagina has called the "soft spot." Rusesabagina's story is well known and formed the basis for the 2004 film *Hotel Rwanda*. He managed to shelter more than 1,200 Tutsi and moderate Hutu in the Hotel Mille Collines, which he managed, while killers roamed outside with guns and machetes. In a BBC *HARDtalk* interview with David Jessel in May 2007, Rusesabagina explained his strategy: he would find what he called the "soft spot" in the perpetrators. "Nobody is totally good or totally evil," he attested.

Rusesabagina described how, at one point, he traveled from his house to the hotel, along with his family and people who had sought refuge in his house. At a roadblock, he was handed a gun and ordered to kill his family and everyone accompanying him; thereafter, he too would be killed. He looked into the eyes of the man who gave this order, while the man proceeded to oversee the killing of others at the roadblock. For five long minutes, Rusesabagina attempted to hold his gaze. He noticed that the man could not withstand it: he had touched this Hutu perpetrator's inner awareness of his own guilt. Eventually, his party was allowed to leave.

Rusesabagina's account may point to possible strategies for genocide intervention, based on a deeper understanding of humiliation and shame. Leaders with genocidal tendencies must, of course, be prevented from taking power, wherever possible. But even democracy offers no guarantees: such leaders may find ways to manipulate democratic mechanisms and exploit democratic freedoms to incite followers, as Hitler did.

Another strategy, therefore, may be to dignify the masses that otherwise serve as "fodder" for the narratives of humiliation into which they are "invited" by humiliation entrepreneurs. Efforts must be made to explain, through the education system and media, that feelings of impurity and dissonance are an inevitable, indeed healthy part of the human condition; they do not require purgation or "cleansing."

This offers some hope amidst the bleakness that sometimes threatens to overwhelm us. Hunter-gatherer cultures, existing up until ten thousand years ago or so, provided a cultural context that promoted cooperation. This was enough time for such cooperation to be partly "hardwired": for genetic adaptation to derive from cultural adaptation. Then, about ten thousand years ago, a cultural context arose that favored war. The intervening millennia, however, were not sufficient for genetic adaptation—so this aspect is *not* hardwired. Soldiers have had to be trained and inculcated to kill their "enemies," since killing is not something that human beings do "naturally" and easily. (We usually forget how much we depend on our expectation that fellow human beings outside our own tribe will not kill us. The global tourism industry, for example, would founder without this expectation!)

We currently inhabit a transitional period that promotes malign aspects drawn from the legacy of the past ten thousand years, such as an orientation toward competition and accumulating material goods; but which also features benign elements derived from the period prior to the rise of agriculture, which is now linked to the similarly benign aspects of an emerging knowledge society. Thus, neither ancient nor modern culture can be said to corrupt or (alternatively) ennoble humans. Rather, certain aspects and elements of these cultures can corrupt, while others exert a positive influence.

I agree with William Ury that for all its negative aspects, globalization—by paving the way for a global knowledge society—may allow us to push toward a more dignified and egalitarian world. We need to become more attentive to this trend, and start channeling it constructively. I call for globalization to be married to *egalization* (the implementation of the human rights call for equal dignity). Such a strategy might allow us to build a decent global village, following the call for a decent society issued by Avishai Margalit.

Egalization must be implemented at all levels, from the global "macro" context to the "micro" contexts of relationships with our families, colleagues, and friends—even within our own psyches. Egalization offers an opportunity to dismantle tyrannical systems and their destructive ways of defining human conduct, including the tyrannical behavior that emanates from deep within us. Another way to frame this is as thesis-antithesis-synthesis. In the *thesis,* subalterns subserviently accept oppression. In the *antithesis,* subalterns violently reject oppression. In the needed *synthesis,* human beings transcend oppression rather than merely rejecting it, and construct thereby a newly dignified world.

In former times, the process stopped at the antithesis stage. Subaltern actors rose up, replaced the tyrant—and maintained the tyrannical system intact. This is also what the *génocidaires* and terrorists of today accomplish. They act like tyrants in their fight against tyrants. They focus on the *what*, not the *how*. In many cases, this flows from an enthusiastic fervor for liberation—from aspirations to greater dignity. In my research, I attach the label "extremists" to those who perpetuate cycles of humiliation rather than seeking to end them. "Moderates," by contrast, are those who have the intellectual and emotional resources to end such cycles.

I see some of these dangers, and also the potential for constructive action, in the present-day "war on terror." If we accept that feelings of subaltern inferiority influence the decision to adopt terrorist methods, it hardly suffices for target populations to triumphantly cry: "Oh, they only hate us because they admire and envy us!"—as if the fact of envy bolsters the targets' superiority. And subalterns who rise to power need to understand that feelings of inferiority are not something to be ashamed of, or to "cleanse." They stem, rather, from a historic evolution that first cultivated hierarchies, including emotional mindsets of inferiority and elite admiration for subaltern actors, only later to delegitimize them. The emotional pain associated with this transformation cannot be healed by violent mayhem, whether terrorist or counterterrorist in nature. It can be healed only by gradually expanding boundaries of a world in which all people have equal rights and access to dignity.

In recent times, few leaders have so exemplified the possibility of such a healing strategy as Nelson Mandela in South Africa. Mandela could have followed the example of Rwanda's Hutu leadership. He would certainly have had the power to unleash genocide on the white elite in South Africa. He did not. One can only agree with Archbishop Desmond Tutu's 1997 comment "to white people of this country: you don't know how lucky you are."[41]

Clearly, post-Apartheid South Africa still faces many challenges. However, the lessons that Mandela taught the world are still relevant. After twenty-seven years in prison, some of his prison guards had become his friends. In short, his strategy was not to kill enemies, but to turn them into partners. Let us accordingly end this chapter with a quote from Mandela himself:

> I always knew that deep down in every human heart, there is mercy and generosity. No one is born hating another person because of the color of his skin, or his background, or his religion. People must learn to hate, and if they can learn to hate, they can be taught to love, for love comes more naturally to the human heart than its opposite. Even in the grimmest times in prison, when my comrades and I were pushed to our limits, I would see a glimmer of humanity in one of the guards, perhaps just for a second, but it was enough to reassure me and keep me going. Man's goodness is a flame that can be hidden but never extinguished.[42]

Notes

1. Lindner, "The Psychology of Humiliation: Somalia, Rwanda/Burundi, and Hitler's Germany."

2. See a deeper discussion in Lindner, "Were Ordinary Germans Hitler's 'Willing Executioners'?" and Lindner, "Humiliation and Reactions to Hitler's Seductiveness in Post-War Germany."

3. See, for example, Lindner, "Avoiding Humiliation"; Lindner, "In Times of Globalization and Human Rights"; Lindner, "Emotion and Conflict"; Lindner, *Making Enemies*.

4. For a comprehensive description, see Ury, *Getting to Peace*.

5. Those interested in pursuing these themes further may consult the author's extensive writings at http://www.humiliationstudies.org/whoweare/evelin02.php.

6. Among the few exceptions are Klein, "The Humiliation Dynamic," and Hartling and Luchetta, "Humiliation: Assessing the Impact of Derision, Degradation, and Debasement."

7. Among others, by Tomkins, *Affect Imagery and Consciousness*, whose work is carried further by Nathanson, *Shame and Pride*.

8. "Dissmell" is a neologism created by Tomkins. If "disgust" is a word indicating bad taste, "dissmell" is the analogue for a bad smell.

9. See, for example, Elias, *The Civilizing Process*.

10. Marks and Mönnich-Marks, "The Analysis of Counter-Transference Reactions as a Means to Discern Latent Interview-Contents."

11. Ibid., para. 12.

12. Scheff and Retzinger, *Emotions and Violence*.

13. Smedslund, "Social Representations and Psychologic."

14. Vogel and Lazare, "The Unforgivable Humiliation: A Dilemma in Couples' Treatment."

15. Lazare, *On Apology*, 262.

16. Lifton, *Super Power Syndrome*.

17. Stern, *Terror in the Name of God*.

18. Hale, "The Role of Humiliation and Embarrassment in Serial Murder."

19. Scheff, *Bloody Revenge: Emotions, Nationalism and War*.

20. See, for example, Lewis, *The Role of Shame in Symptom Formation*, 19.

21. See also Scheff, *Emotions, the Social Bond and Human Reality*, and Smith, *Globalization, the Hidden Agenda*.

22. Volkan, Julius, and Montville, *The Psychodynamics of International Relationships*.

23. Volkan, *Blind Trust*.

24. Staub, *The Psychology of Good and Evil*; Staub, "The Roots of Evil."

25. Margalit, *The Decent Society*.

26. Nisbett and Cohen, *Culture of Honor*.

27. Wyatt-Brown, *Southern Honor*.

28. Miller, *Humiliation and Other Essays*.

29. See, for example, the work done by Barry Posen, "The Security Dilemma and Ethnic Conflict," and Hardin, *One for All*.

30. Ury, *Getting to Peace*, xvii.

31. Miller, *Humiliation and Other Essays*, 175.

32. See, for more detail, Coser, *Masters of Sociological Thought*.

33. Smith, "Organisations and Humiliation," 541–44; Lindner, *Making Enemies*, 28–29.

34. Lindner, *The Psychology of Humiliation*, 351.

35. Jäckel, *Hitler's World View*, 64.

36. Scheff, "Shame in Self and Society," 258.

37. See the first chapters, where Hitler describes his youth and adolescence in *Mein Kampf*.

38. See, among others, Levy, *The Lotus Lovers*.

39. Scheff, *Aggression, Male Emotions and Relations*, 4–5.

40. See Festinger, *A Theory of Cognitive Dissonance*. As to the topic of purity, see, for example, Mary Douglas, *Purity and Danger*.

41. Tutu and Davis, *Moment of Truth,* interview.
42. Mandela, *A Long Walk to Freedom,* 542.

Works Cited

Coser, Lewis A. *Masters of Sociological Thought: Ideas in Historical and Social Context.* 2nd ed. Fort Worth: Harcourt Brace Jovanovich, 1977.

Douglas, Mary. *Purity and Danger: An Analysis of the Concepts of Pollution and Taboo.* London: Ark Paperbacks, 1984.

Elias, Norbert. *The Civilizing Process. Volume 1: The History of Manners. Volume 2: State Formation and Civilization.* Oxford: Blackwell, 1994.

Festinger, Leon. *A Theory of Cognitive Dissonance.* Stanford, Calif.: Stanford University Press, 1957.

Haas, Jonathan. *Warfare and the Evolution of Culture.* Santa Fe, N.M.: Santa Fe Institute, 1998. Available at http://www.santafe.edu/sfi/publications/Working-Papers/98-10-088.pdf. Accessed November 15, 2002.

Hale, Robert L. "The Role of Humiliation and Embarrassment in Serial Murder." *Psychology. A Journal of Human Behaviour* 31, no. 2 (1994): 17–23.

Hardin, Russell. *One for All: The Logic of Group Conflict.* Princeton: Princeton University Press, 1995.

Hartling, Linda M., and Tracy Luchetta. "Humiliation: Assessing the Impact of Derision, Degradation, and Debasement." *Journal of Primary Prevention* 19, no. 5 (1999): 259–78.

Hitler, Adolf. *Mein Kampf.* 1925–26. London: Pimlico, 1999.

Jäckel, Eberhard. *Hitler's World View. A Blueprint for Power.* Cambridge, Mass.: Harvard University Press, 1991.

Klein, Donald C. "The Humiliation Dynamic: An Overview. Viewing the Task of Prevention From a New Perspective I (Special Issue, Section 1)." *Journal of Primary Prevention* 12, no. 2 (1991): 93–121.

Lazare, Aaron. *On Apology.* New York: Oxford University Press, 2004.

Levy, Howard S. *The Lotus Lovers: The Complete History of the Curious Erotic Custom of Footbinding in China.* Buffalo: Prometheus Books, 1992.

Lewis, Helen B. *The Role of Shame in Symptom Formation.* Hillsdale, N.J.: Lawrence Erlbaum Associates, 1987.

Lifton, Robert J. *Super Power Syndrome: America's Apocalyptic Confrontation with the World.* New York: Thunder's Mouth Press, 2003.

Lindner, Evelin G. "Avoiding Humiliation—From Intercultural Communication to Global Interhuman Communication." *Journal of Intercultural Communication, SIETAR Japan* no. 10 (2007): 21–38.

———. "Emotion and Conflict: Why It Is Important to Understand How Emotions Affect Conflict and How Conflict Affects Emotions." In *The Handbook of Conflict Resolution: Theory and Practice,* ed. Morton Deutsch, Peter T. Coleman, and Eric C. Marcus, 268–93. 2nd ed. San Francisco: Jossey-Bass, 2006.

———. "Humiliation and Reactions to Hitler's Seductiveness in Post-War Germany: Personal Reflections." *Social Alternatives* 25, no. 1 (special issue: Humiliation and History in Global Perspectives) (2006): 6–11.

———. "In Times of Globalization and Human Rights: Does Humiliation Become the Most Disruptive Force?" *Journal of Human Dignity and Humiliation Studies* 1, no. 1 (March 2007). Available at http://www.humilliationstudies.upeace.org/.

_____. *Making Enemies: Humiliation and International Conflict.* Westport, Conn.: Greenwood Press, 2006.

_____. "The Psychology of Humiliation: Somalia, Rwanda/Burundi, and Hitler's Germany." Ph.D. diss., University of Oslo, 2000.

_____. "Were Ordinary Germans Hitler's 'Willing Executioners'? Or Were They Victims of Humiliating Seduction and Abandonment? The Case of Germany and Somalia." *IDEA: A Journal of Social Issues* 5, no. 1 (2000). Available at http://www.ideajournal.com/lindner-willing-executioners.html.

Mandela, Nelson R. *A Long Walk to Freedom: The Autobiography of Nelson Mandela.* Boston: Little, Brown, 1994.

Margalit, Avishai. *The Decent Society.* Cambridge, Mass.: Harvard University Press, 1996.

Marks, Stephan, and Heidi Mönnich-Marks. "The Analysis of Counter-Transference Reactions as a Means to Discern Latent Interview-Contents." *Forum Qualitative Sozialforschung / Forum: Qualitative Social* Research [*On-Line Journal*] 4, no. 2 (May 2003). Available at http://www.qualitative-research.net/fqs-texte/2-03/2-03marks-e.htm. Accessed June 17, 2004.

Miller, William Ian. *Humiliation and Other Essays on Honor, Social Discomfort, and Violence.* Ithaca: Cornell University Press, 1993.

Nathanson, Donald L. *Shame and Pride: Affect Sex and the Birth of the Self.* New York: Norton, 1992.

Nisbett, Richard E., and Dov Cohen. *Culture of Honor: The Psychology of Violence in the South.* Boulder, Colo: Westview Press, 1996.

Posen, Barry. "The Security Dilemma and Ethnic Conflict." *Survival* 35, no. 1 (1993): 27–47.

Scheff, Thomas J. *Aggression, Male Emotions and Relations: The Silence/Violence Pattern.* Santa Barbara, Calif., 2005. Available at http://www.soc.ucsb.edu/faculty/scheff/42.html.

_____. *Bloody Revenge: Emotions, Nationalism and War.* Chicago: University of Chicago Press, 1990.

_____. *Emotions, the Social Bond and Human Reality. Part/Whole Analysis.* Cambridge: Cambridge University Press, 1997.

_____. "Shame in Self and Society." *Symbolic Interaction* 26, no. 2 (2003): 239–62.

Scheff, Thomas J., and Suzanne M. Retzinger. *Emotions and Violence: Shame and Rage in Destructive Conflicts.* Lexington, Mass.: Lexington Books, 1991.

Smedslund, Jan. "Social Representations and Psychologic." *Culture & Psychology* 4, no. 4 (1998): 435–54.

Smith, Dennis. *Globalization, the Hidden Agenda.* Cambridge: Polity Press: 2006.

_____. "Organisations and Humiliation: Looking Beyond Elias." *Organization* 8, no. 3 (2001): 537–60.

Staub, Ervin. *The Psychology of Good and Evil: Why Children, Adults, and Groups Help and Harm Others.* Cambridge: Cambridge University Press, 2003.

_____. "The Roots of Evil: Social Conditions, Culture, Personality and Basic Human Needs." *Personality and Social Psychology Review* 3, no. 3 (1999): 179–92.

Stern, Jessica. *Terror in the Name of God: Why Religious Militants Kill.* New York: HarperCollins, 2003.

Tomkins, Silvan S. *Affect Imagery and Consciousness (Volumes I–IV).* New York: Springer, 1962.

Tutu, Desmond, and Sharon Davis. *Moment of Truth.* Interview, "Background Briefing," ABC Radio, May 4, 1997. Available at http://www.abc.net.au/rn/talks/bbing/stories/s10597.htm. Accessed January 1, 2008.

Ury, William. *Getting to Peace: Transforming Conflict at Home, at Work, and in the World.* New York: Viking, 1999.

Vogel, William, and Aaron Lazare. "The Unforgivable Humiliation: A Dilemma in Couples' Treatment." *Contemporary Family Therapy* 12, no. 2 (1990): 139–51.

Volkan, Vamik D. *Blind Trust: Large Groups and Their Leaders in Times of Crisis and Terror.* Charlottesville, Va.: Pitchstone Publishing, 2004.

Volkan, Vamik D., Demetrios A. Julius, and Joseph V. Montville, eds. *The Psychodynamics of International Relationships. Volume 2: Unofficial Diplomacy at Work.* Lexington, Mass.: Lexington Books, 1991.

Wyatt-Brown, Bertram. Southern *Honor: Ethics and Behavior in the Old South.* New York: Oxford University Press, 1982.

8

Evolution, Primates, and Subaltern Genocide

E. O. SMITH

The incident took place in February 1974 and marked the beginning of the end of the Kahama community. A raiding party of three adult males and one adult female from the Kasakela community hiked for over half an hour into Kahama country, where they happened upon a member of the Kahama community. The three males attacked quickly, catching the unsuspecting Kahama male, biting him and stamping on him. Soon the victim stopped struggling and sat hunched over on the ground. Suddenly he attempted to run away, but he was caught by the leg and pulled to the ground. Now all the members of the Kasakela raiding party, including the female, joined in the attack, pounding the prostrate victim repeatedly. One or more of the aggressors ripped the skin from the victim's leg with their teeth. The attack ended as quickly as it had begun. Two months later the victim was seen again. His spine and pelvis were protruding. He had an unhealed gash on his inner thigh, likely the spot where his skin was ripped in the attack. The nails had been torn off his fingers. One toe was partially severed. He had lost part of an ear. He was emaciated. After that sighting, he was never seen again.

This is not an instance of a genocidal attack among humans, but rather an attack by members of a larger, socially dominant group of chimpanzees (based on the demography of the group, and in particular the number of adult males) on members of a smaller, less dominant group in the Gombe Stream National Park in Tanzania.[1] The incident suggests that humans are not the only primates capable of systematic group attack and killing of nongroup members. Consideration of, and comparison with, our closest nonhuman relatives may provide useful insights into genocidal behavior in general, and subaltern genocide in particular. Are humans, for example, the only animal species in which some groups experience "oppression" and seek to gain "revenge" and achieve "liberation" by waging genocide against their "oppressors"? To the extent that humans exhibit such behavior, can we account for it with culture and learned behavior alone? Or is there an evolutionary basis for this behavior?

A reasonable question is: "So what if there are commonalities between humans and nonhumans in the expression of certain types of aggressive behavior?" And additionally, "What difference does it make if genocide has an evolutionary or biological basis or not?" It is important to understand that the strategies developed to control genocide might be different from those employed today, if it could be shown that there was at least a partial evolutionary or biological basis to this aggressive behavior. An evolutionary perspective on human aggression might therefore stimulate new thinking about the formation and implementation of social policy, incorporating an acceptance of the underlying genetic and hence evolutionary basis of our aggressive behavior. Using an evolutionary approach, it might be possible to identify certain sociopolitical and ecological situations where genocide may occur, and at the very least prepare a humanitarian response if it occurs.

An Evolutionary Primer

Many critics of the application of evolutionary theory to human behavior are vigorous adherents to the Standard Social Science Model (SSSM) of explanation. The central theme of the SSSM is that differences between people result from differing environmental conditions, not genetic differences between populations or individuals. Unfortunately, adherents of the SSSM are misinformed about the relationship between genes and behavior. Rather than playing a rigidly deterministic role in shaping behavior, genes may exert more subtle influences—which feel like urges from within that have positive feelings attached to them, as opposed to rigid cause-and-effect relationships. The widespread acceptance of the SSSM is based on its moral appeal rather than on empirical fact. The SSSM has been carefully critiqued,[2] but its appeal lies in its strong stand against explaining differences between races, sexes, or individuals as exclusively the outcome of underlying biological differences. In its most extreme form, the SSSM holds that humans are plastic and the contingencies of the environment shape and channel our behavior with no input from our genetic heritage in explaining modern human variation.

This model has been important in combating social injustices. Supporters of the SSSM are opposed to racism and sexism; by definition, those who challenge the moral superiority of SSSM are labeled "biological determinists." This characterization of all non-SSSM adherents as determinists is patently wrong. Moreover, SSSM adherents argue that those who challenge the SSSM are attacking the basic human behavioral plasticity that is the cornerstone of their view of human nature. This "learning" view of human behavior favored by ardent devotees of SSSM is the intellectual product of the renowned psychologist John B. Watson:

> Give me a dozen healthy infants, well-formed, and my own specified world to bring them up in and I'll guarantee to any one at random and train him to become any type of specialist I might select—doctor, lawyer, artist, merchant-chief, and yes, even beggar-man and thief, regardless of his talents, penchants, tendencies, abilities, vocations, and the race of his ancestors.[3]

Before I enter into the details of the argument about an evolutionary basis for genocide, it is important to have a basic understanding of evolutionary theory. Most people feel they have an intuitive grasp of what Darwinian evolution is all about, but it may be beneficial to review some basic principles. Readers with a solid background in Darwinian thinking are invited to skip ahead to the section "Comparative Data."

Darwin 101

Darwin's central thesis consists of three major points and can be summarized as follows. Where competition exists for scarce resources, those organisms most fit to survive and reproduce will do so in greater numbers than those less fit. Darwin's ideas were not completely novel when he wrote *On the Origin of Species,* and they seem almost absurdly simple today. But there is much more here than first meets the eye. The first aspect of Darwin's theory is that competition is a fundamental aspect of life; it occurs when two or more individuals require the same resources and those resources are in limited supply. Competition exists at several different levels in biological communities, but for our purposes intraspecific competition is of considerable importance.

Intraspecific Competition

Organisms encounter competition from members of their own species, and it is common among animals as well as humans. Intraspecific competition among humans takes a variety of forms, and it is not always the "main event, winner-take-all" strategy that is most successful. Deception, bluffing, and false advertising are all important alternative competitive strategies—very often the strategies that are played out in human subaltern genocide in order to initiate a discourse of resistance and sometimes active rebellion.[4] The first thing to do in understanding competition in an evolutionary sense is to attempt to identify the cause of the original conflict—although identification of the contested resource is not as easy as it may seem at first blush.

Most Fit to Survive

Winning at evolution means more than simply surviving. In fact, survival alone does not even get you entered in the competition. What you really want to do is to maximize your genetic representation in future generations. Is that the same as maximizing the number of children that you have? That is partially the case—but the real definition of fitness has to do with the number of your genes that are present in the next generation.

When one thinks about measuring fitness, the renowned evolutionary biologist W. D. Hamilton (1936–2000), called by some the most distinguished Darwinian since Darwin, suggested that there are two components that must be taken into account.[5] First, there is your direct fitness, the number of your offspring that survive and reproduce. Remember that the only way to win at the game of evolution is to ensure that your genes reach the next generation, producing offspring that in turn produce offspring. By becoming a grandparent, you win at the game of evolution. However, the production of massive numbers of offspring that fail to reach maturity is not a winning strategy in evolution; nor is producing offspring that reach maturity but do so too slowly to make an impact in subsequent generations. It does not matter in the evolutionary calculus how many children you have if none of them reach sexual maturity and mate.

The production of offspring is not the only way one can get genes into subsequent generations. On average, you share about fifty percent of your genes with a full sibling, someone who has the same mother and father as you. This means that if your full sibling has children that survive and reproduce, then you are also winning at the game of evolution without reproducing yourself. Hamilton called this indirect fitness, and it is the outcome of the reproductive efforts of those to whom you are related. Imagine that you are actually helping yourself in the game of evolution if your sibling produces offspring that reproduce—even if you never see them or interact with them, or even know their names. Your total fitness is thus composed of your direct fitness plus your indirect fitness. In most cases, your indirect fitness will not exceed your direct fitness, but it is conceivable that it might.[6] And since it is *total lifetime fitness* that is significant, one could make a relative judgment about fitness based on current reproductive output that would be totally incorrect. This is particularly important to keep in mind for a long-lived species such as our own.

Greater Numbers of Survivors

The final piece of the short version of Darwinian evolution emphasized that where competition exists for scarce resources, those organisms that are most fit survive and reproduce in greater numbers than those that are less fit. It means that while individuals live and die, it is a species that undergoes extinction. Not all individuals with certain characteristics favorable to a particular environment will necessarily survive and reproduce; there are many non-Darwinian factors (unpredictable environmental change, random chance, and so on) that can affect survival. What Darwin meant is that if you possess characteristics that are fitness-enhancing in a particular environment, you will survive in greater numbers than those not possessing those favorable characters.

So is there some absolute number of individuals possessing a particular phenotype that must survive in order for you to win at evolution? How many grandchildren must you have to ensure that you are a winner in evolutionary terms? Must you produce 1.8, 2.4, 4, or even 7 offspring to "win"? Unfortunately, there is no absolute number that ensures you will win in the competitive arena of evolution. The only thing you must do is to produce more viable offspring that reproduce themselves than your local competition. It is not the number of offspring produced by competitors that are distantly removed, but ones with whom you compete daily.

Exactly What Is Evolution?

Evolution is one of the central concepts in biology, and because its definition is so simple and elegant, people are easily deceived into thinking that it is something it is not. The concept of evolution is widely deployed, yet there is a fundamental problem with how it is used. For example, many assume that evolution is somehow progressive. To most people, if something is evolving, there is an unstated assumption that it is improving. Of course, what constitutes improvement is another matter entirely.

The word evolution has its origin in Latin *evolvere*, means to unfold or unfurl. Nowhere in its definition is there a notion that progress is an inherent part of evolution. The hypothesis that there was some driving force in organisms that moved them in a unilinear manner toward perfection can be traced to Jean-Baptiste-Pierre-Antoine de Monet, Chevalier de Lamarck (1744–1829), and his idea of the inheritance of acquired characteristics. The notion that organisms are moving inexorably toward perfection has many implications that are beyond the scope of this chapter, most notably in current ideas about intelligent design and religion. However, it was Herbert Spencer (1820–1903) who suggested that social evolution was comparable to biological evolution and that human societies progressed from undifferentiated hordes into complex civilizations. Ideas about the progressive nature of evolution still hold considerable power in the common conception of evolution. In fact, Darwin did not refer to evolution in the *Origin* until the last page, the last paragraph, the last sentence, and the final word of his book:

> There is grandeur in this view of life, with its several powers, having been originally breathed by the Creator into a few forms or into one; and that, whilst this planet has gone cycling on according to the fixed law of gravity, from so simple a beginning endless forms most beautiful and most wonderful have been, and are being evolved.[7]

So if evolution is not progressive, what is it? As used in evolutionary anthropology, and for that matter in virtually all of science, evolution simply describes genetic changes in organisms over time. The definition has no hidden assumptions about organisms progressing to forms that are increasingly better adapted to their local environment. Genetic changes could produce forms that are better able to exploit their local environment; but just as easily, evolution can produce forms less able to survive. From a statistical perspective, the odds are that species extinction is much more likely than survival.

If this view of evolution is correct, what factors will bring about these genetic changes over time? There are four forces that can cause changes in gene frequency or produce evolutionary change in a population. Natural selection, the differential production and survival of offspring, is the force that most frequently comes to mind. It is certainly important, but the others deserve careful consideration as well. Mutation, the physical alteration of heritable genetic material, is the source of new genetic material in the population and that new genetic material can have positive, negative, or neutral effects. Rather than characterizing mutations as good or bad, it is best to think of them as having potential for both. Gene flow, the migration of fertile individuals and their subsequent reproduction, or the transfer of gametes between groups of individuals, is a lesser known agent of evolutionary change, but one that has had considerable importance in the evolution of early humans and their diffusion from Africa. Finally, there are changes in the genetic makeup of populations that are due to random events that have nothing to do with the process of organisms becoming better adapted to their environment, and this is called genetic drift.

Another evolutionarily important concept with which almost everyone has a passing familiarity is adaptation. This is the outcome of natural selection, since such selection is the only evolutionary force that can "choose" one phenotype over another. It is important to remember that natural selection is an evolutionary force that does not "know" if an organism possesses an underlying genotype that will be more successful than other genotypes in the population. Natural selection can only "see" the variation expressed in the phenotype. An individual could be the carrier of the most adaptive trait imaginable in a particular environment; but if it is not expressed, it cannot be selected. When we speak about an organism being "adapted" to its environment, we are really saying that it possesses a suite of traits or characteristics, expressed in the phenotype, that increase its fitness relative to individuals without those traits. We can talk about both process and outcome: about an organism becoming adapted to its environment, and about an organism possessing adaptations to an environment.

Underlying Assumptions of Darwinian Evolution

First, for a character or trait to be called Darwinian, there must be some phenotypic variation in the population under study. A phenotypic trait is one that is observable, and is the outcome of an interaction between the underlying genetic basis and the environment. What is of particular concern here is that there must be variation in the expression of the trait. Without variation in phenotype there would be no raw material on which natural selection could operate.

The genetic basis for all traits, whether they are expressed phenotypic traits or unexpressed traits, is the genotype. Not all of the genetic variation present in an organism is expressed in the phenotype. The variation in phenotype can be due to underlying genetic variation, as well as variation introduced by the environment. Indeed, the second assumption that must be met before a trait can be considered a Darwinian trait is that some proportion of the phenotypic variation must be due to underlying genetic variation. This is not the same as saying a trait is genetically determined, just that a proportion of the variation in the phenotype is due to underlying variation in the genes. That one can see variation in genetically identical offspring demonstrates that not all variation is due to genes.

Finally, to be considered Darwinian, a trait must have some effect on the fitness of the individual possessing it. While many traits fulfill this condition, a nontrivial number are simply adaptively neutral. These neutral traits are maintained in populations because there is no selection pressure against them.[8] Without fitness consequences for the possessor, no trait can be called a Darwinian trait; while perhaps interesting to specialists in genetics and evolutionary biology, the discussion of neutral traits is beyond the scope of this chapter.

Comparative Data

I have attempted to lay the foundation for the serious consideration that there are aspects of modern human behavior that should be called Darwinian evolutionary traits. Indeed, an evolutionary perspective has been enormously helpful in understanding such disparate aspects of human behavior as our reproductive strategies,[9] our parenting behavior,[10] and our tendency toward aggression, violence, and warfare.[11]

This perspective is important if we are to assess the possibility that genocide in general, and subaltern genocide in particular, may have an evolutionary basis. My goal in this section is to present comparative data on intraspecific killing in other animals, and to evaluate its importance for our discussion of subaltern genocide. The data are restricted to mammals, and to cases of individuals killing members of their own species in particular. (While intraspecific killing is well known in birds, insects, and fish, I have excluded those data based on their presumed phylogenetic distance from humans. I have also excluded cases of interspecific predatory behavior.)

I categorize intraspecific killing into three types: infanticide,[12] intragroup killing, and intergroup killing. Infanticide is a fascinating behavior: at first glance it seems to run counter to Darwinian principles, but on further examination it can be seen as a classic Darwinian trait.[13] Male infanticide in animals is a straightforward fitness-maximizing strategy whereby males will attack and kill infants sired by other males. The net result of the loss of a dependent infant is that mothers soon return to a sexually receptive state. This type of infanticide typically occurs in species where males immigrate between groups, but it has also been observed in species lacking male migration.[14] Female infanticide is also observed in a variety of animals; typically, the killing of dependent offspring of other females helps to secure additional resources for the perpetrator's offspring. Classifying killings into those perpetrated against members of a social group by members of that group, as distinct from killings perpetrated by nongroup members, also seems relevant. Given that genocide involves the killing of members of one group by members of another, differentiating among the types of lethal aggression seen in mammals seems justified if we are to search for examples that inform our study.

While chimpanzees are the primary focus of this comparative analysis, it is important to note that there are many other primate species, as well as other mammalian species, that form coalitions in order to enhance dominance status, gain access to estrus females, or gain access to preferred food resources. Most of the research on coalitions has been done on nonhuman primates, but there is good evidence that such diverse animals as South and Central American coatimundis, African spotted hyenas, and Atlantic spotted dolphins form coalitions for a variety of reasons. (See Table 8.1.) While the comparative data are instructive, they still leave unanswered questions. If coalition formation is as widespread as it appears among primates, and is as important in chimpanzee society as the field research indicates, then what does that mean for us? An in-depth discussion of coalition formation in humans is far beyond the scope of this paper, but there seem to be some interesting parallels, particularly with the behavior of wild chimpanzees.

Both male and female chimpanzees form temporary as well as long-term coalitions in both the field and captive conditions. Such coalitions seem to be important for both males and females, but for different reasons. Captive, group-living female chimpanzees as well as male chimpanzees form coalitions, but the functions of these coalitions seem to differ dramatically, with males forming coalitions in order to increase status while female coalitions are formed for protection from male aggression.[15] Oddly, however, female chimpanzees have been reported to form such coalitions in the natural setting at only one research site.[16] This suggests that female chimpanzees, like males, have the behavioral potential to engage in such interactions, but do so only when particular demographic and ecological conditions are present. While the precise reasons females engage in coalitions against males in the Budongo Forest, Uganda, are unclear, it may be that by participating in such coalitions, females reduce the levels of future aggression.[17]

In contrast, male chimpanzees routinely form coalitions that have been observed at several different field sites. Chimpanzee males form dyadic as well as triadic coalitions to enhance or maintain dominance status.[18] On one occasion, in the Kasakela chimpanzee community in the Gombe Stream National Park, the existing alpha male was overthrown by a team of two brothers (Figan and Faban) that left Figan as the top-ranking male.[19] Another coalitionary dominance takeover was observed in the M group in the Mahale Mountains of Tanzania. A deposed alpha male who had remained in the vicinity but some distance from his previous group took advantage of the death of one of the three dominant resident males and allied himself with the less dominant of the two remaining males and ultimately reasserted his alpha dominance position.[20]

Central to the question of genocide are observations of intergroup killing. If there is a parallel to human genocide among animals and in particular primates, it is likely the coalitionary killing observed in chimpanzees (*Pan troglodytes*).[21] Coalitionary attacks have also been reported in white-faced capuchin monkeys (*Cebus capucinus*) and spider monkeys (*Ateles geoffroyi yucatanensis*), but these are much rarer occurrences and do not appear to have the same underlying motivation as seen in chimpanzees. The real question is whether coalitionary killing in chimpanzees is truly homologous with human genocide; or whether certain attributes of human genocide serve to clearly differentiate our behavior from that of our closest primate relatives. The reports of intergroup killing are summarized in Table 8.2.

TABLE 8.1 CASES OF COALITIONARY KILLING BY ADULT NONHUMAN PRIMATES

Species	Common Name	Location	Details	Reference
Cebus capucinus	White-faced capuchin	Lomas Barbudal Biological Reserve, Costa Rica	1. a♂ wounded and evicted from group, later attacked again by group members and killed. 2. Lone nongroup ♂ (2–3 yr) was attacked by several group member males including adults, subadult, and juveniles. Victim was severely injured and died the next day.	(Gros-Louis et al. 2003)
Ateles geoffroyi	Spider monkey	Otoch Maàx Yetel Kooh, Mexico	1. Young adult ♂ (6–7 yr) group member attacked by three adult ♂ group members and killed.	(Valero et al. 2006)
Pan troglodytes	Chimpanzee		1. Prime adult ♂ of Kahama community (Godi) attacked by six adult ♂♂, adolescent ♂, and adult ♀ members of Kasakela. Godi suffered severe wounds, never seen again following attack, presumed dead. 2. Adult ♂ of Kahama community (Dé) attacked by three adult ♂ and one adult ♀ member of Kasakela. Dé suffered severe wounds and survived the attack, but was assumed to have died as result of attack. 3. Old adult ♂ of Kahama community (Goliath) was attacked by three adult ♂♂, and one adolescent ♂ members of Kasakela. Goliath suffered severe wounds, never seen again following attack, presumed dead.	(Goodall et al. 1979)

Species	Common Name	Location	Details	Reference
Pan troglodytes	Chimpanzee	Gombe Stream Reserve, Tanzania	1. Prime adult ♂ of Kahama community (Charlie) was presumably killed by party of five adult ♂♂ of Kasakela community. No details of attack available, but Charlie's body found two days later at Kahama Stream. 2. Prime young adult ♂ of Kahama community (Sniff) was attacked by three adult ♂♂ and one adolescent ♂ members of Kasakela. Sniff suffered severe injuries, seen the day after attack unable to move, never seen again, presumed dead. 3. Old adult ♀ of Kahama community (Madam Bee) attacked by four adult ♂♂ of Kasakela community. Madam Bee suffered severe injuries and died five days after the attack.	(Goodall 1986)
Pan troglodytes	Chimpanzee	Budongo Forest, Uganda	1. Prime adult ♂ of Sonso community (Zesta) was attacked by at least two adult ♂♂ of the Sonso community. Zesta suffered fatal injuries and died at the scene of the attack. (Suggested reason for attack was intra-community male sexual competition.)	(Fawcett and Muhumuza 2000)
Pan troglodytes	Chimpanzee	Kibale National Park, Uganda	1. Low ranking adult ♂ of the Ngogo community (GRA) was attacked by at least seven other adult ♂♂ of the Sonso community. GRA was held down during the attack by three adult ♂♂ but not completely immobilized. GRA suffered severe wounds, but survived attack only to die a week or so later from his wounds. (Suggested hypotheses include retribution for past behavior, contests over a status, or sexual access.)	(Watts 2004)

168

Species	Common Name	Location	Details	Reference
Pan troglodytes	Chimpanzee	Kibale National Park, Uganda	1. Adult ♂ from another community was feeding with other group members (at least two ♀♀ with infants, one adult ♂, one juvenile) when the adult ♂ was attacked and killed by five adult ♂♂ of the Ngogo community.	(Watts et al. 2006)
			2. Adult ♂ from Wantabu community was attacked by sixteen adult and three adolescent ♂♂ of the Ngogo community. Attacking ♂♂ did not press the attack continuously. Different ♂♂ participated. Wantabu ♂ died within ten minutes of start of attack.	
			3. Adult ♂ from another community was attacked by eight Ngogo ♂♂. Both adults and adolescents participated. Injured adult ♂ left area and was not seen again, presumed dead.	
			4. Adult ♂ from Sebitoli was presumably killed by ten ♂♂ from the Kanyawara community. The attack was not witnessed, but victim was found already dead, surrounded by Kanyawara ♂♂	
			5. Juvenile ♂ (from neighboring community) was attacked by ≈ eight Ngogo ♂♂. The victim suffered severe wounds, but was not followed after the attack and presumably died.	

Species	Common Name	Location	Details	Reference
Pan troglodytes	Chimpanzee	Gombe Stream Reserve, Tanzania	1. Juvenile ♂ (≈10 yr) from the Kalande community was attacked by three adult ♂♂ from the Kasekala community. Victim suffered severe injuries which were presumably fatal, although he was not seen after the attack. 2. Adolescent ♂ (≈12–14 yr) of the Mitumba community was found dead. Suffered wounds that were consistent with those administered during chimpanzee attacks. Males from adjacent community Kasekala were within 1 km of site of victim's body.	(Wilson et al. 2004)
Pan troglodytes	Chimpanzee	Mahale Mountains National Park, Tanzania	1. Six adult ♂♂ members of K group killed between 1969 and 1980. Sobongo and Kamemanfu killed by M group ♂♂. All ♂♂ that disappeared were healthy and not senile.	(Nishida and Kawanaka 1985)
Pan troglodytes	Chimpanzee	Mahale Mountains National Park, Tanzania	1. Adult ♂ (Ntologi) of M group was found dead in center of M group territory dead. His death followed numerous coalitionary attacks by former subordinates after his defeat as α ♂ of M group	(Nishida 1996)

Table 8.2 Examples of Species Who Routinely Form Coalitions

Species	Common Name	Details	Reference
Macaca thibetana	Tibetan macaques	Males form coalitions to maintain dominance rankings against lower ranking males or immigrants.	(Berman et al. 2007)
Macaca mulatta	Rhesus monkeys	Matrilineal kin relations are the basis of coalitions to maintain dominance rank.	(Kutsukake and Hasegawa 2005)
Cercopithecus aethiops	Vervet monkeys	Females formed coalitions to accelerate integration into a new group.	(Hauser et al. 1986)
Cebus capucinus	Capuchin monkeys	Females form coalitions against other females as well as males to maintain dominance hierarchy.	(Manson et al. 1999; Perry 1997; Vogel et al. 2007)
Cercopithecus mitis	Blue monkeys	Females form coalitions with other group females to defend territorial boundaries.	(Cords 2002)
Papio cynocephalus	Savanna baboons	Female coalitions important in determining dominance relationships and access to resources.	(Silk et al. 2004)
Crocuta crocuta	Spotted hyenas	Males form coalitions to rise in status in female dominated heterosexual groups.	(East and Hofer 2001; Szykman et al. 2003)
Nasua narica	White-nosed coatis	Kin-related individuals form bands and direct aggressive behavior toward nongroup unrelated individuals.	(Gompper et al. 1997)
Stenella frontalis	Atlantic spotted dolphins	Formed coalitions of young males for social play.	(Herzing and Johnson 1997)

There are several important things to note about Table 8.2. The most obvious is that there is a decided mismatch in competitive abilities between aggressor and victim. Killing in nonhuman primates is not an individual effort, and more importantly there has been no instance of lethal dyadic aggression observed among any adult apes. This is not to say that there is not aggression between and among individuals, but when it escalates to the level of lethal force, individuals give way to coalitions. In order to kill another, coalitions of individuals are implicated, not single individuals.

Second, an examination of the primates that have been observed engaging in coalitionary killing reveals a strong bias toward chimpanzees. There has been considerable energy expended among primatologists to explain this bias,[22] and a detailed discussion of the ecological as well as social factors involved in chimpanzees' disproportionate levels of lethal coalitionary aggression is beyond the scope of this paper. Suffice it to say that many feel it has to do with the high degree of male philopatry[23] and female migration between male coalitionary bands; but a completely satisfactory explanation remains elusive.

Finally, a careful examination of the coalitionary data for chimpanzees shows that it is males that are the most frequent perpetrators of fatal aggression. It is true that females may participate in these episodes,[24] but they are virtually never the initiators. Males are also the most frequent targets of these lethal aggressive coalitions, especially those from neighboring communities. What emerges is a picture of groups of male chimpanzees periodically patrolling the boundaries of their territory, looking for intruders. When they encounter members from other groups, there is a nontrivial probability that some sort of aggressive encounter will ensue, and in a few cases these encounters have escalated in lethal aggression. It appears that this coalitionary killing occurs when the probability of injury to the initiator is low, and is most likely when the killing is carried out by a group of individuals.

So What About Subaltern Genocide?

We now return to the question posed at the beginning of this chapter. Are humans the only animal species in which oppressed groups seek to gain revenge and liberation by waging genocide against their oppressors? It is clear that chimpanzees engage in coalitionary killing which has on occasion resulted in the extinction of one group at the hands of another; but does this coalitionary killing among chimpanzees exhibit some of the same patterns and dynamics as *subaltern* genocide in humans?

As one might expect, the answer to that question is complicated. Two factors suggest that chimpanzees do not engage in behavior that is directly comparable to human genocide. First, as we have seen, lethal aggression in chimpanzees is not an individual event, but neither is genocide typically committed by single individuals. Among chimpanzees, coalitions of individuals in all observed cases were the perpetrators of the attacks. Second, the attacks are opportunistic and seem to occur only when the cost of the attack to the perpetrator is low and the likelihood of success is high. Certainly, any historian of human genocide will recognize these as major differences.

Given our understanding of chimpanzee behavior, then, it seems likely that the answer to my question is "yes": humans *are* the only animal species in which oppressed groups seek to gain revenge and liberation by lethal aggression against their oppressors. One of the critical points of the discussion is the behavior of groups. The coalitions among chimpanzee males have some extraordinary properties (e.g., longevity of associations, mutual support, sharing of resources), but there seems to be a lack of coordinated action of entire groups. Interestingly, some primatologists have speculated that there may be an element of revenge among chimpanzees, a characteristic motivating factor in subaltern genocide.

Robert Trivers, in his seminal paper on the evolution of reciprocal altruism,[25] used the term "moralistic aggression" to identify a type of behavior that would ensure that an altruist would not continue to engage in such behavior in the absence of reciprocation, to frighten a non-reciprocator with injury, or in extreme cases to kill, injure, or exile a non-reciprocator.[26] It has been suggested that "elements of revenge may enter into it (*the attack*) as may dissatisfaction about the cost/benefit balance of the relationship (e.g., lack of reciprocation). It is these more complex, cognition-based emotions that we most clearly associate with the human sense of justice and morality."[27] Chimpanzees have been characterized as the only species to exhibit revenge where individuals "tend to intervene against individuals who intervene against themselves."[28] Instead of risking injury by retaliating against more dominant individuals, subordinate chimpanzees often wait for opportunities to attack more dominant individuals while they are engaged in conflicts with others.[29] So if chimpanzees are capable of engaging in behavior that we could label as revenge, it is possible that their behavior may have more in common with subaltern genocide than it initially appears.

Like our primate relatives, there certainly exists the potential in modern humans to commit violent coalitionary aggressive behavior, and that potential has a distinctly evolutionary basis. Humans have the genetic potential to act in ways that have been favored by natural selection and evolution, and in some cases that means committing lethal acts against other humans. In most cases, humans lack the physical strength to engage in lethal hand-to-hand combat as do chimpanzees, and hence must rely on tools for our aggressive encounters—which makes our aggressive behavior more deadly than that of any nonhuman. Given that we all have the evolutionary predisposition to commit lethal violence under certain circumstances, why is there variation in the expression of this capacity? Why are not all humans genocidal? What are the constraints that limit the expression of this evolved capacity?

Here we must invoke two additional factors to explain our behavior: our experience during sensitive developmental periods in our early life, and the sociocultural and environmental circumstances in which we find ourselves as adults. It is certainly a widely accepted fact that aggressive behavior expressed in adulthood is influenced by the type of environment in which we grow up, and that the environment has many subtle elements including parents, siblings, early educational experiences, different parenting practices, and so on.[30] This developmental underpinning of aggressive behavior has been well studied by social scientists, and while there is much left to understand, it is clear that growing up in an environment where critical resources (food, shelter, care, comfort) are limited and unpredictable contributes significantly to the likelihood of the expression of uncontrolled aggressive and antisocial behavior as an adult. But is a particular type of early experience the final arbiter of adult behavior? Absolutely not.

Even though individuals may have had a developmental experience that enhances the probability that they will commit violent acts, the last ingredient must also be in place, and that is a sociocultural and environmental situation that allows for the expression of that behavior. There are some environmental conditions that are particularly favorable for the expression of genocide, but these conditions are not sufficient by themselves to cause it.

Conditions Promoting Genocide

Xenophobia

One of humans' great adaptations is a reliance on culture as a fundamental determinant of our social behavior. Humans are successful because we live in groups and have developed cultural traits that enhance the benefits of group living. But there is a cost to sociality, and that is prejudice and intolerance toward nongroup members. It is clear that in our evolutionary past, xenophobia was adaptive and fitness-enhancing. We can imagine that nongroup members posed a threat for a variety of reasons, not the least of which was their potential for commandeering critical resources (food, territory, mates), their potential for providing misinformation about the location of necessary future resources (locations of water holes, game paths, salt licks), and their potential challenge to other cultural beliefs (symbolic identity, supernatural powers) by polluting them with outside influences. It is relatively easy to imagine that the chance meeting of two proto-human bands could have a violent outcome.

On the other hand, we do not greet all strangers with violence and hostility. The difference seems to be in the recognition of kin relationships and immediate inferred intent. Anthropologists have long been interested in rituals and greetings between humans because it is in the context of these encounters that potentially lethal interactions can occur but often do not. For example, among the Tuareg, nomads living in the Western Sahara, encounters between individuals are rare but are culturally defined. Since visibility in the desert is generally good (save for the occasional simoon or scirocco), it is usually quite easy to spot another traveler in the distance. Assessment of the intentions of a stranger begins immediately upon sighting. First, there is an assessment of the posture and riding style of the other, the type of camel, the direction of travel, and so on. Closer approach calls for an escalation of threat assessment techniques and finally, when the two individuals are literally within arm's reach of each other, they start to identify common kin relations.[31] Such rituals of greeting and assessment have long been the providence of anthropologists,[32] and such research has demonstrated not only the importance of first impressions, but the ability of strangers to identify kin relations as a way of avoiding conflict.

The differential treatment of those to whom we are genetically related has a long and distinguished evolutionary history, ranging from bees and wasps to naked mole rats and to the apes. Since we share some proportion of our genes with our siblings, cousins, aunts, uncles, and so on, it behooves us to treat them differently than we would a totally unrelated individual. This differential treatment of relatives enhances our own indirect fitness, as previously discussed.

It is interesting to see how our reliance on culture has amplified and elaborated this potential. Our culture allows us to share fundamental aspects of group identity (kinship, if you will) and in turn to treat members of our group as our kin, whether or not genetic relatedness exists. Hence we have moved beyond the level of groups of individuals who are genetically related, to larger coalitions that rely on culture to trick us into believing all our group members are kin. This trickery has been extraordinarily important in the course of human evolution because it allowed individuals who were not related to form alliances and coalitions that would have been impossible based solely on true kinship. As I have suggested, the cost of this trickery is a widespread intolerance for "nonkin" individuals, but that cost is no different than without trickery. Our xenophobic response to nongroup members was certainly adaptive during the course of our evolution, but what was once highly adapted has proven to be quite costly in modern society. In fact, one would predict that the greater the degree of kin recognition among members of a coalition or alliance, the greater the tendency would be to fight in support of other group members. Rephrasing slightly, it may be that the more susceptible to the trickery of evolution, the greater the potential for intergroup aggression.[33]

Limited Availability of High Value Concentrated Resources

External environmental and social factors also contribute to creating an environment in which subaltern genocide could flourish. In addition to our xenophobic tendencies, living in an environment where there are limited high value resources is likely to exacerbate any predispositions we might have. We know that the distribution of resources plays a vital role in the behavior of our nonhuman primate relatives, and it is the lack of access to critical resources that dictates much of human behavior as well. Subaltern groups are often characterized by their lack of access to critical resources, and it has been suggested that much of the humiliation and envy they suffer is directly attributable to differential resource allocation.[34]

Other Individual and Social Problems

Other individual factors have also been implicated in the likelihood of the occurrence of genocide (e.g., relative importance of social status and authority, degree of acceptance of social identity and acceptance of in-group and out-group boundaries, susceptibility to social influence). In addition, authors have noted that a destabilizing political crisis will also enhance the probability of genocide.[35] While it is unlikely that any of these contributing factors would inevitably lead to populations committing genocide, the confluence of several of them has often proven sufficient.

Relevance of the Comparative Data

It is clear that when environmental conditions are encountered that tip the cost-benefit equation toward benefits, both long and short term, chimpanzees as well as humans are capable of lethal aggression. While genocide as a behavioral practice has been viewed as a struggle between the powerful and powerless,[36] from a chimpanzee's perspective it is clear that any individual will take advantage of an opportunity to enhance its reproductive success. If you are male, it is by recruitment of females, or if you are a female it is by accumulation of resources which can be translated into more or healthier offspring.

The real value of the comparative data is to demonstrate the capacity of all individuals to commit lethal violence under the right set of circumstances. Chimpanzees are particularly calculating in this regard, and only kill conspecifics when the probability of success is high and the risk of injury is low. For chimpanzees, it is not a question of individual fighting ability, but of the combined fighting abilities of a coalition of individuals against a single victim. If this cost/benefit assessment is an intrinsic part of the expression of lethal levels of aggression in primates, then it should not surprise us that humans follow similar paths. This is to say that under the right set of developmental, ecological, and social conditions we all can express violent aggressive potential, as well as extreme submission; it simply takes a particular set of circumstances to elicit the behavior. A culture characterized by rigid status differentials and dominance relationships, widespread poverty, highly concentrated wealth among a small group of individuals, and clearly and rigidly divided cultural groups are conditions that provide the environment in which the human capacity for lethal aggression might be played out. Those individuals who are most disenfranchised economically, politically, and socially are likely to be the perpetrators.

An evolutionary perspective would predict that where such conditions exist, subaltern genocide is a possibility. Moreover, our comparative and evolutionary perspective also suggests that subaltern genocide is possible where groups of people assess the probabilities of success (lethal aggression against the oppressor) and failure (risk of fatal injury) and those probabilities tip in favor of aggression. To state it more bluntly, subaltern genocide is not an inevitable consequence of oppression, but the potential for lethal aggression among the oppressed against the oppressors is a part of every human's behavioral potential. When placed in a particular set of ecological, social, and political conditions, any individual is capable of subaltern genocide.

The Darwinian approach to genocide has a number of strengths that should make it relevant to genocide scholars. It is clear that humans have a long and distinguished evolutionary history of intraspecific violence. Lethal aggression is the ultimate expression of the capacity, but, as I have noted, it is not inevitable. If we can identify situations where there exist significant differences in allocation of resources, dominance and oppression of minority populations, exaggeration and emphasis on cultural themes of nationalism and distrust of nongroup members, then it may be possible to head off genocide before it starts. Failure to fully recognize that all humans have the capacity for genocide will undoubtedly resign us to witness its horror again.

What can we say about an evolutionary perspective on subaltern genocide? An evolutionary perspective tells us that in order to understand something that has such deep historical roots as seen in various forms of genocide, we need to look at the larger picture of human evolution to make any sense out of this seemingly maladaptive behavior. Over evolutionary time, organisms have been favored by natural selection to act in ways that allowed them to survive, reproduce, and see that their offspring reproduced. Any anatomical, physiological, or behavioral trait that aided in the process was carried along with genes into the next generation. Human ancestors who were slightly more willing to aid a relative, even if they recognized the relationship or not, were actually helping their own genes survive. We need not impute conscious choice in the decision-making process to give aid to another; it is simply that those who did offer aid to relatives survived in greater numbers than those who did not. Once the practice of aiding kin was established, it provided a powerful set of rules that would guide much of human behavior.

We also know that because an individual human is no match for a variety of the predators present during our evolutionary history, the only way that humans could be successful was to band together into small groups where they could enjoy considerable advantage over many other larger and stronger animals. In addition, social living provided immense advantages in other competitive arenas with larger groups dominating smaller groups, and groups developing a host of social customs that fostered intragroup loyalty and intergroup hostility. It is easy to imagine that individuals who were the most articulate and persuasive would enjoy high status along with individuals who possessed certain cognitive or physical skills that enhanced the welfare of all individuals in the group. It is also easy to imagine that occasionally there existed a conspiracy of factors creating an environment that was favorable for genocide. Historically, the powerful have generally succeeded in eliminating the less powerful, but there are occasions when the less powerful have banded together to carry out lethal aggression against their oppressors. We have reviewed the evidence that coalitions are an important part of the social fabric for many primate societies and in particular chimpanzees. We have also noted the potential for chimpanzees to engage in coalitionary killing both within their own group but more often of males from other groups. This is not surprising if one accepts the Darwinian argument that any of us have the potential to commit lethal aggression under the right circumstances. To think that the social forces that shape society preclude any particular segment from the predisposition to commit lethal aggression is naïve at best. The important point of this chapter is that we all have the potential to engage in genocide, subaltern or not, under the right set of circumstances.

It should come as no surprise that the oppressed have turned on their oppressors with astonishing ferocity. Where circumstances favor the expression of genocide, we should always be mindful of the potential for the expression of subaltern genocide with considerable rapidity if circumstances allow it. Recognizing the panhuman nature of our behavioral potential for lethal aggression should alert us to the possibility that any human group, if placed in the right environmental, political, and social circumstances, can commit astonishingly brutal behavior.

So what conclusions can be drawn from this discussion of lethal aggression in chimpanzees and its relevance to human subaltern genocide? To answer the questions initially posed: Are humans the only animal species in which some groups wage genocide against their oppressors? It seems that while there are similarities to coalitionary killing in chimpanzees, subaltern genocide among humans is an elaboration on a theme rather than something that is fundamentally distinct from chimpanzee behavior. We know that subaltern genocide may be motivated by similar fundamental impulses, but it is often an individual behavior in humans, and never a behavior committed by single individuals among chimpanzees. No instances of dyadic lethal encounters have ever been recorded among chimpanzees. Of course, our use of weapons changes the cost/benefit ratio of such interactions to allow for individuals to carry out lethal aggression with considerably reduced risk of harm when compared to chimpanzees. It is also reasonable to conclude that human culture and our reliance on learned behavior have shaped and molded the evolutionary predispositions into the forms of genocide seen today. While there is no gene for genocide, there is strong evidence that there are evolutionary predispositions that we share with our closest primate relatives that allow for the expression of this type of violent aggressive behavior, and these predispositions have been elaborated in the context of human culture.

Notes

1. Goodall, *The Chimpanzees of Gombe*, 507–10.
2. Tooby and Cosmides, "The Psychological Foundations of Culture."
3. Watson, *Behaviorism*, 82.
4. Scott, *Weapons of the Weak*.
5. Hamilton, "The Genetical Evolution of Social Behaviour. I" and "The Genetical Evolution of Social Behaviour. II."
6. Imagine the case of one sibling in a large family entering the priesthood. In doing so this individual foregoes the possibility of any direct fitness, but his overall fitness could be considerably greater than zero due to the indirect fitness effects of the reproductive efforts of his siblings.
7. Darwin, *On the Origin of Species By Means of Natural Selection or the Preservation of Favoured Races in the Struggle for Life*, 445.
8. Charlat, Ballard, and Mercot, "What Maintains Noncytoplasmic Incompatibility Inducing Wolbachia in Their Hosts," 322–30; Joshi, Castillo, and Mueller, "The Contribution of Ancestry, Chance, and Past and Ongoing Selection to Adaptive Evolution," 147–62; Pyle and Richmond, "Genetic Basis of Aristal Morphology in *Drosophila Melanogaster* and Its Correlation with Behavior," 297.
9. Betzig, *Despotism and Differential Reproduction*; Betzig, Mulder, and Turke, *Human Reproductive Behaviour*; Chisholm, *Death, Hope, and Sex*; Ellison, *Reproductive Ecology and Human Evolution*; Short, "On the Evolution of Human Reproduction," 5.

10. Campbell, *A Mind of Her Own*; Daly and Wilson, *The Truth about Cinderella*; Ellis and Bjorklund, *Origins of the Social Mind*.

11. Buss and Shackelford, "Human Aggression in Evolutionary Psychological Perspective," 605; van der Dennen, *The Origin of War*; Wrangham and Peterson, *Demonic Males*; Wrangham, Wilson, and Muller, "Comparative Rates of Violence in Chimpanzees and Humans," 14.

12. I have excluded infanticide from these analyses because it is clear that there are very different evolutionary strategies in play when it comes to killing of particular infants.

13. Hausfater and Hrdy, *Infanticide: Comparative and Evolutionary Perspectives*; van Schaik and Janson, *Infanticide by Males and Its Implications*.

14. Species include Mongolian gerbils (*Meriones unguiculatus*), wild rabbits (*Oryctolagus cuniculus*), Hanuman langurs (*Presbytis entellus*), meadow voles (*Microtus pennsylvanicus*), howler monkeys (*Alouatta palliata*), lions (*Panthera leo*), crab-eating macaques (*Macaca fascicularis*), chacma baboons (*Papio ursinus*), chimpanzees (*Pan troglodytes*), brown bears (*Ursus arctos*), as well as a variety of other rodents, mammals, and birds.

15. Baker and Smuts, "Social Relationships of Female Chimpanzees," 227; de Waal, "Sex Differences in the Formation of Coalitions Among Chimpanzees," 239.

16. Newton-Fisher, "Female Coalitions Against Male Aggression in Wild Chimpanzees of the Budongo Forest," 1589.

17. Ibid., 1591.

18. Nishida and Hosaka, "Coalition Strategies among Adult Male Chimpanzees of the Mahale Mountains, Tanzania"; Riss and Goodall, "The recent rise to the alpha-rank in a population of free-living chimpanzees," 134; Watts, "Reciprocity and Interchange in the Social Relationships of Wild Male Chimpanzees," 343.

19. Riss and Goodall, "The Recent Rise to the Alpha-Rank in a Population of Free-Living Chimpanzees," 137.

20. Nishida, "Review of Recent Findings on Mahale Chimpanzees."

21. Wrangham, "Evolution of Coalitionary Killing," 1.

22. Roscoe, "Intelligence, Coalitional Killing, and the Antecedents of War," 485; Wilson, Wallauer, and Pusey, "New Cases of Intergroup Violence among Chimpanzees in Gombe National Park, Tanzania," 523; Watts, "Intracommunity Coalitionary Killing of an Adult Male Chimpanzee at Ngogo, Kibale National Park, Uganda," 507; Wilson and Wrangham, "Intergroup Relations in Chimpanzees," 363; Wrangham, "Evolution of Coalitionary Killing," 2.

23. In the study of animal behavior, philopatry (Greek, "home-loving") is the tendency of an animal to return to or remain in a specific location in order to breed or feed. Philopatry can manifest itself in several ways, and can be applied to more than just the area in which an animal was born. Species that return to their birthplace in order to breed are said to exhibit natal philopatry. Species that return in consecutive years to the same breeding site or territory exhibit breeding philopatry or site fidelity. Philopatry is generally believed to be an adaptation to a specific set of environmental circumstances.

24. See the example in the first paragraphs of this chapter.

25. Reciprocal altruism is a form of altruism in which one organism provides a benefit to another without any immediate compensatory benefit, but with the expectation that the altruistic act will be repaid in the future.

26. Trivers, "The Evolution of Reciprocal Altruism," 35.

27. de Waal, "The Chimpanzee's Sense of Social Regularity and Its Relation to the Human Sense of Justice," 342.

28. de Waal and Luttrell, "Mechanisms of Social Reciprocity in Three Primate Species," 114.

29. Ibid., 115.

30. Anderson and Bushman, "Human Aggression," 27; Cairns, "Aggression from a Developmental Perspective"; Constantino, "Early Relationships and the Development of Aggression in Children," 259; Ramirez, "Hormones and Aggression in Childhood and Adolescence," 621; Tremblay, "The Development of Aggressive Behaviour During Childhood," 129.

31. Youssouf, Grimshaw, and Bird, "Greetings in the Desert," 797.

32. Firth, "Verbal and Bodily Rituals of Greeting and Parting"; Goffman, *The Presentation of Self in Everyday Life.*

33. Brannigan, "Criminology and the Holocaust," 257. See Cashdan, "Ethnocentrism and Xenophobia," 761, for an interesting but incomplete test of this hypothesis.

34. Kamola, "The Global Coffee Economy and the Production of Genocide in Rwanda," 571; Niazi, "The Ecology of Genocide in Rwanda," 223.

35. Woolf and Hulsizer, "Psychosocial Roots of Genocide," 101.

36. Freeman, "Puritans and Pequots," 278; Longman, "Genocide and Socio-Political Change," 18; Longman, "Empowering the Weak and Protecting the Powerful," 49; Mirkovic, "Ethnic Conflict and Genocide," 191; Ndikumana, "Institutional Failure and Ethnic Conflicts in Burundi," 29; Newbury, "Understanding Genocide," 73; Uvin, "Ethnicity and Power in Burundi and Rwanda," 253.

Works Cited

Anderson, Craig A., and Brad J. Bushman. "Human Aggression." *Annual Review of Psychology* 53, no. 1 (2002): 27–51.

Baker, Kate C., and Barbara B. Smuts. "Social Relationships of Female Chimpanzees: Diversity Between Captive Social Groups." In *Chimpanzee Cultures,* ed. R. W. Wrangham, W. C. McGrew, F. B. M. de Waal, and P. G. Heltne, 227–42. Cambridge, Mass.: Harvard University Press, 1994.

Berman, Carol M., Consuel Ionica, and Jinhua Li. "Supportive and Tolerant Relationships among Male Tibetan Macaques at Huangshan, China." *Behaviour* 144, no. 6 (2007): 631–61.

Betzig, Laura L. *Despotism and Differential Reproduction: A Darwinian View of History.* New York: Aldine, 1986.

Betzig, Laura L., Monique Borgerhoff Mulder, and Paul Turke, eds. *Human Reproductive Behaviour: A Darwinian Perspective.* Cambridge: Cambridge University Press, 1988.

Brannigan, Augustine. "Criminology and the Holocaust: Xenophobia, Evolution, and Genocide." *Crime & Delinquency* 44, no. 2 (1998): 257–76.

Buss, David M., and Todd K. Shackelford. "Human Aggression in Evolutionary Psychological Perspective." *Clinical Psychology Review* 17, no. 6 (1997): 605–19.

Cairns, Robert B. "Aggression from a Developmental Perspective: Genes, Environments and Interactions." In *Genetics of Criminal and Antisocial Behaviour,* ed. G. R. Bock and J. A. Goode, 45–56. New York: Wiley, 1996

Campbell, Anne. *A Mind of Her Own: The Evolutionary Psychology of Women.* New York: Oxford University Press, 2002

Cashdan, Elizabeth. "Ethnocentrism and Xenophobia: A Cross-Cultural Study." *Current Anthropology* 42, no. 5 (2001): 760–65.

Charlat, Sylvain, J. W. Ballard, and H. Mercot. "What Maintains Noncytoplasmic Incompatibility Inducing Wolbachia in Their Hosts: A Case Study from a Natural *Drosophila Yakuba* Population." *Journal of Evolutionary Biology* 17, no. 2 (2004): 322–30.

Chisholm, James S. *Death, Hope, and Sex: Steps to an Evolutionary Ecology of Mind and Morality.* Cambridge: Cambridge University Press, 1999.

Constantino, John N. "Early Relationships and the Development of Aggression in Children." *Harvard Review of Psychiatry* 2, no. 5 (1995): 259–73.

Cords, Marina. "Friendship among Adult Female Blue Monkeys (*Cercopithecus mitis*)." *Behaviour* 139, nos. 2–3 (2002): 291–314.

Daly, Martin, and Margo Wilson. *The Truth about Cinderella: A Darwinian View of Parental Love.* New Haven: Yale University Press, 1998.

Darwin, Charles R. *On the Origin of Species By Means of Natural Selection or the Preservation of Favoured Races in the Struggle for Life.* London: J. Murray. 1859.

de Waal, Frans B. M. "The Chimpanzee's Sense of Social Regularity and Its Relation to the Human Sense of Justice." *American Behavioral Scientist* 34, no. 3 (1991): 335–49.

————. "Sex Differences in the Formation of Coalitions among Chimpanzees." *Ethology and Sociobiology* 5, no. 4 (1984): 239–55.

de Waal, Frans B. M., and Lesleigh M. Luttrell. "Mechanisms of Social Reciprocity in Three Primate Species: Symmetrical Relationship Characteristics or Cognition?" *Ethology and Sociobiology* 9, nos. 2–4 (1988): 101–18.

East, Marion L., and Heribert Hofer. "Male Spotted Hyenas (*Crocuta crocuta*) Queue for Status in Social Groups Dominated by Females." *Behavioral Ecology* 12, no. 5 (2001): 558–68.

Ellis, Bruce J., and David F. Bjorklund. *Origins of the Social Mind: Evolutionary Psychology and Child Development.* New York: Guilford Press, 2005.

Ellison, Peter T., ed. *Reproductive Ecology and Human Evolution.* New York: Aldine de Gruyter, 2001.

Fawcett, Katie, and Geresomu Muhumuza. "Death of a Wild Chimpanzee Community Member: Possible Outcome of Intense Sexual Competition." *American Journal of Primatology* 51, no. 4 (2000): 243–47.

Firth, Raymond. "Verbal and Bodily Rituals of Greeting and Parting." In *The Interpretation of Ritual: Essays in Honour of A. I. Richards,* ed. J. S. La Fontaine and A. I. Richards, 1–38. London: Tavistock Publishers, 1972.

Freeman, Michael. "Puritans and Pequots: The Question of Genocide." *New England Quarterly* 68, no. 2 (1995): 278–93.

Goffman, Erving. *The Presentation of Self in Everyday Life.* Harmondsworth: Penguin, 1971.

Gompper, Matthew E., John L. Gittleman, and Robert K. Wayne. "Genetic Relatedness, Coalitions and Social Behaviour of White-Nosed Coatis, *Nasua narica.*" *Animal Behaviour* 53, no. 4 (1997): 781–97.

Goodall, Jane. *The Chimpanzees of Gombe: Patterns of Behavior.* Cambridge, Mass.: Harvard University Press, 1986.

Goodall, Jane, Adriano Bandora, Emilie Bergmann, Curt Busse, Hilali Matama, Esilom Mpongo, Ann Pierce, and David Riss. "Intercommunity Interactions in the Chimpanzee Population of the Gombe National Park." In *The Great Apes,* ed. D. A. Hamburg and E. R. McCown, 13–53. Menlo Park, Calif.: Benjamin/Cummings Publishing Co., 1979.

Gros-Louis, Julie, Susan Perry, and Joseph H. Manson. "Violent Coalitionary Attacks and Intraspecific Killing in Wild White-Faced Capuchin Monkeys (*Cebus capucinus*)." *Primates* 44, no. 4 (2003): 341–46.

Hamilton, William D. "The Genetical Evolution of Social Behaviour. I." *Journal of Theoretical Biology* 7, no. 1 (1964a): 1–16.

_____. "The Genetical Evolution of Social Behaviour. II." *Journal of Theoretical Biology* 7, no. 1 (1964b): 17–52.

Hauser, Marc D., Dorothy L. Cheney, and Robert M. Seyfarth. "Group Extinction and Fusion in Free-Ranging Vervet Monkeys." *American Journal of Primatology* 11, no. 1 (1986): 63–77.

Hausfater, Glenn, and Sarah Blaffer Hrdy, eds. *Infanticide: Comparative and Evolutionary Perspectives.* Hawthorne, N.Y.: Aldine Publishing Co., 1984.

Herzing, Denise L. and C. M. Johnson. "Interspecific Interactions between Atlantic Spotted Dolphins (*Stenella frontalis*) and Bottlenose Dolphins (*Tursiops truncatus*) in the Bahamas, 1985–1995." *Aquatic Mammals* 23, no. 2 (1997): 85–99.

Joshi, Amitabh, Robinson B. Castillo, and Laurence D. Mueller. "The Contribution of Ancestry, Chance, and Past and Ongoing Selection to Adaptive Evolution." *Journal of Genetics* 82, no. 3 (2003): 147–62.

Kamola, Isaac A. "The Global Coffee Economy and the Production of Genocide in Rwanda." *Third World Quarterly* 28, no. 3 (2007): 571–92.

Kutsukake, Nobuyuki, and Toshikazu Hasegawa. "Dominance Turnover Between an Alpha and a Beta Male and Dynamics of Social Relationships in Japanese Macaques." *International Journal of Primatology* 26, no. 4 (2005): 775–800.

Longman, Timothy P. "Empowering the Weak and Protecting the Powerful: The Contradictory Nature of Churches in Central Africa." *African Studies Review* 41, no. 1 (1998): 49–72.

_____. "Genocide and Socio-Political Change: Massacres in Two Rwandan Villages." *Issue* 23, no. 2 (1995): 18–21.

Manson, Joseph H., Lisa M. Rose, Susan Perry, and Julie Gros-Louis. "Dynamics of Female-Female Relationships in Wild *Cebus capucinus:* Data from Two Costa Rican Sites." *International Journal of Primatology* 20, no. 5 (1999): 679–706.

Mirkovic, Damir. "Ethnic Conflict and Genocide: Reflections on Ethnic Cleansing in the Former Yugoslavia." *Annals of the American Academy of Political and Social Science* 548 (November 1996): 191–99.

Ndikumana, Leonce. "Institutional Failure and Ethnic Conflicts in Burundi." *African Studies Review* 41, no. 1 (1998): 29–47.

Newbury, David. "Understanding Genocide." *African Studies Review* 41, no. 1 (1998): 73–97.

Newton-Fisher, Nicholas E. "Female Coalitions Against Male Aggression in Wild Chimpanzees of the Budongo Forest." *International Journal of Primatology* 27, no. 6 (2006): 1589–99.

Niazi, Tarique. "The Ecology of Genocide in Rwanda." *International Journal of Contemporary Sociology* 39, no. 2 (2002): 223–48.

Nishida, Toshisada. "The Great Chimpanzee Ruler Killed by a Coalition of Previous Group Mates: Cruel Political Dynamics in Wild Chimpanzees." *Asahi-Shimbun* (Osaka, Japan), January 31, 1996.

_____. "Review of Recent Findings on Mahale Chimpanzees: Implications and Future Research Directions." In *Chimpanzee Cultures,* ed. R. W. Wrangham, W. C. McGrew, F. B. M. de Waal, and P. G. Heltne, 373–96. Cambridge, Mass.: Harvard University Press, 1994.

Nishida, Toshisada, and Kazuhiko Hosaka. "Coalition strategies among Adult Male Chimpanzees of the Mahale Mountains, Tanzania." In *Great Ape Societies,* ed. W. C. McGrew, L. F. Marchant, and T. Nishida, 114–34. New York: Cambridge University Press, 1996.

Nishida, Toshisada, and Kenji Kawanaka. "Within-Group Cannibalism by Adult Male Chimpanzees." *Primates* 26, no. 3 (1985): 274–84.

Perry, Susan. "Male-Female Social Relationships in Wild White-Faced Capuchins (*Cebus capucinus*)." *Behaviour* 134, nos. 7–8 (1997): 477–510.

Pyle, D. W., and R. C. Richmond. "Genetic Basis of Aristal Morphology in *Drosophila melanogaster* and Its Correlation with Behavior: Selection for Increased and Decreased Aristal Branching." *Behavior Genetics* 9, no. 4 (1979): 297–308.

Ramirez, J. M. "Hormones and Aggression in Childhood and Adolescence." *Aggression and Violent Behavior* 8, no. 6 (2003): 621–44.

Riss, David C., and Jane Goodall. "The Recent Rise to the Alpha-Rank in a Population of Free-Living Chimpanzees." *Folia Primatologica* 27, no. 2 (1977): 134–51.

Roscoe, Paul. "Intelligence, Coalitional Killing, and the Antecedents of War." *American Anthropologist* 109, no. 3 (2007): 485–95.

Scott, James C. *Weapons of the Weak: Everyday Forms of Peasant Resistance.* New Haven: Yale University Press, 1985.

Short, Roger. "On the Evolution of Human Reproduction." In *Proceedings of the Australasian Society for Human Biology No. 1: Perspectives In Human Biology,* ed. N. W. Bruce, L. Freedman, and W. F. C. Blumer, 5–21. Nedlands, Western Australia: Australasian Society for Human Biology, 1988.

Silk, Joan B., Susan C. Alberts, and Jeanne Altmann. "Patterns of Coalition Formation by Adult Female Baboons in Amboseli, Kenya." *Animal Behaviour* 67, no. 3 (2004): 573–82.

Szykman, Micaela, Anne L.Engh, Russell C. van Horn, Erin E. Boydston, Kim T. Scribner, and Kay E. Holekamp. "Rare Male Aggression Directed toward Females in a Female-Dominated Society: Baiting Behavior in the Spotted Hyena." *Aggressive Behavior* 29, no. 5 (2003): 457–74.

Tooby, John, and Leda Cosmides. "The Psychological Foundations of Culture." In *The Adapted Mind: Evolutionary Psychology and the Generation of Culture,* ed. J. Barkow, L. Cosmides, and J. Tooby, 19–136. New York: Oxford University Press, 1992.

Tremblay, Richard E. "The Development of Aggressive Behaviour during Childhood: What Have We Learned in the Past Century?" *International Journal of Behavioral Development* 24, no. 2 (2000): 129–41.

Trivers, Robert L. "The Evolution of Reciprocal Altruism." *Quarterly Review of Biology* 46, no. 1 (1971): 35–57.

Uvin, Peter. "Ethnicity and Power in Burundi and Rwanda: Different Paths to Mass Violence." *Comparative Politics* 31, no. 3 (1999): 253–71.

Valero, Alejandra, Colleen M. Schaffner, Laura G. Vick, Filippo Aureli, and Gabriel Ramos-Fernandez. "Intragroup Lethal Aggression in Wild Spider Monkeys." *American Journal of Primatology* 68, no. 7 (2006): 732–37.

van der Dennen, Johan M. G. *The Origin of War: The Evolution of a Male-Coalitional Reproductive Strategy, Vols. 1 & 2.* Groningen, Netherlands: Origin Press, 1995.

van Schaik, Carel, and Charles H. Janson, eds. *Infanticide by Males and Its Implications.* Cambridge: Cambridge University Press, 2000.

Vogel, E. R., S. B. Munch, and C. H. Janson. "Understanding Escalated Aggression over Food Resources in White-Faced Capuchin Monkeys." *Animal Behaviour* 74, no. 1 (2007): 71–80.

Watson, John B. *Behaviorism*. New York: The People's Institute Publishing Co., 1925.

Watts, David P. "Intracommunity Coalitionary Killing of an Adult Male Chimpanzee at Ngogo, Kibale National Park, Uganda." *International Journal of Primatology* 25, no. 3 (2004): 507–21.

———. "Reciprocity and Interchange in the Social Relationships of Wild Male Chimpanzees." *Behaviour* 139, nos. 2/3 (2002): 343–70.

Watts, David P., Martin Muller, Sylvia J. Amsler, Godfrey Mbabazi, and John C. Mitani, "Lethal Intergroup Aggression by Chimpanzees in Kibale National Park, Uganda." *American Journal of Primatology* 68, no. 2 (2006): 161–80.

Wilson, Michael L., William R. Wallauer, and Anne E. Pusey. "New Cases of Intergroup Violence among Chimpanzees in Gombe National Park, Tanzania." *International Journal of Primatology* 25, no. 3 (2004): 523–49.

Wilson, Michael L., and Richard W. Wrangham. "Intergroup Relations in Chimpanzees." *Annual Review of Anthropology* 32, no. 1 (2003): 363–92.

Woolf, Linda, and Michael Hulsizer. "Psychosocial Roots of Genocide: Risk, Prevention, and Intervention." *Journal of Genocide Research* 7, no. 1 (2005): 101–28.

Wrangham, Richard W. "Evolution of Coalitionary Killing." *Yearbook of Physical Anthropology* 42 (1999): 1–30.

Wrangham, Richard W., and Dale Peterson. *Demonic Males: Apes and the Origins of Human Violence*. Boston: Houghton, Mifflin and Co., 1996.

Wrangham, Richard W., Michael L. Wilson, and Martin N. Muller. "Comparative Rates of Violence in Chimpanzees and Humans." *Primates* 47 (2006): 14–26.

Youssouf, Ibrahim Ag, Allen D. Grimshaw, and Charles S. Bird. "Greetings in the Desert." *American Ethnologist* 3, no. 4 (1976): 797–824.

9

"When the Rabbit's Got the Gun"
Subaltern Genocide and the Genocidal Continuum

Adam Jones

I n seminal essays published in 2002 for collections edited by Jeanette Mageo and Alexander Hinton, the anthropologist Nancy Scheper-Hughes described her provocative concept of a "genocidal continuum." Derived from her long-standing anthropological research—"a concern with popular consent to everyday violence"—Scheper-Hughes described "a multitude of 'small wars and invisible genocides'" occurring in various "normative social spaces." Institutional settings (jails, old-age homes, and the like) were especially prone to violent acts and relationships that contained at least a kernel of genocide, in the sense that they exhibited in a smaller-scale or more localized form some of the same ideological and symbolic frameworks, similar patterns of demonization and scapegoating, and exclusions from the sphere of social obligation as fully fledged genocidal outbreaks. They also pointed to the way that a genocidal potential was latent and pervasive in societies, available for activation in mass-killing campaigns. These "less dramatic, *permitted*, everyday" acts and atrocities were tied to the human capacity for "social exclusion, dehumanization, depersonalization, pseudo-speciation, and reification that normalize atrocious behavior and violence toward others." Given the presence of these ideological and institutional features of our environment, Scheper-Hughes argued that we must "exercise a defensive hyper-vigilance, a hypersensitivity" to the "*genocidal capacity*" of human beings; and recognize how strategies of marginalization, anathematization, and exclusion "make participation (under other conditions) in genocidal acts possible, perhaps more easy than we would like to know."

Some of the more directly or destructively violent manifestations of Scheper-Hughes's "genocidal continuum" approach or even cross the threshold of genocide as it is broadly understood. For example, she explores the "social cleansings" of thousands of street children, prostitutes, and transgendered people in urban areas of Latin America and elsewhere—cleansings carried out by selective murder on a substantial scale. Her framework also seems highly useful in exploring structural and institutional forms of violence, including genocidal and "gendercidal" violence.[1] In this chapter, I seek to apply the notion of a "genocidal continuum" to subaltern genocide—looking at latent, symbolic, and

TABLE 9.1 THE CONTINUUM OF SUBALTERN GENOCIDE

	Symbolic/ Performative Aggression		Individual/ Local Atrocity		Mass atrocity
Context	(1) Subaltern popular culture	(2) Subaltern interaction with dominant culture	(3) Niches of subaltern dominance	(4) Local and/ or temporary unrest	(5) Generalized and/or protracted conflict
Content	Songs, writings (incl. slogans, graffiti, pamphlets), jokes, gossip, rumors, curses/vulgarities, children's stories	"Everyday forms of resistance" (Scott); inversion rituals (carnivals, bacchanalias, etc.); individual hate crimes and hate-influenced crimes	Patterned and pervasive acts of physical and sexual assault; torture, murder; local (micro) regimes and rituals of domination, degradation, humiliation, dehumanization	Riots, pogroms, witch-hunts, vigilante campaigns, genocidal massacres	Systematic campaigns of genocide and crimes against humanity; generalized (macro) regimes of genocide and mass atrocity with a subaltern-inflected "foundation myth"

localized expressions as well as overt, systematic, and massively destructive ones (see Table 9.1).

Many subaltern motifs at points (1) and (2) on the continuum take the form of what the Yale political scientist James Scott called "acts of everyday resistance" deploying "weapons of the weak."[2] Often there is an added element of ritualized play or performance, symbolized, for example, by the radical symbolic inversions of the world's "carnival" traditions. Many of these originated as managed forms of libidinal release through fiesta—a "safety valve" for a manifestly unjust social order. To the extent that such performances are politically coherent, they serve a cathartic or wish-fulfillment function—somewhat similar to the minor "androcidal" strain of feminist science fiction touched on below in this chapter.

Accordingly, I do not wish to overstress the "proto-genocidal" character of certain ritual forms and expressions. However, it would be equally unwise to dismiss this dimension as merely marginal or purely symbolic. At particular times, and in particular contexts where the dominant-subaltern relationship is destabilized or inverted, the consequences may be explosively violent and destructive. At points (3), (4), and (5) on the continuum as sketched in Table 9.1, real-world and physical consequences increase notably. The scale of atrocity may be substantial: riots and pogroms[3] inflicted on "middleman" groups and other privileged minorities the world over; acts of terrorism and suicide-bombing against western civilians by humiliated, vengeful subaltern actors of the Global South; the rape and gang-rape of white prisoners by black inmates in U.S. prisons; and the murder and mutilation of Afrikaner farmers and their families in South Africa.

The following sections of the chapter provide examples of symbolic/performative acts and institutions along the continuum of subaltern genocide, followed by more directly violent ones, including mass atrocity. I consider the theoretical and practical implications of the framework, including those for genocide prevention, in the conclusion.

Performance

Carnivals and Curses

"Always new, always changing, always multivalent,"[4] carnival is one of the most remarkable and complex of human ritual expressions. At its heart is a "parodistic and profane inversion of canonized values"[5] and sacrosanct social relationships: slaves parade as masters, women as men, poor as rich. In colonial New Amsterdam (New York) in the seventeenth century, slave carnivals "included symbolic role reversals . . . in which blacks dressed in their masters' clothing and rode their masters' horses," together with "the election of black kings and judges." On the face of it, this symbolically evoked the deepest fears of overlords—fears of overthrow, annihilation, and usurpation by the dark subaltern masses. Yet by confining this subaltern expression within strict temporal and physical boundaries, and by making cathartic inversion contingent on quotidian servitude, subaltern status was confirmed and ritually *renewed*. "Disorder implies order," as David Brion Davis points out; and Saturnalia and similar rituals "reinforced the basic structures of authority."[6] From another perspective, however—that of subaltern actors—they kept vividly alive the vision of a utopian reversal of fortune.[7]

Fundamental to this constraining and confining of the subaltern is the confinement of that utopian dream, for fear that the licentious and subversive aspects of carnival may break their bonds, finding expression as orgiastic violence against oppressors. German psychologist Florenz Christian Rang located, in carnival's "will to frenzy," the threat of the "terrible outbreak of human rabidity. . . . In the mystery ritual of masked nocturnal dances and rebellious frenzy there is performed every despicable act, every murder, every form of excess that licentiousness and lunacy have dared to dream."[8] The rhetoric here may be exaggerated, but there does seem to be a combustibility at the heart of carnival. It is well captured by the greatest scholar of subaltern codes of resistance and rebellion, James C. Scott. He describes carnival as "something of a lightning rod for all sorts of social tensions and animosities," both "a festival of the physical senses" and "a festival of spleen and bile." Carnival is "the outcome of social conflict, not the unilateral creation of elites" as a social safety-valve; "what is striking historically about carnival is not how it contributed to the maintenance of existing hierarchies, but how frequently it was the scene of open social conflict."[9]

Scott has provided an unparalleled, almost anthropological catalogue of symbolic forms of resistance, born of subaltern oppression and frustration and the complex negotiations with hegemonic actors. Several of these have a carnival-like dimension. For example, victories by black athletes over white ones "legitimately allowed the black community to vicariously and publicly savor" a rare niche of subaltern dominance:

> The fight between Jack Johnson and Jim Jeffries (the "White hope") in 1910 and Joe Louis's subsequent career, which was aided by instant radio transmission of the fights, were indelible moments of reversal and revenge for the black community. "When Johnson battered a white man (Jeffries) to his knees, he was the symbolic black man taking out his revenge on all whites for a lifetime of indignities." . . . In the flush of their jubilation, blacks became momentarily bolder in gesture, speech, and carriage, and this was seen by much of the white community as a provocation, a breach of the public transcript.[10]

Scott also points to the phenomenon of *schadenfreude* ("joy at the misfortunes of others"), which may be palpable when social relations are dramatically inverted. "This represents a wish for negative reciprocity, a settling of scores when the high shall be brought low and the last shall be first." Finally, Scott reminds us of the institution of the *elaborate curse*. This is "an open prayer" which embodies "an intricate and lovingly ornate vision of revenge," as with this example collected in the Deep South of the United States, some decades after the abolition of slavery:

> I pray that death and disease shall be forever with them and that their crops shall not multiply and their cows, their sheep, their hogs and all their living possessions shall die of starvation and thirst. . . . I pray that their friends shall betray them and cause them loss of power, of gold and of silver, and that their enemies shall smite them until they beg for mercy, which shall not be given then. . . . O Man God, I ask you for all these things *because they have dragged me in the dust and destroyed my good name; broken my heart and caused me to curse the day that I was born.* So be it.[11]

Scott notes, incidentally, that the curse was cited by African American writer Alice Walker as an explanation for "why many blacks were not much interested" in anti-nuclear activism during the 1980s: "Their 'hope for revenge' made them look on nuclear destruction brought about by a white-ruled world with equanimity if not malevolent pleasure. One has, she implies, no right expecting civic spiritedness from those whose experience of community has mostly been that of victims."[12]

Androcidal Feminism

Males may feel grateful that the subaltern status of females worldwide has so rarely prompted women to inflict violence upon men *as such*—certainly not on a large scale. However, there are plenty of examples in the historical and sociological record of women's participation in large-scale violence against out-group pop-ulations—women, men, and children alike. The torture of captives was a female monopoly in many Native American tribes. Kurdish women in the Armenian genocide, female Nazi camp officials, and Rwanda's notorious female *génocidaires* all attest to women's ready involvement in violence, including genocide, when they are permitted and encouraged to participate. An element of subaltern geno-cide is sometimes evident in such female-inflicted violence. The female *génocid-aires* of Rwanda, it seems, were regularly inspired by the same subaltern hostilities and humiliations experienced by Hutu men, translating to "a gendered jubilation at the comeuppance" of Tutsi women,[13] depicted as Rwanda's sexual elite (see chapter 6). Closer investigation of the dynamics of female-inflicted violence in situations of localized subaltern dominance (point (3) on the continuum) may be merited, especially to discern whether violence meted out to males contains an element of pent-up subaltern frustration.

For present purposes, however, my interest lies in the fringe of female cul-tural performances that may be called "androcidal feminism." These cultural products envisage, and usually depict as desirable, a world cleansed of men and masculinities. Possibly the most notorious work of 1960s feminist agitprop is Valerie Solanas's *SCUM Manifesto*, recently reissued with a long and informa-tive introduction by Avital Ronell.[14] Solanas circulated on the margins of Andy Warhol's cultural "Factory" in the mid-to-late 1960s. Aside from an appearance in one of Warhol's films and a failed attempt at publishing a play, she worked on the manifesto of the "Society for Cutting Up Men"—SCUM—exploring her vision of a world stripped by mass extermination and systematic cultural effacement, of men and putatively masculine traits. Solanas is also notorious for shooting Warhol very nearly to death (and wounding another man) in an attack originally aimed at her (male) publisher. She served three years in prison for the crime, and after her release lived destitute and schizophrenic in San Francisco, dying there in 1988.

In her fascist-inflected *SCUM Manifesto*,[15] Solanas wrote that men are "defi-cient, emotionally limited . . . cripples." They "want to be squashed, stepped on, crushed and crunched, treated as the curs, the filth that they are, have their repul-siveness confirmed. . . . Just as humans have a prior right to existence over dogs by virtue of being more highly evolved and having a superior consciousness, so women have a prior right to existence over men. The elimination of any male is, therefore, a righteous and good act, an act highly beneficial to women as well as an act of mercy."[16] Possibly, direct acts of elimination would be "academic," Solanas railed, given that men were busy engineering their own annihilation through "wars and race riots," "becoming fags," and "obliterating themselves through drugs." It was the destiny of any surviving males to "exist out their puny days dropped out on drugs or strutting around in drag or passively watching the high-powered female in action, fulfilling themselves as spectators, vicarious livers or breeding in the cow pasture with the toadies, or they can go off to the nearest friendly suicide center where they will be quietly, quickly, and painlessly gassed to death."[17]

The reactions to Solanas's *Manifesto* ranged from predictable hostility and contempt to amusement, and even a surprising degree of praise and admiration. Four decades after its appearance, the *Manifesto* still crackles and cackles with the "castrative glee" born of what Ronell has termed Solanas's "primal sense of injury." The *Manifesto* was flung into the public domain as "payback . . . to all shameless woman-hating manifestos" ever issued, Ronell writes. This sense of the value of the subaltern scream or counter-scream—albeit from a psychologically distressed individual—may explain the significant support and solidarity that feminists displayed after Solanas's attempted murder of two men. The well-known radical feminist writer Robin Morgan lobbied for her release from jail. Ti-Grace Atkinson, the New York president of the National Organization for Women (NOW), praised Solanas as the "first outstanding champion of women's rights," and feminist lawyer Florynce Kennedy likewise declared her "one of the most important spokeswomen of the feminist movement."[18] The subaltern genocidal fantasy of the *Manifesto* retains a place in the pantheon of women's studies. I have, after all, been citing from a new and handsome edition, published by a mainstream-left publisher (Verso), and introduced by a noted New York professor.

We may also note, in this context, the androcidal strain in feminist science-fiction utopias, most prominently exemplified by the books of Joanna Russ. In Russ's 1975 novel *The Female Man,* the hero Jael "has turned her body into a killing-machine through plastic surgery and metal implants," according to Jeanne Cortiel, and directed it to explicitly androcidal ends. Jael "uses her hatred and vindictiveness [toward men] as an instrument in a violent resolution of the sex-antagonism and the reappropriation of her sense of self." "Murder is my one way out," Jael declares. "For every drop of blood shed there is restitution made; with every truthful reflection in the eyes of a dying man I get back a little of my soul." Cortiel, who calls *The Female Man* "probably the most outstanding feminist science fiction novel of the decade," depicts these androcidal themes as "a celebration of Jael's physical power, an atrocious violation of the male body" that mirrors the violation of women implicit, for Russ, in patriarchal sexual relations. "Mercilessly destroying the male body, she transfers women's physical and psychological pain to him."[19]

Atrocity

In shifting from the symbolic/performative to the atrocious, we court two dangers. One, examined in greater detail below, is that we ignore the qualitative connections between the genres. The other, paradoxically, is that we *too easily* assume a causal connection between the points on the continuum—that subaltern fantasies and imaginings "prime" a genocidal situation. I believe they frequently do, but this needs to be argued and supported in given cases, and clear demonstrations of cause and effect may prove elusive.

Regardless, we have witnessed in this volume numerous instances of subaltern identifications fueling genocidal outcomes. The cases examined below seem, for the most part, clear examples of qualitatively similar atrocities spawned by subaltern hatred, envy, and vengefulness—though without assuming the proportions and systematic character normally associated with full-blown genocidal campaigns.

"Understandably Very Angry": Jews over Germans

We saw in the introduction to this volume that Nazism was animated by a phantasmagorical vision of the world-dominating Jew as single-mindedly dedicated to the destruction of the German people. As the Nazi holocaust unfolded in Europe, however, the intensity of its violence prompted an extreme ideology of vengeance among many Jews—leading, in a small number of cases, to coherent plans for the obliteration of Germany, and violence on a significant scale.

There is an analytical issue to confront in addressing the cases of Jewish subaltern violence against Germans as such. To what extent is it legitimate to depict actions by a self-identified Jewish person as motivated by his or her Jewishness (and thus, in the context of wartime Europe, the subaltern status that attached to it)? Consider the most detailed manifesto for the annihilation of Germans as a people: *Germany Must Perish!* a 1941 book by the American Jewish writer Theodore N. Kaufman. Writing to press the United States to enter the war, in a work published a few months before the nation did so, Kaufman likened Germans to "savage beast[s]," "wild animals," and "poisonous reptiles." The German state, which had "forfeit[ed] its own national life" by seeking to destroy others, had to be extinguished. And Germans themselves should be exterminated—not by anything so repugnant as "massacre and wholesale execution," but through a meticulous campaign of "Eugenic Sterilization." This could only "be considered a great health measure promoted by humanity to immunize itself *forever* against the virus of Germanism."[20]

It is hardly surprising that Joseph Goebbels, seizing a golden propaganda opportunity, promoted Kaufman in Germany as a powerful figure of international Jewry, and "the quintessential representation of the mentality of 'the enemy.'"[21] But like Valerie Solanas in 1960s New York, Kaufman was a socially marginal figure—nothing more than "an independent, *understandably very angry* Jewish writer," as Jeffrey Herf writes (emphasis added). Moreover, in *Germany Must Perish!* Kaufman in no way positioned himself as a Jewish commentator who was especially concerned about the Nazi threat to Jews. Thus, wherever one might locate such wild fantasies on the genocidal continuum, it is uncertain whether they could reasonably be situated along a continuum of *subaltern* genocide.

Where an explicit element of violent Jewish revenge was present, however, a subaltern framing may be demonstrably valid. One such case concerns the deaths of tens of thousands of German prisoners at the end of World War II and in its immediate aftermath. In his controversial book *An Eye for an Eye: The Story of Jews Who Sought Revenge for the Holocaust,* journalist John Sack examined how the Office of State Security in Kattowitz, Poland, with its network of hundreds of detention centers, fell under the control of predominantly Jewish officers. Many were Auschwitz survivors. These Jews, Sack writes (in his sometimes melodramatic style), "felt their blood boiling, or their muscles curling, or their bones aching with hate for the German murderers." They unleashed that hatred "in 1945 [by killing] a great number of Germans: not Nazis, not Hitler's trigger men, but German civilians, German men, women, children, babies, whose 'crime' was just to be Germans."

Much of the violence displayed the subaltern codes that are familiar from the discussion in chapters 1 and 2. One female administrator of a network of prisons and detention centers "saw that she could turn the hierarchy of Auschwitz upside-down." Specific punishments emphasized and symbolized the victory of the previously oppressed. At the Schwientochlowitz camp, Shlomo Morel presided over a murderous regime founded on ubiquitous assaults and atrocities against German captives: "The guards put the Germans into a doghouse, beating them if they didn't say 'Bow wow.' They got the Germans to beat each other . . . they raped the German women . . . and trained their dogs to bite off the German men's genitals at the command of 'Sic!' . . . In time, three-fourths of the Germans at Shlomo's camp were dead."[22]

This was probably the largest real-world example of a subaltern-genocidal tendency in postwar Jewish violence against German civilians. It was not, however, the most remarkable one. That designation belongs to Nakam (Revenge), the organization studied by Tom Segev in *The Seventh Million: The Israelis and the Holocaust*. Nakam, founded by the former partisan fighter Abba Kovner at war's end, was based in Europe, with a presence in the Jewish émigré community in Palestine. Kovner eventually rallied dozens of mostly younger Jewish fighters to his call for a revenge that "had to precisely equal the dimensions of the crime. Kovner therefore set [the deaths of] six million German citizens as his goal. He thought in apocalyptic terms: revenge was a holy obligation that would redeem and purify the Jewish people."

The plan was to be implemented through mass poisonings of water systems in a number of German cities; agents were actually dispatched to waterworks in Nuremberg and Hamburg to prepare for the introduction of toxins brought from Palestine. Soldiers of the Jewish Brigade of the Haganah assisted in procuring the poison. Its shipment to Europe was interrupted, however—likely derailed by other Jewish leaders who strongly disapproved of the plot's extremism—and Kovner switched to "Plan B": "to poison several thousand former SS men in the American army's POW camps." Segev notes that Kovner's followers had considerable difficulty adjusting to the change in plan: "They all believed they were going to kill six million Germans and now were being told to satisfy themselves with a thousand." Arsenic-laced flour was in fact introduced at one camp, seriously sickening a number of prisoners; Kovner pointed triumphantly to rumors that 400 had died.

In addition, a large number of Jewish killing teams roamed postwar Germany and other countries, summarily executing alleged Nazi war criminals and sometimes innocent civilians. All these guerrilla/terrorist forces explicitly positioned themselves as Jewish avengers and subaltern exacters of revenge. They included leading figures in the post-independence Israeli armed forces, one of whom—chief of staff Haim Laskov—justified the "acts of revenge" as follows: "When it comes down to it, we lost the war. We lost six million Jews. Anyone who hasn't seen those places, the concentration camps and crematoriums, can never understand what they did to us. *Because we were weak, and did not have our own country, and did not have power, we avenged. . . .* I'm sorry to say that we did not liquidate very many."[23]

Subaltern Hate Crimes and "Market-Dominant Minorities"

It is impossible to gauge accurately the scale of crimes committed by subaltern actors which could be classified as "hate crimes." Black-on-white violence in the United States, considered below in the context of prison sexual assault, offers a point of entry into the phenomenon. While issuing a strong warning about the "motley collection of white supremacists and rightist extremist groups [which] has eagerly made black-on-white violence a wedge issue in their crusade to paint blacks as the prime racial hatemongers in America," Earl Ofari Hutchinson, the African American director of the National Alliance for Positive Action, acknowledged that "more whites than ever are the targets of racially motivated attacks by blacks." In an article headlined "Why Are Black Leaders Silent on Black Hate Crimes?" Hutchinson wrote:

> True, some of the attacks against whites by blacks are for their money and valuables. Others are revenge assaults by blacks for real or imagined racial insults. It is equally true that the vast majority of violent crimes against whites are committed by other whites, while the vast majority of violent crimes against blacks are committed by other blacks. Yet even after discounting crimes that are hastily and erroneously tagged as racially motivated, many blacks do attack whites because they are white. A Justice Department study in 1998 confirmed that nearly 20 percent of the hate crimes examined were committed against whites by black attackers. And the Southern Poverty Law Center has noted that black-on-white violence soared during the 1990s.[24]

As Hutchinson suggests, and as James Morsch has explored more systematically,[25] isolating the motive of racial or ethnic hatred in a given conflict interaction or criminal act may be difficult. But a modest proposition seems sustainable: that many acts of criminal assault committed by minority actors, against majority or minority actors, seem to contain an element of hatred toward majorities, born of subaltern anger, frustration, and humiliation. We will see this expressed powerfully below in the case of prison sexual assaults. Many if not most of these attacks can be classed as "hate crimes" for their explicit dimension of subaltern vengeance and racial subjugation.[26]

Perhaps the most visible subaltern hate crimes in the contemporary North American experience occurred during the Los Angeles riots of 1992, following the acquittal of white policemen accused in the beating of black motorist Rodney King. In some black neighborhoods, "everybody that came through here that was not black was in trouble," according to a gang member quoted in the *Los*

Angeles Times—which noted that "white people . . . are suddenly afraid of being judged by the color of their skin."[27] Images of a white trucker pulled out of his cab and brutally beaten by black youths were eclipsed by the siege against Korean American residents. This also contained a pronounced dimension of subaltern rage. According to the *New York Times,* Korean Americans had become "overwhelmingly dominant" in the commercial life of Watts and other predominantly black neighborhoods: "Across much of the poorest area of the city, the only shops to buy groceries or liquor or gasoline, or to have clothes cleaned or a car repaired, are owned by Korean immigrants. Korean merchants had become a lightning rod for the discontent of some black residents. Many blacks in Los Angeles have remained poor as, one after another, immigrant groups have arrived and climbed past them to prosperity."

Attacks on Korean persons and property spiraled throughout poor neighborhoods. "It's illogical, but it's convenient to target the Koreans," said a member of the city's Human Relations Commission. "Why were they burning the businesses that serve them? Why has that anger not been vented at the educational system that has failed them? Why weren't the employment offices burned to the ground?" One ethnic Korean described the events in terms pungent with the racial tensions afflicting Korean/African American relations: "I think the black people are jealous of the Koreans," he said. "They're lazy; we are working hard. They're not making money; we are making money."[28] Kyeyoung Park's research similarly found that "Koreans value themselves and explain their successes in terms of having 'more culture' (family unity, ethnic solidarity, education) than blacks." Interestingly, "Blacks also present Koreans as having more culture than themselves," which meshes with some of the dynamics of subaltern envy and humiliation explored by Evelin G. Lindner in this volume (see chapter 7).[29]

Prison Rape in the United States

For decades, the subject of male rape in prison and other settings was one of the last human rights "taboos."[30] The issue received limited scholarly and media attention, but no systematic study by leading human rights organizations until the investigation that produced, in 2001, the Human Rights Watch report *No Escape: Male Rape in U.S. Prisons.*[31] While vividly depicting the rampant sexual violence against (and by) males in the world's most populous prison system, *No Escape* also stressed a little-known element: the heavy concentration of white males among victims, and black and Latino males among the perpetrators. This was, moreover, no simple correlation (e.g., with black and Latino overrepresentation in prison populations). Rather, a *powerful strain of subaltern revenge* underpinned many such attacks. "Inter-racial sexual abuse is common *only* to the extent that it involves white non-Hispanic prisoners being abused by African Americans or Hispanics," HRW noted. The organization's own findings confirmed "past studies [that] have documented the prevalence of black on white sexual aggression in prison." One black inmate offered his thoughts on the targeting of whites for sexual attack:

> Most [blacks] feel that the legal system is fundamentally racist and officers are the most visible symbol of a corrupt institution & with good reason. . . . Blacks know whites often associate crime with black people. They see themselves as being used as scapegoats. . . . So is it any wonder that when a white man comes to prison, that blacks see him as a target.

> Stereotypes are prevalent amongst blacks also that cause bad thinking. The belief that all or most white men are effete or gay is very prevalent, & that whites are cowards who have to have 5 or 6 more to take down one [black] dude. . . . Whites are prey and even a punk will be supported if he beats up a white dude.[32]

A selection of inmate testimonies gathered by HRW attested to the special vulnerability of inmates seen as representatives of the hegemonic regime outside prison walls, when they are confined in institutional settings where the rules are inverted and subaltern actors hold sway. The configuration here is close to that of the Jewish-German camp dynamic sketched in the previous section. The subaltern agents, though, are not in positions of official responsibility. They merely exploit an anarchic environment, in which guards do little or nothing to prevent physical and sexual attack, to create a localized hierarchy in which rape (often gang rape) serves as an explicit and vengeful message of political triumph and racial subjugation. Inmates offered further insights into the dynamic:

> In my experience having a "boy" (meaning white man) to a negro in prison is sort of a "trophy" to his fellow black inmates. And I think the roots of the problem go back a long time ago to when the African Americans where [sic] in the bonds of slavery. They have a favorite remark: "It ain't no fun when the rabbit's got the gun, is it?"

> Gangs of black and spanish inmates are very angry at free-world white people for a variety of reasons, and this results in an attitude of vengeance towards white people in prisons.

> Why prison sexual assault occurs: Part of it is revenge against what the non-white prisoners call, "The White Man," meaning authority and the justice system. A common comment is, "y'all may run it out there, but this is our world!" More of it I think is the assaulters own insecurities and them trying to gain some respect in their peer group by showing that they "are a man."[33]

"Y'all may run it out there, but this is our world." The message seems closely parallel with the one transmitted to other dominant populations in contexts of subaltern hegemony, like the white farmers of post-Apartheid South Africa. Their plight constitutes the final case of subaltern atrocity explored in this chapter.

A Genocide of Afrikaner Farmers?

In his 1999 novel *Disgrace*, Nobel Prize–winning author J. M. Coetzee describes the gang rape of Lucy, a rural white woman living alone, whose father, David, is the novel's central character. David pleads with Lucy to abandon her isolated settlement. She refuses, though she knows it means her rapists are likely to return—probably regularly. "I think I am in their territory," Lucy says. "They will come back for me. . . . But . . . what if *that* is the price one has to pay for staying on? Perhaps this is how they look at it; perhaps that is how I should look at it too. They see me as owing something. They see themselves as debt collectors, tax collectors. Why should I be allowed to live here without paying?"

"They want you for their slave," her father protests. "Not slavery," Lucy replies. "Subjection. Subjugation."[34]

There are echoes here of the decisions made, and self-justifications offered, by individuals throughout history in the crisis conditions of war and genocide. A bargain may be struck with the subaltern-turned-oppressor—highly disadvantageous, perhaps, but permitting one to survive, and perhaps to remain in one's home and native land. Whether the option is made available, however, varies from case to case. In many instances in the history of genocide, and in some rural areas of post-apartheid South Africa, it has not been offered. Assault, massacre, and mutilation have reigned.

The post-1994 death toll of South African farmers in the killing campaign dubbed *Plaasmoorde* (farm murders) in Afrikaans now approaches 2,000. Most victims are white; most perpetrators are poor, young black males. Allegations have swirled of official complicity in the killings—of "an orchestrated, government-sanctioned attempt to purge South Africa of White landowners, as has already happened in Zimbabwe"[35]—but these are unproven. Regardless of whether an organized political dimension is evident, though, a retributive element clearly is present: "revenge, fueled by racism and envy" is primary in the estimation of the *Sunday Times,* though subaltern frustration and humiliation seem equally likely sources.[36] In the "post-Apartheid" period, patterns of wealth and property ownership have altered only at a glacial pace, and white farmers are viewed by many as an obstacle to agrarian justice. South African theology professor B. J. van der Walt describes the dynamic in a way that corroborates Evelin Lindner's emphasis on subaltern humiliation (chapter 7 in this volume):

> Many black people (or their parents) have been humiliated on farms in different ways by (racist) white farmers, *inter alia* by the way in which farmers spoke to them (even to older people among them) or the way they withheld fair wages from them. Such things probably hurt black people even more deeply than it would whites . . . because it brings shame on them and causes them to feel unworthy, it erodes their human dignity. Something like this can in no other way be put right but that the honour of the injured person has to be restored. Since this does not happen the feeling of shame and inferiority changes to anger and eventually revenge by oneself or a mediator (e.g. one's children) who help one to revenge the disgrace. The revenge is determined by the extent to which your family member's honour was injured by the farmer, the humiliation experienced. Therefore it is sometimes cruel without anything being robbed. Revenge is facilitated further because (white) farmers belong to the "out-group," that is, not to their own group towards whom the murderer has a sole obligation.[37]

As this account suggests, the element of subaltern rage seems evident in acts of "extreme violence, including rape, torture and physical mutilation" that regularly accompany the farm murders, including in cases where theft of property does not take place.[38] "There is a motive of hate crimes [present]" in many such attacks, according to Greg Stanton, current president of the International Association of Genocide Scholars. "These people [victims] are tortured, murdered in ways that are dehumanizing."[39]

Extensions and Implications

In this closing section, I consider some of the implications for genocide studies of the materials and perspectives presented in this chapter. This serves also as an informal conclusion to the volume. Many of the themes relevant to the continuum of subaltern genocide point additionally to the place of subaltern genocide in comparative genocide studies.

A prominent theme in genocide studies, and throughout this volume, is the role of *millenarian and utopian ideologies*. These surely have a particular piquancy for those at the bottom of the social ladder. Lepore emphasizes that the ritual humiliations and mutilations meted out by perpetrators of subaltern genocide are intended to be not only destructive, but *restorative*: in the case of Native American atrocities, they were meant "to restore their world to a balance, to recover it from the chaos into which it had been falling ever since the English first arrived."[40] In the present volume, for example, both Nicholas Robins's chapter and my own (chapter 2) show how conquered and dispossessed indigenous populations harked back to a "golden age" of self-rule and cultural integrity in fomenting their great rebellions against colonial rule. The golden age is usually one of social justice and egalitarianism prior to the imposition of unjust, unequal social structures and relationships. We have seen in this volume subaltern actors mobilized by similar ideologies under the Khmer Rouge and Hutu Power in Rwanda. There is nothing uniquely or distinctively subaltern about millenarianism and utopianism. But they do seem to have swept a number of subaltern populations as bottom-up phenomena. Even when they are imposed by leadership figures who are hardly drawn from subaltern ranks—they include Inca royal descendants in the Andean case, and elite, foreign-educated intellectuals like Pol Pot and his cohorts in Cambodia—such ideologies have to be made persuasive to subaltern populations, if the masses are part of the scheme of revolutionary mobilization. Accordingly, the message is usually shaped to harness the power of their frustrations and humiliations, and marshal them to the millenarian project.

These comments touch on the broader relationship between *leaders and followers* in genocide and subaltern genocide. It is impossible to gauge, in the cases examined in this chapter ranging from "pure" performance to mass atrocity, what precise role is played by leadership figures, and exactly how significant they are in the overall equation. Surely, they are always present. But the leaders need not be drawn from *state* ranks—though state involvement is sometimes seen as so essential to genocide that it is a core element of many scholarly definitions of genocide. Recent political science contributions to genocide studies, notably by

Benjamin Valentino, Manus Midlarsky, and Scott Straus, have placed renewed emphasis on state direction and top-down mobilization.[41] Close attention to subaltern genocide framings, however, suggests that in addition to top-down mobilizations, proto-genocidal worldviews may be *organically constructed from below*, to a significant and sometimes predominant extent, and that these may be essential to the "successful" waging of a genocidal campaign.

One can, for example, question Valentino's claim that in Cambodia, certain "communist elites seem to have created new social categories for their victims out of whole cloth"—as with the "new people" under the Khmer Rouge, "a completely manufactured social group consisting of businessmen, city dwellers, foreigners, and virtually anyone with an education."[42] Valentino is correct that the categories were constructed and shaped far beyond the subaltern realm. But even in this extreme case of top-down mobilization, the antipathies associated with the social categories *did* long preexist Khmer Rouge propaganda. The communists did not invent urban-rural, literate-illiterate, worker-farmer, and rich-poor distinctions. Inchoate prejudices, stereotypes, and hostilities may need to be mobilized and directed in order to reach their full virulent potential. But leaders and "violence entrepreneurs" may also be plowing fertile ground among marginalized or dispossessed populations.

Mahmood Mamdani emphasizes this point in *When Victims Become Killers*, the work of genocide studies that has taken the most explicit note (albeit in passing) of a subaltern genocidal framing. Analysis of the Rwandan holocaust that "presents the genocide as exclusively a state project and ignores its subaltern and 'popular' character" is misplaced, writes Mamdani, in a passage cited in the introduction. The "salient political fact" for him is "that the genocide was carried out by subaltern masses, even if organized by state functionaries."[43] Perhaps, then, the genocidal dynamic is best viewed as a *dialectic*, in which leadership is vital, but not necessarily statist in nature, and to which followers make distinctive—sometimes primary, often decisive—contributions. Among those contributions, as Nicholas Robins has pointed out to me,[44] is shaping leaders themselves: in the Andean revolts that Robins studies in chapter 1, "the leaders were considerably more conservative than their followers," who "projected" their dreams and aspirations onto the leaders and seem to have radicalized those leaders' programs and ideologies thereby.

A prominent theme in the recent genocide-studies literature has been a growing emphasis on the *dynamism and contingency* of genocidal processes. The findings of this chapter, and a number of earlier ones in the book, validate attention to these nuances—rather than assuming that genocides are long planned and consistently implemented across time and space. This may assist in developing models of subaltern genocide, and of the evolution of subaltern genocidal ideologies. For example, at both performative and atrocious points on the genocidal continuum, annihilatory discourses and strategies may be most evident at the earliest stage of a given movement, when humiliation and disempowerment may be felt most keenly. At the level of performance, for example, the institution of carnival moved from a genuinely subversive institution, one often perceived as a threat to the social order, to the far more tightly managed, commercialized, and politically neutered productions of today.[45] Likewise, with regard to the "androcidal" strain in feminist theory and literature, it is difficult to imagine Valerie Solanas's vengeful fantasies of subjugating and exterminating the male sex receiving today the warm response accorded them by some movement leaders in the 1960s.

In subaltern atrocity, likewise, an explosive dimension—or perhaps, echoing Nicholas Robins's analysis in chapter 1, an *implosive* one—is often evident. The mood of Jewish vengeance against Germans, for example, which found murderous expression in certain prison camps and vigilante campaigns, dissipated rapidly. Certainly, the type of official or semi-official support for a campaign of mass poisoning is difficult to conceive of beyond the immediate aftermath of World War II. With regard to the broader mass movements studied in this volume, the tendency of revolutionary radicalism to give way to factionalism and reaction, or to evaporate when the next planting season comes, has been well noted by scholars of revolutions.

The genocidal impetus of such processes does not necessarily end at this point—the reactionary phase, for example, may be far bloodier than the radical one. But the distinctively *subaltern* dimension may be absent, suggesting its greater influence and predominance at earlier stages of rebellions and revolutionary upheavals. James Scott alludes to something of this dynamic in the final sentence of his masterful *Domination and the Arts of Resistance,* speaking of the moment when "hidden transcripts" of subaltern resistance finally explode into the public sphere. "If the results seem like moments of madness," Scott writes, "if the politics they engender is tumultuous, frenetic, delirious, and occasionally violent, that is perhaps because the powerless are so rarely on the public stage and have so much to say and do when they finally arrive."[46]

On the other hand, one must be alive to a countervailing tendency: the growing *radicalization over time* of the types of movements (fascistic/dictatorial, millennial-revolutionary) that often produce genocidal outcomes. Something of this is evident, for example, in the great peasant revolts of the Andean highlands studied by Nicholas Robins, and in twentieth-century cases such as the Ottoman Young Turks, Hutu Power in Rwanda, and possibly the Khmer Rouge in Cambodia. Might these genocidal trajectories reflect a substantially greater degree of *top-down* mobilization of subaltern masses, and might subaltern movements that are more extreme at an earlier stage be substantially more *bottom-up* in their origins and orientation, representing explosive outbursts by frustrated populations? Is leadership drawn from subaltern ranks (rather than imposed from without) more prominent in earlier-cresting rather than later-cresting genocidal movements? Or do "late developers" reflect the rise of subaltern actors through the ranks to positions of dictatorial authority, where they are able to inflict acts of class vengeance? Something of this latter dynamic might be evident in the great violence associated with the French revolutionary suppression of the Vendée rebels (1791–94), or the destruction of Soviet "kulaks," and resisting peasants more generally, by predominantly industrial workers of mostly subaltern (peasant) origins.[47]

The study of subaltern genocide may also help to illuminate the relationship between *terrorism and genocide,* an area of some controversy in the genocide studies field. Scholars such as Juergen Zimmerer have called for drawing clear distinctions between these phenomena.[48] Others, though, perceive a core genocidal impetus in many acts of "freelance" terrorism, notably the attacks on New York and Washington on September 11, 2001. The combustible elements of oppression, humiliation, resentment, and envy that are so palpable in most cases of subaltern genocide are no less central to terrorism, and to the sympathy or outright support that some terrorist acts evoke—if they can be cast persuasively as acts of subaltern revenge. As Amy Chua points out, "The September 11 attacks were an act of revenge by the weak against the powerful, motivated by tremendous feelings of humiliation and inferiority." The perpetrators, she adds, came "from countries that in their own eyes had been raped and humiliated by the West."[49]

Terrorism is too often defined by its freelance, "franchise," and small-cell variants. Equally relevant, however, is *state* terrorism and its connection to genocide. Certain state-terrorist campaigns of recent decades—Indonesia in 1965–66, Guatemala under the generals in the 1970s and 1980s—are now widely accepted as cases of genocide. Often, the terrorist strategy is meant to cow and cull subaltern populations, and to erode their support for rebellious forces. The genocidal killing may then become tit-for-tat, as the oppressed adopt the methods of their oppressors: the vicious rounds of mutual racial killing at key points in the Haitian liberation struggle offer a particularly vivid example of this dynamic.

As the terrorist example indicates, *humiliation and envy* are central to many genocidal processes, and may be particularly powerful forces in cases of subaltern genocide, proto-genocidal violence, and symbolic performances containing a genocidal kernel. Intimately related to these founts of genocidal, proto-genocidal, and quasi-genocidal action are the anathematization, humiliation, and frequently mutilation of victims. This *inscription of atrocity,* at once symbolic and cruelly substantive, reminds us that distinctions drawn between "performance" and "atrocity" in the genocidal continuum are to some degree an analytical convenience. Atrocity *is* in part performance: a communicative act. "Ritual cruelty," within this scheme, "is a symbolic language that can be 'read' and then 'translated' into spoken or written language"[50] (see further discussion in chapters 1 and 6).

As Christopher Taylor's work has shown, here and elsewhere, this atrocious inscription is often decisively gendered, and this points to the potential interest of investigating links between *gender and subaltern genocide.* As one example, my work on gendercide (gender-selective mass killing) suggests that subaltern males are perceived by hegemonic males and females alike as the greatest threat to their security.[51] The depiction of the subaltern male is uniquely incendiary. He is on the one hand subjugated and despised, but also viewed as powerful, volatile, potentially history-altering: consider the portrait of the male "superpredator" in U.S. discourse on urban public safety during the 1990s, or that of the Islamist terrorist (or illegal immigrant) today.[52]

How parallel are perceptions in cases of subaltern-fueled mass violence? Do the males who overwhelmingly predominate as perpetrators of subaltern genocide (and all other genocides) perceive hegemonic males as the greatest threat, to be targeted selectively and disproportionately for murder and other severe violence? Additionally, does the sexual "prize" status that attaches to dominant-group women in many instances of subaltern genocide represent a special threat to women thus positioned—as in Rwanda in 1994 (chapter 6), or German territories under Soviet invasion and occupation (chapter 3)?

The Rwandan example may also lead us to ask whether subaltern females are more likely to participate in campaigns of genocide and mass violence that carry a high degree of resonance with popular masses, as opposed to narrower, more elitist campaigns. (The high representation of women in guerrilla armies versus national armies may provide some clues here.) If women *are* more likely to participate as perpetrators in such contexts, is this because subaltern genocides offer special avenues of activity, achievement, and aggrandizement for women? Are the emancipatory justifications for subaltern campaigns especially attractive to women who seek a specifically gendered liberation? Do female perpetrators, as in Rwanda, display a special desire to assist in attacks on *women* from the hegemonic group, as revenge for gendered feelings of humiliation?[53]

Lastly, what of children as gendered subjects of analysis?[54] Are they more or less likely to be targeted in subaltern than in other forms of genocide? And—thinking of the chilling use of child killers in Cambodia, Rwanda, and elsewhere—are they more likely to be perpetrators?

Essential to genocide studies from the beginning have been *strategies of prevention and intervention.* It is perhaps fitting to conclude with some considerations of the possible relevance of the continuum of subaltern genocide for such strategies.

Attention to this continuum helps to highlight vulnerable groups who may otherwise be sidelined—especially when they occupy positions of privilege, such as the "market-dominant minorities" studied by Amy Chua and others. A certain moral tone-deafness has occluded empathy for such victims. This was evident, for example, in the blasé or even celebratory response of hundreds of millions of people worldwide to the September 11 attacks. It was exploited by Hutu Power in Rwanda to obscure the systematic character of the genocide against Tutsi (depicted instead as self-defense against a population that was seeking to reestablish its recently lost hegemony). It also explains much of the cultural numbness to large-scale victimization of adult males in genocidal situations. Whatever their position in a given social and political equation, men are likely to be viewed not only as militarized, as has long been recognized, but as members of a globally hegemonic gender class—thus, not as "innocent civilians" or potential subjects of humanitarian intervention.[55]

Attention to the subaltern strand of genocide tends to evoke a less idealized and romanticized image of subaltern actors. A pressing task is to construct framings of subaltern genocide that acknowledge the morally plausible element of campaigns for freedom and liberation, against oppression and injustice—while also recognizing that atrocious and even genocidal tendencies may result from such initiatives. One is therefore called on to identify such tendencies as early as possible in a genocidal process—and for scholars to approach past genocides of this type with equal seriousness and dispatch, for the lessons they may hold.[56]

Moreover, close attention should be paid to institutional environments and social "niches" where subaltern actors may exercise local and/or temporary hegemony (point (3) on the continuum of subaltern genocide sketched in Table 9.1). If it is true, as Kofi Annan has suggested, that genocide occurs when even a single person is targeted "not for what [s]he has done, but because of who [s]he is,"[57] then genocidal actions short of full-scale exterminatory campaigns may well qualify—and subaltern actors may sometimes hold the upper hand in these encounters.

Notes

1. See the discussion of "gendercidal institutions" in Jones, *Gendercide and Genocide*; the case studies collected on the Gendercide Watch web site, http://www.gendercide.org; also, Jones, "Genocide and Structural Violence: Charting the Analytical Terrain," paper presented at the conference of the International Association of Genocide Scholars, Sarajevo, Bosnia, and Herzegovina, July 10, 2007.

2. See Scott, *Weapons of the Weak*; also Scott, *Domination and the Arts of Resistance*; Scott, *The Moral Economy of the Peasant*.

3. Brass, *Riots and Pogroms*.

4. Crowley, "The Sacred and the Profane in African and African-Derived Carnivals."

5. Lachmann, Eshelman, and Davis, "Bakhtin and Carnival," 125.

6. Davis, *Inhuman Bondage*, 130–31. Christopher Hill likewise notes "certain set occasions" in medieval England when "the social hierarchy and the social decencies could be turned upside down. It was a safety valve: social tensions were released by the occasional *bouleversement;* the social order seemed perhaps that much more tolerable." Hill, *The World Turned Upside Down*, 16–17.

7. "The provocative, mirthful inversion of prevailing institutions and their hierarchy as staged in the carnival offers a permanent alternative to official culture—even if it ultimately leaves everything as it was before." Lachmann et al., "Bakhtin and Carnival," 125.

8. Quoted in ibid., 127.

9. Scott, *Domination and the Arts of Resistance*, 173–74, 181. Another example of the phenomenon is the Hindu festival of Holi, which according to Maria Masri "involv[ed] the ebullient hurling of coloured powder at one's social superiors. It is intended to subvert, temporarily, the Hindu caste hierarchy, turning the world upside-down and putting the Shudras [lower caste pastoral groups] on top. By the 1930s Holi, now a seven-day event, had become the main festival of north Indian bazaars and remains one of the most popular festivals of India today." Masri, *Vishnu's Crowded Temple*, 123.

10. Ibid., 41, citing Al-Tony Gilmore, *Bad Nigger!: The National Impact of Jack Johnson*.

11. Quoted in Scott, *Domination and the Arts of Resistance*, 41–43. Emphasis added.

12. Ibid., 43n49.

13. Jones, "Gender and Genocide in Rwanda," in *Gendercide and Genocide*, 123.

14. Solanas, *SCUM Manifesto*.

15. Dana Stevens points to "the fascist moments in Solanas's text," including "her quasi-Futurist love for the politics of pure destruction" and "references to the 'degenerate

art' produced by male artists." See her review on Bookslut.com, July 2004, http://www.
bookslut.com/nonfiction/2004_07_002814.php.

16. Solanas, *SCUM Manifesto,* 35–36, 80.

17. Ibid., 67, 70.

18. All quotes from Ronell, "Deviant Payback," 10, 15.

19. All quotes from Cortiel, "Acts of Violence." For more on these feminist utopias
and related sub-genres, see Larbalestier, *The Battle of the Sexes in Science Fiction.*

20. Kaufman, *Germany Must Perish!,* 13, 90, 93–94.

21. Herf, *The Jewish Enemy,* 111–12. Something of the same quandary arises with
regard to Henry Morgenthau, the only American Jewish member of Franklin Roosevelt's
wartime cabinet, who proposed a radical scheme (the "Morgenthau Plan") for the dein-
dustrialization of Germany and the transfer of millions of Germans to the Soviet Union as
forced laborers. See Bassiouni, *Crimes against Humanity in International Criminal Law,* 38.
Morgenthau was closely involved in relief efforts for Jews during the war (see his entry in the
U.S. Holocaust Memorial Museum's online Holocaust Encyclopedia, http://www.ushmm.
org/wlc/article.php?lang=en&ModuleId=10007408), so he can reasonably be assumed to
have been knowledgeable about the Jewish plight and sympathetic to it. This may account
for the disparaging depiction of his plan, by Morgenthau's colleague Henry Stimson, as
"Semitism gone wild for vengeance" (quoted in Bass, *Stay the Hand of Vengeance,* 167).
But one should by no means casually adopt this framing of Morgenthau's actions. He
himself seems to have avoided a direct linkage (though this may have been smart politics
in an antisemitic era). Moreover, non-Jewish figures in the Allied camp vocally supported
Morgenthau's plan, while others crafted their own variations on the Carthaginian theme.

22. Sack, *An Eye for an Eye,* 47, 87, 106. See also the discussion (including of Sack's
book) in Piotrowski, *Poland's Holocaust,* 58–65. As an intriguing and possibly relevant
coda, when new generations of Israelis reached adolescence in the 1960s and 1970s, one
of the most popular cultural products they seized upon was a series of pornographic
novels, sold at kiosks, depicting Jews and other victims in Nazi concentration-camp
settings. See Glasner-Heled, "Reader, Writer, and Holocaust Literature," 109–33. The
plots of this so-called "Stalag" genre "frequently concluded with the male characters
exacting revenge on their tormentors by raping and killing them." See "Documentary
Looks at Nazi Porn in Israel."

23. Segev, *The Seventh Million,* 142, 145, 149; emphasis added. Similar feelings of
weakness and paralysis afflicted the Palestinian Jewish community "when the extermination
of the Jews was at its height." Moshe Kleinman, editor of the World Zionist Organization
paper *Haolam,* declared his willingness "to impose on the German people a boundless
measure of suffering and torture to be endured for hundreds of years, until their heavy
sins are burned away and purified." But he was perceptive enough to recognize that this
desire for vengeance was born of subaltern despair—*"the desperate cry of the miserable and
oppressed,* those powerless to protect themselves, [who] demand vindication for their blood
and *humiliation* from the conscience of the world and long, at least in their imaginations,
to see 'the revenging of the blood of thy servants.'" Quoted in Segev, *The Seventh Million,*
150–51; emphasis added.

24. Earl Ofari Hutchinson, "Why Are Black Leaders Silent on Black Hate Crimes?"25.
See, e.g., Morsch, "The Problem of Motive in Hate Crimes," 659–89.

26. Moreover, hoax reporting of hate crimes is quite common. Often, such actions
can themselves be considered hate crimes; subaltern men and women are frequently the
perpetrators, whether they aim to draw attention to themselves, a wider cause, or both. See,
e.g., "When a Hate Crime Isn't a Hate Crime: Racial Hoaxes on College Campuses," 52.

27. Cited in D'Souza, *The End of Racism*, 403.

28. Mydans, "A Target of Rioters, Koreatown is Bitter, Armed and Determined."

29. Park, "Use and Abuse of Race and Culture," 497.

30. Del Zotto and Jones, "Male-on-Male Sexual Violence in Wartime."

31. Human Rights Watch, *No Escape*.

32. Ibid., 35, 73.

33. Quoted in Human Rights Watch, *No Escape,* 215–17.

34. Coetzee, *Disgrace*, 158–59.

35. SkyNews report on YouTube, http://www.youtube.com/watch?v=v2E9oz4dfLs, posted July 19, 2006.

36. Moynahan, "Farms of Fear."

37. van der Walt, "A Shame versus a Guilt-Oriented Conscience."

38. Moynahan, "Farms of Fear."

39. Stanton interviewed on "Carte Blanche," South African television clip, undated (available from the author; write to adam.jones@ubc.ca).

40. Lepore, *The Name of War*, 119.

41. Straus, *The Order of Genocide*; Midlarsky, *The Killing Trap*; Valentino, *Final Solutions*.

42. Valentino, *Final Solutions,* 19.

43. Mamdani, *When Victims Become Killers*, 8, 185.

44. Robins, personal communication, March 19, 2008. See also the important discussion of "Leadership and Division," in Robins, *Native Insurgencies and the Genocidal Impulse in the Americas*, 108–41.

45. After abolition in Brazil, reports Alma Guillermoprieto, "the newly free blacks were a constant source of irritation for the conservative elite defeated in the fight over slavery, and at no time more so than during carnival, when their boisterous presence on the streets amounted to a provocation. By the turn of the century carnival had become the staging ground for a new battle fought between the proponents of a 'civilized' celebration and the recalcitrantly 'African' blacks. A flurry of police regulations and restrictions sought to limit or eliminate the black influence on carnival. African drum sessions were prohibited. With an eye to keeping black revelers up on the hills, many regulations specified that only 'certain types' of carnival associations could parade down Rio's principal streets." Guillermoprieto explores how this conservative opinion found its echo among "the emerging class of black artisans, skilled laborers and professionals" who also "want[ed] to distance themselves from the drums and the chants and all the native music's tribal connotations," leading by the early twentieth century to the advent of "the civilized black carnival the white world had been waiting for." Guillermoprieto, *Samba*, 24–25.

46. Scott, *Domination and the Arts of Resistance,* 227.

47. See Viola, *The Best Sons of the Fatherland*.

48. See, e.g., Zimmerer, "From the Editors: Genocidal Terrorism?," 379–87.

49. Chua, *World on Fire*, 256.

50. Taylor, *Sacrifice as Terror*.

51. See Jones, *Gendercide and Genocide*.

52. On the "Superpredator" motif, see Hayden, "The Myth of the Super-Predator." For vivid evidence of the overlap of gender with race/culture/religion in the "war on terror," see the short video pastiche *The Planet of the Arabs,* posted (at the time of writing) to Google Videos.

53. See Jones, "Gender and Genocide in Rwanda."

54. The principal theorist of children as subjects in genocide is R. Charli Carpenter; see, e.g., her article, "Surfacing Children," 428–77.

55. See Carpenter, *"Innocent Women and Children"*; Jones, "Genocide and Humanitarian Intervention"; Jones, "Straight as a Rule," 451–69.

56. Elsewhere along the genocidal continuum, this might prompt greater attention to (and critical engagement with) hate speech that accompanies and masquerades as emancipatory discourse—whether this takes the form of the racial bigotry afflicting some African American activism or the bludgeoning misandry of Andrea Dworkin's feminist writings, permeated with "a primitive abhorrence of men, so blatant and compulsive that it obviates [a] pretense to critical analysis" (Mullarkey, "Hard Cop, Soft Cop," reviewing Dworkin's *Intercourse*).

57. Kofi Annan, quoted in "A Genocide Begins with the Killing of One Man," Everything2.com, http://everything2.com/index.pl?node_id=1493745.

Works Cited

Bass, Gary Jonathan. *Stay the Hand of Vengeance: The Politics of War Crimes Tribunals.* Princeton: Princeton University Press, 2000.

Bassiouni, M. Cherif. *Crimes Against Humanity in International Criminal Law.* The Hague: Kluwer Law International, 1999.

Brass, Paul R., ed. *Riots and Pogroms.* New York: New York University Press, 1996.

Carpenter, R. Charli. *"Innocent Women and Children": Gender, Norms and the Protection of Civilians.* London: Ashgate, 2006.

———. "Surfacing Children: Limitations of Genocidal Rape Discourse." *Human Rights Quarterly* 22, no. 2 (May 2000): 428–77.

Chua, Amy. *World on Fire: How Exporting Free Market Democracy Breeds Ethnic Hatred and Global Instability.* New York: Anchor Books, 2004.

Coetzee, J. M. *Disgrace.* London: Penguin, 2005.

Cortiel, Jeanne. "Acts of Violence: Representations of Androcide." In *Demand My Writing: Joanna Russ/Feminism/Science Fiction* (Liverpool: Liverpool University Press, 1999) .

Crowley, Daniel J. "The Sacred and the Profane in African and African-Derived Carnivals." *Western Folklore* 58, nos. 3/4 (Summer 1999): 223–28.

Davis, David Brion. *Inhuman Bondage: The Rise and Fall of Slavery in the New World.* New York: Oxford University Press, 2006.

Del Zotto, Augusta, and Adam Jones. "Male-on-Male Sexual Violence in Wartime: Human Rights' Last Taboo?" Paper presented at the annual convention of the International Studies Association, New Orleans, March 23–27, 2002. Available at http://adamjones.freeservers.com/malerape.htm.

"Documentary Looks at Nazi Porn in Israel." United Press International dispatch, September 6, 2007. http://www.upi.com/Entertainment_News/2007/09/06/Documentary_looks_at_Nazi_porn_in_Israel/UPI-50001189125300/.

D'Souza, Dinesh. *The End of Racism.* New York: Free Press, 1995.

"A Genocide Begins with the Killing of One Man," Everything2.com. http://everything2.com/index.pl?node_id=1493745.

Glasner-Heled, Galia. "Reader, Writer, and Holocaust Literature: The Case of Ka-Tzetnik." *Israel Studies* 12, no. 3 (2007): 109–33.

Guillermoprieto, Alma. *Samba.* London: Bloomsbury, 1991.

Hayden, Tom. "The Myth of the Super-Predator." CommonDreams.org (from *Los Angeles Times*), December 14, 2005. http://www.commondreams.org/views05/1214-26.htm.

Herf, Jeffrey. *The Jewish Enemy*. Cambridge, Mass.: Harvard University Press, 2006.

Hill, Christopher. *The World Turned Upside Down: Radical Ideas during the English Revolution*. London: Penguin, 1972.

Human Rights Watch. *No Escape: Male Rape in U.S. Prisons*. New York: Human Rights Watch, 2001.

Hutchinson, Earl Ofari. "Why Are Black Leaders Silent on Black Hate Crimes?" Salon.com, March 6, 2000. http://archive.salon.com/news/feature/2000/03/06/hate/index.html.

Jones, Adam, ed. *Gendercide and Genocide*. Nashville: Vanderbilt University Press, 2004.

_____. "Genocide and Humanitarian Intervention: Incorporating the Gender Variable." *Journal of Humanitarian Assistance* (online), February 2002. http://jha.ac/articles/a080.htm.

_____. "Straight as a Rule: Heternormativity, Gendercide, and the Non-Combatant Male." *Men and Masculinities* 8 (2006): 451–69.

Kaufman, Theodore N. *Germany Must Perish!* Newark: Argyle Press, 1941.

Lachmann, Renate, Raoul Eshelman, and Marc Davis. "Bakhtim and Carnival: Culture as Counter-Culture." *Cultural Critique* 11 (Winter 1988–89): 125.

Larbalestier, Justine. *The Battle of the Sexes in Science Fiction*. Middletown, Conn.: Wesleyan University Press, 2002.

Lepore, Jill. *The Name of War: King Philip's War and the Origins of American Identity*. New York: Vintage Books, 1999.

Mamdani, Mahmood. *When Victims Become Killers: Colonialism, Nativism, and the Genocide in Rwanda*. Princeton: Princeton University Press, 2001.

Masri, Maria. *Vishnu's Crowded Temple: India since the Great Rebellion*. London: Penguin Books, 2007.

Midlarsky, Manus I. *The Killing Trap: Genocide in the Twentieth Century*. Cambridge: Cambridge University Press, 2005.

Morsch, James. "The Problem of Motive in Hate Crimes: The Argument against Presumptions of Racial Motivation." *Journal of Criminal Law and Criminology* 82, no. 3 (1991): 659–89.

Moynahan, Brian. "Farms of Fear." *Sunday Times Magazine*, April 2, 2006.

Mullarkey, Maureen. "Hard Cop, Soft Cop." *The Nation*, May 30, 1987. Available at http://www.maureenmullarkey.com/essays/porn1.html.

Mydans, Seth. "A Target of Rioters, Koreatown is Bitter, Armed and Determined." *New York Times*, May 3, 1992.

Park, Kyeyoung. "Use and Abuse of Race and Culture: Black-Korean Tensions in America." *American Anthropologist* 98, no. 3 (1996): 492–99.

Piotrowski, Tadeusz. *Poland's Holocaust: Ethnic Strife, Collaboration with Occupying Forces and Genocide in the Second Republic, 1918–1947*. London: McFarland and Company, 2007.

The Planet of the Arabs. http://video.google.com/videoplay?docid=-600397827976179049.

Robins, Nicholas. *Native Insurgencies and the Genocidal Impulse in the Americas*. Bloomington: Indiana University Press, 2005.

Ronell, Avital. "Deviant Payback: The Aims of Valerie Solanas." Introduction to Valerie Solanas, *SCUM Manifesto* (London: Verso, 2004), 1–31.

Sack, John. *An Eye for an Eye: The Story of Jews Who Sought Revenge for the Holocaust*. 4th ed. N.p., 2000.

Scott, James C. *Domination and the Arts of Resistance: Hidden Transcripts*. New Haven: Yale University Press, 1992.

_____. *The Moral Economy of the Peasant: Rebellion and Subsistence in Southeast Asia*. New Haven: Yale University Press, 1977.

_____. *Weapons of the Weak: Everyday Forms of Peasant Resistance*. New Haven: Yale University Press, 1986.

Segev, Tom. *The Seventh Million: The Israelis and the Holocaust*. New York: Holt, 2000.

Solanas, Valerie. *SCUM Manifesto*. London: Verso, 2004.

Straus, Scott. *The Order of Genocide: Race, Power, and War in Rwanda*. Ithaca: Cornell University Press, 2006.

Taylor, Christopher C. *Sacrifice as Terror: The Rwandan Genocide of 1994*. Oxford: Berg, 1998.

Twaddle, Michael, ed. *Expulsion of a Minority: Essays on the Ugandan Asians*. London: Athlone Press, 1975.

Valentino, Benjamin A. *Final Solutions: Mass Killing and Genocide in the 20th Century*. Ithaca: Cornell University Press, 2004.

van der Walt, B. J. "A Shame versus a Guilt-Oriented Conscience." Available at http://www.aspecten.org/teksten/IS2005/Walt_Workshop.pdf.

Viola, Lynne. *The Best Sons of the Fatherland: Workers in the Vanguard of Soviet Collectivization*. New York: Oxford University Press, 1987.

"When a Hate Crime Isn't a Hate Crime: Racial Hoaxes on College Campuses." *Journal of Blacks in Higher Education* 22 (1998): 52.

Zimmerer, Juergen. "From the Editors: Genocidal Terrorism? A Plea for Conceptual Clarity." *Journal of Genocide Research* 8, no. 4 (2006): 379–87.

Biographical Notes

Editors

NICHOLAS A. ROBINS is a lecturer in the Department of History at North Carolina State University. He holds a Ph.D. in Latin American Studies from Tulane University. He is author of *Priest-Indian Conflict in Upper Peru: The Generation of Rebellion, 1750–1780*; *Native Insurgencies and the Genocidal Impulse in the Americas*; *Genocide and Millennialism in Upper Peru: The Great Rebellion of 1780–1782*; *The Culture of Conflict in Modern Cuba*; *Mesianismo y Semiótica Indígena en el Alto Perú: La Gran Rebelión de 1780–1782*; and *El mesianismo y la rebelión indígena: La rebelión de Oruro en 1781*. He is also editor of *Conflictos Políticos y movimientos sociales en Bolivia* and *Cambio y continuidad en Bolivia: etnicidad, cultura e identidad*, as well as numerous articles.

ADAM JONES is Associate Professor of Political Science at the University of British Columbia, Okanagan, Canada. From 2005 to 2007, he was postdoctoral fellow in the Genocide Studies Program at Yale University. He is the author or editor of a dozen books, including *Genocide: A Comprehensive Introduction*; *Crimes against Humanity: A Beginner's Guide*; and *Gender Inclusive: Essays on Violence, Men and Feminist International Relations*. He serves as executive director of Gendercide Watch (www.gendercide.org), a Web-based educational initiative that confronts gender-selective atrocities against men and women worldwide. He is also senior book review editor of the *Journal of Genocide Research*. Personal web site: http://adamjones.freeservers.com. Email: adam.jones@ubc.ca.

Authors

ALEXANDER LABAN (ALEX) HINTON is Director of the Center for the Study of Genocide and Human Rights and Associate Professor of Anthropology and Global Affairs at Rutgers University, Newark. He is the author of *Why Did They Kill? Cambodia in the Shadow of Genocide* and five edited or co-edited collections: *Genocide: Truth, Memory, and Representation*; *Night of the Khmer Rouge: Genocide and Democracy in Cambodia*; *Annihilating Difference: The Anthropology of Genocide*; *Genocide: An Anthropological Reader*; and *Biocultural Approaches to the Emotions*. He is currently working on several other projects, including an edited volume, *Local Justice*, a book on 9/11 and Abu Ghraib, and a book on the politics of memory and justice in the aftermath of the Cambodian genocide.

ERIC LANGENBACHER is Visiting Assistant Professor and Director of Special Programs in the Department of Government, Georgetown University, where he teaches courses on comparative politics, political culture, and political films. He has also taught at George Washington University and in Buenos Aires, Argentina. His book manuscript *Memory Regimes and Political Culture in Contemporary Germany* is currently under review. His research interests center on political culture, collective memory, political institutions, and public opinion in Europe and the United States.

EVELIN G. LINDNER is an interdisciplinary social scientist. She holds two Ph.D.s, in social medicine and social psychology. In 1996, she began her research on humiliation and its role in genocide and war. This research conducted from 1997 to 2001 involved more than 200 interviews with people implicated in or knowledgeable about Rwanda, Somalia, and Nazi Germany. Lindner is currently concentrating on planned books and articles on humiliation, as well as establishing the Human Dignity and Humiliation Studies network as an international platform for further work on the subject. She is affiliated with the Columbia University Conflict Resolution Network, New York; the University of Oslo, Department of Psychology, Norway; and the Maison des Sciences de l'Homme, Paris; and she teaches in Southeast Asia, the Middle East, Australia, and other places globally.

DAVID B. MACDONALD holds a Ph.D. in International Relations from the London School of Economics. He is the author of *Balkan Holocausts? Serbian and Croatian Victim-Centered Nationalism and the War in Yugoslavia* and *Identity Politics in the Age of Genocide: The Holocaust and Historical Representation.* Formerly a Senior Lecturer in Political Studies at the University of Otago, he now teaches political science at the University of Guelph.

E. O. SMITH is Emeritus Professor of Anthropology at Emory University. He received his Ph.D. from Ohio State University, where his dissertation research focused on the evolutionary basis of social play in rhesus monkeys. He has done fieldwork with nonhuman primates in Micronesia as well as in Africa. His fieldwork has been supported by the National Science Foundation, the World Wildlife Fund, the International Union for the Conservation of Nature, and the Leakey Foundation. Smith has also done research with captive nonhuman primates at the Yerkes National Primate Center, and has received funding from the National Institutes of Health and the National Institute on Drug Abuse. He is the author *When Culture and Biology Collide* and more than seventy-five journal articles, abstracts, and other publications; and the editor of *Social Play in Primates, Private Ecology and Human Origins, Evolutionary Medicine,* and Evolutionary Medicine and Health. His current research centers on the application of evolutionary theory to the behavior of modern humans.

CHRISTOPHER C. TAYLOR is Professor in the Department of Anthropology and Social Work at the University of Alabama–Birmingham. His research specialties are symbolic anthropology, medical anthropology, and political anthropology. He conducted fieldwork in Rwanda from 1983 to 1985, in 1987, and again in 1993–1994 at the outset of the genocide. The experience is described in his book *Sacrifice as Terror: The Rwandan Genocide of 1994.* He has also published *Milk, Honey and Money: Changing Concepts in Rwandan Healing.*

Index